The Franciscan monk, humanist, and physician François Rabelais, who flourished in sixteenth-century France, is widely considered as the Renaissance's greatest comic writer. His work – including most notably *Gargantua* and *Pantagruel* – continues to enthral readers with its complex and delicately crafted humor. "Rabelaisian" and "Gargantuan" have entered the lexicon but are often misunderstood; this *Companion* explains the literary and historical reality behind these notions. It provides an accessible account of Rabelais's major works and the contextual information and conceptual tools needed to understand the author and his world. The most up-to-date book on Rabelais to be designed specifically for English-speaking audiences, the *Companion* is intended to enable a broad spectrum of readers both to appreciate and to enjoy Rabelais. With a detailed guide to further reading and a chronology, and with all quotations given in translation, this is an ideal guide for students and scholars of French and comparative literature.

JOHN O'BRIEN is Professor of French Renaissance Literature at Royal Holloway, University of London. He is the author of *Anacreon Redivivus* (1995) and the coeditor of *Remy Belleau, "Les Odes d'Anacréon"* (1995), *Distant Voices Still Heard* (2000), *La "familia" de Montaigne* (2001), and most recently of *Theory and the Early Modern* (2006). His current projects involve the relationship between law, fiction, and narrative, and between speculation, the imagination, and the grotesque in early modern French literature.

A complete list of books in the series is at the back of this book.

THE CAMBRIDGE
COMPANION TO
RABELAIS

EDITED BY
JOHN O'BRIEN
Royal Holloway, University of London

CAMBRIDGE
UNIVERSITY PRESS

CAMBRIDGE UNIVERSITY PRESS
Cambridge, New York, Melbourne, Madrid, Cape Town, Singapore,
São Paulo, Delhi, Dubai, Tokyo, Mexico City

Cambridge University Press
The Edinburgh Building, Cambridge CB2 8RU, UK

Published in the United States of America by Cambridge University Press, New York

www.cambridge.org
Information on this title: www.cambridge.org/9780521687287

First published 2011

Printed in the United Kingdom at the University Press, Cambridge

A catalogue record for this publication is available from the British Library

Library of Congress Cataloguing in Publication data
The Cambridge companion to Rabelais / edited by John O'Brien.
p.   cm. – (Cambridge companions to literature)
Includes bibliographical references and index.
ISBN 978-0-521-86786-3 – ISBN 978-0-521-68728-7 (pbk.)
1. Rabelais, François, ca. 1490–1553? – Criticism and interpretation.
I. O'Brien, John, 1954–
PQ1694.C36   2011
843′.3 – dc22   2010041664

ISBN 978-0-521-86786-3 Hardback
ISBN 978-0-521-68728-7 Paperback

To the memory of
Malcolm Bowie (1943–2007)
friend, scholar, intellectual, luminary
Ta plume vole au ciel pour être quelque signe

CONTENTS

CONTRIBUTORS

BARBARA C. BOWEN is Professor of French and Comparative Literature Emerita, Vanderbilt University. British-born, but a U.S. resident since 1962, she is the author of *The Age of Bluff: Paradox and Ambiguity in Rabelais and Montaigne* (1972) and *Enter Rabelais, Laughing* (1988) as well as articles on Rabelais, Montaigne, French, Italian, and neo-Latin Renaissance comic literature (farces, short stories, jokes), and P. G. Wodehouse.

RICHARD COOPER is Professor of French and Fellow and Vice-Principal of Brasenose College, Oxford. He is the author of *Rabelais et l'Italie* (1991) and *Litterae in Tempore Belli* (1997) and editor of the poetry of Jean du Bellay and Marguerite de Navarre (both 2007). Well known for his work on Rabelais, his other research interests are in the relations between France and Italy in the Renaissance, Court festivals, Renaissance antiquarians and Renaissance manuscript painting.

FRANÇOIS CORNILLIAT teaches French literature at Rutgers University. His work focuses mostly on matters of rhetoric and poetics, and in particular on the evolving status of poetry from the fifteenth to the sixteenth century. He is the author of *"Or ne mens": Couleurs de l'éloge et du blâme chez les "Grands Rhétoriqueurs"* (1994) and of *Sujet caduc, noble sujet: La poésie de la Renaissance et le choix de ses "arguments"* (2009). He has edited, with Richard Lockwood, the volume *Èthos et pathos: Le statut du sujet rhétorique* (2000), and published several articles in *Études Rabelaisiennes*: "On Words and Meaning in Rabelais Criticism" (vol. 35, 1998); "On Sound Effects in Rabelais" (part 1, vol. 39, 2000; part 2, vol. 42, 2003).

MARIE-LUCE DEMONET is Professor at the Centre d'Études Supérieures de la Renaissance, of which she was the director from 2003 to 2007, and a member of the Institut Universitaire de France. Specializing in the connections between literature, languages, and semiotic theories, she has published *Les Voix du signe* (1992) and *Logique et littérature à la Renaissance* (co-editor, 1994) as well as several books and conferences on Montaigne (*Montaigne et la question de l'homme*, ed., 1999; *A plaisir: Sémiotique et scepticisme chez Montaigne*, 2002; *L'Écriture du scepticisme chez Montaigne*, coeditor, 2003). She is also interested in questions of poetry and semiotics in the works of Rabelais and has organized two conferences on this author to date, *Rabelais et la question du sens* (2000, publication forthcoming; coeditor) and *Les Grands Jours de Rabelais en Poitou* (2006). Since 1998, she has hosted a website offering transcriptions of French Renaissance texts (www.cesr.univ-tours.fr/Epistemon) and is the founder and director of the CESR "Bibliothèques Virtuelles Humanistes" program. Her current projects include two books on the status of fiction and the conception of signs during the Renaissance.

EDWIN DUVAL is Professor of French at Yale University. He has written on a wide range of Renaissance authors – Rabelais, Marot, Marguerite de Navarre, Scève, Montaigne, and d'Aubigné – and his books include a three-volume study of form and meaning in Rabelais. He is currently working on relations between musical structure, poetic form, and logical articulation in French Renaissance lyric.

FLOYD GRAY is Professor of French Emeritus at the University of Michigan and the author of articles and books on French literature of the sixteenth and seventeenth centuries, notably *Le Style de Montaigne* (1958), *Rabelais et l'écriture* (1974), *La Poétique de du Bellay* (1978), *La Balance de Montaigne: Exagium/essai* (1982), *La Bruyère amateur de caractères* (1986), *Montaigne bilingue: Le latin des "Essais"* (1991), *Rabelais et le comique du discontinu* (1994), *Gender, Rhetoric, and Print Culture in French Renaissance Writing* (2000), and *La Renaissance des mots* (2008). In addition, he edited Albert Thibaudet's *Montaigne* (1963) and *Socrate* (2008), an *Anthologie de la poésie française du XVIe siècle* (1967), Rabelais's *Gargantua* (1995) and *Pantagruel* (1997).

NEIL KENNY is Reader in Early Modern French Literature and Thought at the University of Cambridge. Among his publications are *The Palace of Secrets: Béroalde de Verville and Renaissance Conceptions of Knowledge* (1991), *The Uses of Curiosity in Early Modern France and Germany* (2004), *An Introduction to Sixteenth-Century French Literature and Thought: Other Times, Other Places* (2008), and, as editor, *Philosophical Fictions and the French Renaissance* (1991). He is currently researching early modern relationships between tenses and death.

ULLRICH LANGER is Professor of French at the University of Wisconsin and former Senior Fellow at the Institute for Research in the Humanities (Madison). He is editor of the *Cambridge Companion to Montaigne* (2005) and *Au-delà de la "Poétique": Aristote et la littérature à la Renaissance / Beyond the "Poetics": Aristotle and Early Modern Literature* (2002). He is author of various books, including *Vertu du discours, discours de la vertu* (1999), *Perfect Friendship* (1994), and *Divine and Poetic Freedom: Nominalist Theology and Literature in France and Italy* (1990). His latest book, *Penser les formes du plaisir littéraire à la Renaissance*, was published in 2009.

JOHN O'BRIEN is Professor of French Renaissance Literature at Royal Holloway, University of London. He is the author of *Anacreon Redivivus* (1995) and the coeditor of *Remy Belleau, "Les Odes d'Anacréon"* (1995), *Distant Voices Still Heard* (2000), *La "familia" de Montaigne* (2001) and most recently of *Theory and the Early Modern* (2006). His current projects involve the relationship between law, fiction, and narrative, and between speculation, the imagination, and the grotesque in early modern French literature.

WES WILLIAMS is a Lecturer in French at the University of Oxford and Fellow and Tutor of St. Edmund Hall. He is the author of *Pilgrimage and Narrative in the French Renaissance: The Undiscovered Country* (1998) and he continues to explore travel narratives of various kinds across the period. He has just completed a book on monsters and their meanings from, roughly, Rabelais to Racine (by way of Shakespeare, Montaigne, and a few others). He also works on European film and contemporary theater.

ACKNOWLEDGMENTS

I wish to record my thanks to Linda Bree and Maartje Scheltens of Cambridge University Press: they have been helpful and encouraging, wise and forbearing, and it has been a pleasure working with them.

A NOTE ON THE TEXT

References to Rabelais's work included in the text are to *The Complete Works of François Rabelais*, Donald Frame, trans. (Berkeley: University of California Press, 1991), abbreviated *F* followed by the page number(s); and to Rabelais, *Œuvres complètes*, Mireille Huchon with François Moureau, eds., Bibliothèque de la Pléiade (Paris: Gallimard, 1994), abbreviated *H* followed by the page number(s).

1483	Likely date of birth of Rabelais, the son of Antoine Rabelais, seneschal of Lerné. Tradition holds that François is born at La Devinière, a farmhouse owned by his father to the south of Chinon in the Loire valley.
1494	Former (putative) date of Rabelais's birth.
1500	Erasmus publishes his *Adages*. This work will increase in size over successive editions.
1511	Rabelais reputed to have been a novice in the Franciscan priory of La Baumette, near Angers. Erasmus publishes *Praise of Folly*.
1515	François I succeeds to the throne of France.
1516	Sir Thomas More publishes *Utopia*. Erasmus publishes his edition of the Greek New Testament and *The Education of the Christian Prince*.
1517	Luther nails his ninety-five theses to the door of Wittenberg Church.
1520	Rabelais is known at this date to have been a monk at the Franciscan priory of Le Puy-Saint-Martin, at Fontenay-le-Comte. He studies Greek with his fellow priest, Pierre Lamy (or Amy), and moves in the humanist circles of André Tiraqueau (1480–1558).
1521	Rabelais sends a letter to Guillaume Budé (1468–1540), the leading French humanist of his day. Although the letter is in Latin, it contains much Greek and shows Rabelais's commitment to the "New Learning."

1523	The Greek books of Rabelais and Lamy are confiscated by their religious superiors, only to be returned a year later. However, Lamy leaves the monastery.
1524	Rabelais supplicates the Pope, Clement VII, and receives permission to change from the Franciscans to the Benedictines. He transfers to the Benedictine Abbey of Maillezais in Poitou. He is protected by Geoffroy d'Estissac and comes to know the poet and chronicler Jean Bouchet. At the beginning of Tiraqueau's *De legibus connubialibus* (*On the Laws of Marriage*), published the same year, he writes a Greek poem in praise of the author, just as Lamy writes a poem in praise of Rabelais and his translation of book 2 of Herodotus (now lost). Three years later, Rabelais is granted permission to hold ecclesiastical benefices.
1526	From the priory of Ligugé, Rabelais writes a verse epistle to Bouchet. It will be published in the latter's *Epistres morales et familieres* (*Moral and Familiar Letters*) of 1545.
1528–30	Possible stay in Paris for medical (and legal?) studies. Two children (later legitimized by the Pope) are dated to this period in Rabelais's life.
1529	Pierre de Lille, in his *Tria calendaria* (*Triple Calendars*), mentions a translation of Lucian by Rabelais, a monk of Maillezais.
1530	François I founds the Royal College, later to become the Collège de France. It is headed by Guillaume Budé. Rabelais registers as a student in the Faculty of Medicine at Montpellier. He attends an anatomy lesson given by Rondelet and gains his Bachelor of Medicine degree in November of the same year.
1531	He lectures at Montpellier on Hippocrates and Galen.
1532	In January, he performs with colleagues in a farce, *The Man Who Married a Dumb Wife*. In June, he publishes the second volume of Manardi's *Medical Letters*, with a dedicatory letter to Tiraqueau. In August, he follows this up with publications of Latin translations of treatises by Hippocrates and Galen, with a dedication of one major treatise to Geoffroy d'Estissac. In November, he is appointed a doctor at the

Hôtel-Dieu (Hospital) in Lyons and writes to Erasmus. The end of the year brings a spate of publications. *Pantagruel* is published in Lyons. At the same time, the *Grandes et inestimables chronicques (Great and Invaluable Chronicles)*, of which Rabelais at the very least wrote the table of contents and perhaps the whole work, and the *Pantagrueline Prognostication* for 1533 and the *Almanach for the Year 1533*, signed by Rabelais, also appear.

1534   Stays in Rome as a doctor in the entourage of Cardinal Jean du Bellay (1492–1560), who, together with his brother Guillaume, Lord of Langey (1491–1543), now acts as Rabelais's patron. Later that year, Rabelais publishes Marliani's *Topography of Ancient Rome*, with a dedicatory letter to the Cardinal. In October of the same year the "affaire des placards" occurs: posters condemning the Mass are put up in Paris and other towns. Repression of Reformers follows.

1535   *Gargantua* published. Rabelais suddenly leaves his post in Lyons and stays in Rome for a second time, returning home in mid-1536. Requests the Pope, Paul III's, absolution from apostasy (since he has left the monastery of Maizellais without permission) and transfer to another Benedictine monastery. The *Pantagrueline Prognostication* for 1535 and the *Almanach for the Year 1535* are published.

1536   The Pope grants Rabelais leave to practice medicine and to transfer to Jean du Bellay's Benedictine Abbey of Saint-Maur-des-Fossés. Helps secularize the abbey and becomes a secular priest there. Death of Erasmus.

1537   Receives his degree of Doctor of Medicine at Montpellier; he lectures on Hippocrates and conducts an anatomy lesson.

1538   Publication of the *Disciple of Pantagruel*, a source of inspiration for Rabelais in *Book 4*.

1539   Accompanies Guillaume du Bellay, now Governor of Piedmont, to Turin. The first of several visits over the next 3 years.

1542   Publication of the revised editions of *Gargantua* and *Pantagruel*. Rabelais mentioned as a beneficiary in Guillaume du Bellay's will.

1543	Rabelais is present at the death of Guillaume du Bellay. The same year, death of Geoffroy d'Estissac. The Sorbonne includes *Gargantua* and *Pantagruel* on its list of censored books.
1545	Jean du Bellay's secretary, François Bribart, is burned at the stake. The Council of Trent convenes, continuing its sessions with intermissions up to 1564.
1546	*Book 3* published. It is included on a new list of censored books. Rabelais leaves France for Metz, then part of the Holy Roman Empire, where he stays for about a year as town doctor.
1547	Goes to Rome as doctor to Cardinal du Bellay. Death of François I; accession of Henri II.
1548	First version of *Book 4*. Rabelais works on a revised edition during 1550.
1549	Death of Marguerite de Navarre, to whom Rabelais had dedicated *Book 3*. Rabelais composes the *Shadow Battle* (*Sciomachie*), an account of the celebrations organized by Jean du Bellay in Rome for the birth of Henri II's second son, Louis. Rabelais returns to France.
1551	Rabelais is granted the benefices of Meudon and Saint-Christophe-du-Jambet. Does not reside.
1552	Publication of revised editions of *Book 4* and *Book 3*.
1553	Probable date of Rabelais's death.
1562	Publication of *The Ringing Island (L'Isle sonnante)*.
1564	Publication of *Book 5*, which includes most of *The Ringing Island*. The Council of Trent concludes its sessions. It deems Rabelais's writings heretical and places them on the Index of Prohibited Books.

I

Introduction

Prologue

Most illustrious topers, and you, most precious poxies – for to you, not to others, my writings are dedicated – Alcibiades, in Plato's dialogue entitled *The Symposium*, praising his master Socrates, inconvertibly the prince of philosophers, among other things says he is like the Sileni.   (F3/H5)

Prologues fulfil a conventional role in early modern works. When they are addressed to a reader, as here, their aim is to explain and justify the work that immediately follows, highlighting its novel features and attempting to arouse the reader's interest and gain his or her sympathy. It is a rhetorical technique known as *captatio benevolentiae*, literally "the capturing of good will." By those standards, the opening lines of the prologue of *Gargantua* far from fit this pattern, yet they present a set of features characteristic of Rabelais's work as a whole: a narrator who directly hails the reader; that reader addressed in scurrilous terms; a speech that then switches register and makes extensive reference to a classical text. From the threshold of the text – before even chapter 1 begins – the narrator introduces us to a world whose prime features are contradiction, tension, brought about, in this case, by the sudden change of cultural registers, the implicit characterization of the reader, the abolition of authorial distance, and the *rapprochement* between the narrator and his public. The reader is thrown headlong into a literary universe that can easily give rise to bafflement and confusion. It is worth emphasizing at the outset that such tensions are not incidental aspects of Rabelais's writing, but standard components. All conventional niceties governing the relationship between the author and the reader are set aside; and the effect is defamiliarization.

We need to draw a distinction between defamiliarization and alienation as forms of distance separating us from a writer five centuries old. Historical distance inevitably exists between our own time and Rabelais's. And various features of his fictional universe, familiar to him and his audience, feel alien-ating to us: obvious instances are the often bawdy humor, the references to bodily functions, and the extensive use of allusions to contemporary and classical literature of an unusually wide range assuming that the reader is versed in medicine, theology, philosophy, the natural sciences, and politics, as well as history, geography, and all literary genres. The purpose of this *Cambridge Companion* is to help present-day readers overcome that sense of alienation and possibly discomfort or even frustration by providing the practical tools they need to acquaint themselves with an unfamiliar intellec-tual landscape. However, even when these practical tools are mastered, so that the text no longer seems so alien, the effect of defamiliarization will still be present. Defamiliarization refers to the way a text continues to defeat our expectations, surprises us, outwits us. It refers to the way that a text rewrites the literary or historical elements it inherits or appropriates and makes con-nections between these elements where no such connections had previously existed. It refers to the way a text takes old, familiar things and reinvigorates them. Defamiliarization takes and breaks our preconceptions, refashions as well as outplays our expectations, and in the process (and *by* this process) sets us down somewhere strange. Unsettling, disconcerting, it opens up new ways of seeing and thinking. It is synonymous with the literary effect. And it is to elucidating that literary effect that this volume is dedicated.

Reading

It is no coincidence that the words "reading Rabelais" occur in the titles of two chapters in this volume and recur directly or indirectly as a theme and a problem in the remainder of the contributions. Reading is to be understood in the widest sense – from the physical act of working through Rabelais page by page attempting to grapple with his inventive language, through questions of interpretation, both specific and general. Every act of reading implies, or ought to imply, the corresponding task of interpretation; deciphering words and meanings is the reader's perennial duty.

Accordingly, when Floyd Gray opens this collection with a description of Rabelais's whole output, he is careful to set it firmly in a framework of reading as such. Gray emphasizes the literary and linguistic dimensions of the works he discusses, insisting on the inextricability of words and things, real-life events and their linguistic counterpart. The temptation to split words from things may be strong, yet it is in their intimate and intricate association that their value and purpose lie, Gray argues. And it is their problematic relationship that continues to delight and puzzle, so much so that to divorce words from things is to misunderstand the literariness of Rabelais's enterprise. "His writing is carefully, artfully structured to avoid transparency and encourage multiple and often conflicting interpretations," Gray states, for questions of fact and fiction "form part of a complex narrative design that conflates them with deliberate and joyous purpose." He demonstrates that even the prologues – as we have seen – cannot be relied upon to provide solid information about the author's intentions, as they themselves are part of the fictional universe they supposedly introduce and do not constitute evidence independent of it. Structure and plot are similarly unhelpful notions if we search only for determinate meanings; digressions abound, impeding the directional flow that is implicit in the Latin etymology of the word "prose," *prorsa oratio*, forward-directed discourse, the onward thrust of prose writing. Erudition piles up, as a verbal equivalent to the giant theme around which Rabelais focuses his work. Gray is clear that the admixture of the comic and the serious presents the most pressing problem for the modern reader. Two options are equally impossible – to search *only* for the "substantific marrow" (F4/H7), or to believe *only* in a world of words, the play of language. It is precisely in the complementarity and tension between these two perspectives that the most fruitful position lies. The double perspective of the comic and the serious is written into the very fabric of Rabelais's literary works: the "prophetic riddle" that closes *Gargantua* is given two contrasting interpretations by the giant and Frère Jean, the first serious and theological, the second comic and parodic. Both characters see the riddle as allegorical, but offer radically different solutions to its meaning. This instance is emblematic of those many episodes in which interpretation and its problems are a fundamental aspect of Rabelais's writing.

Both the prologue to *Gargantua* and the "prophetic riddle" that closes the same book come under further close scrutiny from François Cornilliat. What he draws from his analysis reaffirms what might be termed the principle of simultaneity rather than succession: drinking involves both the comic and the serious; one has to find interpretive solutions to problems while remaining merry. Such episodes represent a steganographic procedure, a term Cornilliat borrows from Mireille Huchon to indicate the degrees of understanding that different readers may derive from any particular passage or incident. Some will take pleasure in the surface message; others prefer its hidden meanings. In which case, the constituent members of Pantagruel's company of friends seem to embody the dialectic incarnated by Socrates in the *Gargantua* prologue – the combination of seriousness and comedy, high and low matter, exterior and interior. Yet Cornilliat is not content with that neat symmetry.

In the final section of his chapter, he makes acute points about the responsibility for interpretation. In particular, he demonstrates that the "revelation" afforded by Bacbuc at the close of *Book 5* does not relieve the inquirers of the duty of interpreting for themselves: "revelation will not suspend, but *activate* a duty to understand ... Whatever interpretation is, it is not a last 'word,' a final result, but an undertaking in search of its own understanding" (author's emphasis). And Cornilliat demonstrates that such understanding becomes progressively harder, not easier, with the antics of Panurge. The Pantagrueline community tolerates his behavior, which nonetheless tends to sully the moral aspect of Pantagruelism, with the result that Rabelais's vision becomes more difficult to circumscribe precisely because it takes serious account of the human dimension.

No reader of Rabelais can fail to acknowledge the vast numbers of quotations, allusions, and references that abound on every page of his writings. Such boundless learning may frankly be daunting to prospective readers. A good annotated edition of the text is a prerequisite; but the reader also needs reliable information about the nature and workings of Rabelais's system of references. Neil Kenny provides exactly that. He opens his contribution by a lucid explanation of the mechanics of Renaissance imitation, showing that imitation implicated both writing and reading in a dynamic process of recreation and had a much greater range of reference and practice than the word "imitation" might suggest today. For these reasons, he prefers to describe this process by "intertextuality," a term that has itself become common currency in criticism since being coined by Julia Kristeva 40 years ago. Kenny usefully reminds us of its advantages, notably that it keeps open the relationship between texts rather than prejudging them by labels such as "source" or "influence." Intertextuality, furthermore, suggests that texts are received by readers against a backdrop of other texts: the reader understands and recognizes a text or set of texts by placing them within the mental store cupboard that is his or her own experience of literature, philosophy, history, and so forth. As its name implies, intertextuality is a dialogue between manifold fragments, a transaction *between* texts, not a static relationship between a cause and an effect.

Rabelaisian intertextuality falls into two categories, for Kenny: "Ancient" and "Modern." He surveys the main subtexts, highlighting the complex system of rethinking and rewriting that characterizes our author's sophisticated handling of all kinds of texts, popular as well as elite. After their nature comes their role, and here Kenny notes two main trends in Rabelais criticism. The first is to view subtexts as keys to an overall interpretation, while the second concentrates on tensions between subtexts. Kenny selects the death of Pan episode in *Book 4* to illustrate the possible intertextual approaches to one specific scene. One reading, indebted to Michael Screech, would regard this incident as an allegory of Christ's death and resurrection. Another, inspired by André Tournon, might emphasize that the allusions in this sequence to the classical Greek writer Plutarch throw up more questions than they comfortably answer. In which case, Rabelais could well be drawing attention, at one remove, to issues such as how texts signify, whether their juxtaposition or association is sufficient to ensure their harmonization, and who in the text has the authority to decide what interpretation of the evidence should prevail. This reflexive dimension of Rabelais – investigating or just setting out the problems of its own interpretation – is an acknowledged aspect of this comic writer's work that has been widely analysed over recent decades, and Kenny is entirely right in drawing attention to its prominence and relevance.

Wes Williams offers a cultural-historical perspective on many of the issues that have engaged our attention up to this point. His topic is Rabelais's bestiary, encompassing the exotic and the monstrous, natural history's equivalent of the comedy of giant size that is a thematic constant in Rabelais's work. At issue in the deployment of animals (dogs, camels, whales . . .) is their signifying function: is the monstrous part of nature, beyond nature, or against nature? This debate has particularly concentrated on the whale (Physeter) episode in *Book 4*, the monster that de-monstrates . . . what, exactly? As the Renaissance understood monster theory, the whale would have been ripe with narrative, ready to unfold its story and significance to the discerning interpreter. The problem is its position in the larger tale of these early modern travelers, Pantagruel and his companions: it is hard to see what the whale betokens, other than the fact that it is a whale, a "work of nature" but not self-evidently a portent, despite Panurge's attempt to link it to biblical antecedents (Leviathan) and classical (Perseus and Andromeda). (Kenny's examination of the problematic clash of subtexts, and the significance which can be derived from them, is fully instanced here.) And even though Pantagruel kills the monster, Williams argues that the giant resists assimilation to the stock myths of epic heroism that would have acted as the standard interpretive yardsticks for such encounters with the monstrous.

It is only when the whale is dead that it becomes subject to the discourses of medicine and money, or metamorphoses into another novelty, an item brought home from abroad to be exhibited in a trophy room as part of a secure, comfortably domesticated species of knowledge (ever-expanding, of course, as trophy collections must be, to give the sense, or the illusion, that knowledge is also on the increase). What Rabelais's text does, for Williams, is to keep in permanent tension the numerous othernesses that Pantagruel

[margin notes: animal/nature; whale; knowledge on the increase]

5

and his friends encounter, and the knowledge that is derived from them by a Western culture of dissection and display: the monster de-monstrates a culture's way of dealing with it by fixing it in a show case, exhibiting it in a museum, relegating it to an epistemic system. Our knowledge stands in place of the Other; our representations supplant the monstrous real. And it is precisely because Rabelais re-enacts this process with increasing regularity in *Book 4* that we are constantly faced by the question of how our intepretive communities tackle the monster in our midst, the otherness we cannot control.

Contexts

Williams's chapter forms the conceptual lynch-pin between contributions that broadly deal with reading and interpretation as puzzles in their own right, and those which focus on historical material, generally identifiable as offshoots of humanism. Rabelais's social and literary background can be gathered from the Chronology in this volume and is further reflected prismatically in those chapters that deal with his intellectual, political, and religious context. Three such chapters fall into this category and they share some common emphases. The founding in 1530 of the Royal College (later to become the Collège de France) and the impetus it gave to humanism is one such emphasis; entwined with it are Rabelais's mockery of the Sorbonne, at that time the Paris Faculty of Theology, his attacks on superstitious religious practices, and his sympathy for the moderate movement of Reform associated with the names of Guillaume Briçonnet and the king's sister, Marguerite de Navarre. Of paramount importance also is the influence of Erasmus (1466/9–1536), the great Dutch humanist who was the author of – among other things – *Praise of Folly* and the *Adages*, and whose presence can be detected in everything from allusions to his works to a shaping part in the theological outlook of Rabelais's works.

The first of the three contextualizing chapters, by Marie-Luce Demonet, tackles Rabelais's humanism, "humanism" being defined here as "humane letters" originally taught by a *umanista*, a tutor of the Greek and Latin Classics. Demonet is careful to set Rabelais firmly within his historical and chronological setting, drawing out his political and religious commitments as part of his intellectual dynamic. Struggles with the Sorbonne, the spread of Reformist teachings in Paris and the central French provinces, and the endeavor to stabilize Gallican principles comprise the backdrop to Rabelais's intellectual evolution, and Demonet stresses the continuation of medieval forms of thinking and writing alongside humanist discoveries:

Aristotelianism is coupled with a renewed interest in Cicero and Pliny; Epicureanism, Skepticism, and Cynicism are added to Platonism and Stoicism; above all, the encyclopedism of Gargantua's letter to Pantagruel and the anti-Abbey of Thélème, both of which represent large-scale programs trying in varying degrees and with variable success to give voice to the strain of ambitious humanism endorsed by Rabelais. By the time of *Book 3* and particularly of *Book 4*, Rabelaisian humanism becomes expressly more combative, with explicit attacks on both Calvin and, contrariwise, the temporal power of Rome. The mixed nature of Rabelais's writing receives emphasis in Demonet's account, with the presence of antiquity balanced against the attraction of enduring forms. Thus Marot rubs shoulders with Erasmus, and medieval adventure stories with narratives imitated from Lucian and Menippean satire; farce and burlesque supply as much material as *The Dream of Poliphile*, while scatological neologisms as well as biblical Hebrew enrich Rabelais's polyglossia.

Two areas call for special comment. The first relates to the place of women. Demonet shows that the Rabelaisian attitude toward women stems from the many-sided traditions he inherited. Medieval misogyny was enshrined in high-culture works such as the *Romance of the Rose* as well as in more popular satires and farces. The Christian tradition, with its idealization of the Virgin and contrasting distrust of the woman as temptress, also had a crucial role to play, and to this can be added legal restrictions on women deriving from Roman Law. The limited role played by women in Rabelais's work has received extensive critical attention and Demonet reviews the evidence for his supposed antifeminism by contextualizing contemporary debates associated with the names of Cornelius Agrippa, Jean Bouchet, André Tiraqueau, Thomas Sebillet, and de Billon. The last two used *Book 3* as the focus for their own contrasting reactions and it is indeed in Panurge's quest that most discussion of women is to be found, particularly in the influential speech of Rondibilis. On the other hand, as Demonet shows, women and female themes are positively colored at key moments in Rabelais: in Thélème, in the use of allegorical characters such as the Chitterlings that puts into question gender polarities, and in the women Rabelais counts among his readers and to whom he dedicates his works. Demonet makes the important point that the views of the narrator or his characters are not simply to be equated with those of Rabelais himself: the biographical fallacy still haunts Rabelais studies and it is especially important to keep such distinctions in mind in such a sensitive area as gender.

The second tradition has a special place for Demonet: classical Cynicism. Diogenes the Cynic, a pupil of Socrates, assumes prominence in *Books*

3 and *4*, and a link is made in the prologue to *Book 4* between Diogenic Cynicism and Pantagruelism, both expressly and indirectly, through the anecdote of Diogenes rolling his barrel during the siege of Corinth. Demonet's point is that Rabelaisian fiction and the Pantagruelism it sustains are themselves back-to-front ventures, undertaken "in a way paradoxical to all philosophers" (*F404/H503*) and yet, like Diogenes himself, creative of their own brand of philosophical ideal and wayward humor. Rabelais's humanism provides him with exact analogies for his own topsy-turvy universe.

In the prologue to *Gargantua*, Rabelais claims that his work contains "some very lofty sacraments and horrific mysteries, concerning [our religion as well as] our political state and our domestic life" (*F4/H7*; translation corrected). Edwin Duval tackles the first of these topics, religion. He regards Rabelais as an Erasmian Christian humanist, someone who took a moderate line between rejection of Catholic beliefs and practices not directly authorized by Scripture and refusal to side with the new orthodoxies of the Reformers. Duval is candid that while this general position is easy to delineate, it is much harder to draw out of Rabelais's work a consistent theological stance, owing to the changing outlook of the writer and his reaction to circumstances, as well as (not least) his comic perspective. The general lineaments are nonetheless clear. In *Pantagruel*, for instance, it is what is left unsaid that is crucial in religious terms. Thus Gargantua and his son both put their faith in God alone, implicitly dispensing with the paraphernalia of priests and the intercessionary power of the Church; communication with God is direct and unmediated. This point comes across clearly even though religion is not the main concern of the book, and its outlook is shared by the Almanachs for 1533 and 1535 which "defin[e] Rabelais's religion as a profoundly skeptical form of Christianity indifferent to things that transcend human experience and hostile to metaphysical speculation of all kinds."

Gargantua extends and deepens Rabelais's hostility to two specific groups and practices: the Sorbonne (the Parisian Faculty of Theology) and monasticism. Rabelais's depiction of "Sorbonicoles" (Sorbonne theologians) culminates in the masterly portrait of Janotus de Bragmardo, in which the theologian's own inept command of language obstructs the very message he is struggling to put across; the building blocks of communication are all in place, but no clear and coherent communication takes place. In this scintillating vignette, Janotus is undermined by the very words that create him on the page, and the deft portrayal – undercutting what it presents – makes Rabelais's satire of the Sorbonne even sharper. Only the portrait of Grosbeak in *Book 4* will achieve the same acuity and memorability.

Monasticism benefits from the opposite kind of portrayal: Frère Jean "condemn[s] his institution through his divergence from it." In truth, as Duval goes on to point out, the monk is an ambivalent figure and far removed from the one-dimensional characters who are elsewhere the object of Rabelais's satire. Duval recognizes that simultaneity of presentation, once again, rather than uniformity of characterization, is at stake; the monk, like his friends the giants, embodies the twofold drive towards seriousness and laughter. It comes as no surprise that this anti-monk is chosen to run an anti-monastery, Thélème, which is underpinned, Duval stresses, by Pauline and Erasmian principles. The monastery's principle of Christian freedom stands in sharp contrast to Panurge in *Book 3*, whose very dress – a Franciscan habit and an earring – points to his enslavement to the letter of the law and his consequent inability to liberate his will by an act of Christian freedom.

The last of Rabelais's indubitably authentic books links religion with politics again. Rabelais here dramatizes, in comically satirical form, the antagonisms that divided the Europe of his time into warring confessional creeds: Fastilent, the Chitterlings, and the Council of Chesil all constitute recognizable religious allusions – to Catholics, Protestants, and the Council of Trent, respectively. The last of these dominates the European religious scene from the 1540s through the 1560s: this council of the Roman Catholic Church, so called from the Italian town of Trente where it met, promotes the Counter-Reformation, a response to the Protestant Reformation. These changed religious circumstances are written into the fabric of Rabelais's work, and in *Book 4*, Duval argues, he attacks two specific targets: the temporal power of the Popes, and the Catholic Mass, contrasting the elaborate ritual of the Eucharist with the direct prayers Pantagruel utters during the storm at sea episode.

Duval emphasizes, in conclusion, that while many critics have noted Rabelais's Erasmian leanings, few have pointed out that religion in his works is linked to political, social, and ethical considerations, rather than explored for its own sake. This is an outlook very much concerned with the human community in the here and now, and the comic vitality to which religious discussion is connected in Rabelais is itself a crucial element in binding that community together.

Ullrich Langer investigates one important aspect of the political world of the first two books in his contribution on the king's political education. In order to distinguish between legitimate kingship and tyranny and to set out the virtues the king was expected to possess, Langer selects as his emblematic reference-point Gargantua's letter to Pantagruel, which is read in line with the Renaissance notion that the son ought to outshine his father. Charity is also a particular injunction for princes (as when Pantagruel befriends

Panurge), and the quirky demands of Pantagruel's entourage demonstrate that they are to be regarded as a group of friends rather than a crowd of flattering courtiers. Similar princely characteristics are displayed during Pantagruel's battle with Werewolf: adopting prudent measures, invoking the help of God, listening to the advice of counsellors, rewarding those who help, and punishing opponents. Even when Pantagruel comically shelters his men from a rainstorm under his tongue, we can see this gesture as an expression of the prince's prudence, Langer argues.

Gargantua likewise supplies plentiful evidence of political education. Once again, war is the test case, as Grandgousier and Gargantua (the good humanist princes) are contrasted with the tyrant, Picrochole. Although the cause of the dispute is trivial (an argument over bread), it betokens larger issues of justice and right conduct for which Langer fills in the background. The precepts of classical moral philosophy are supported by Christian theology, and both stand in contradistinction to the choleric Picrochole, whose very name, meaning "bitter bile," signals his immoderate nature devoid of prudence. Emblematic here is chapter 33 where Rabelais points up the comic disparity between the mighty empire Picrochole builds in his imagination (based on the empire of Alexander the Great), and the tyrant's own petty status as the lord of a local manor near Rabelais's actual place of birth, La Devinière. Langer concedes that the comic outlook of Rabelais's work distorts or relativizes the moral dimension. Thus if Frère Jean is the recipient of royal liberality in the shape of the Abbey of Thélème, he shows himself to be a less than model Christian in the joy he takes in slaying Picrochole's soldiers in the vineyard of the Abbey of Seuillé. At every stage in Rabelais's writing, high moral seriousness is likely to be waylaid by comic anarchy, leaving the reader with the interpretive dilemma of how to account for such disjunctions of character, theme, and tone.

Play and purpose

The term "Rabelaisian," in its standard dictionary sense, is one familiar to all: "joyously coarse or gross" (*Webster's*), "extravagance and coarseness of humour and satire" (*OED*). Schematic as such definitions inevitably are, they do highlight a valuable point: Rabelais is about laughter. Barbara C. Bowen and Richard Cooper take up that perspective, from complementary angles. The former underlines, at the very outset, how limited the common or garden view of Rabelais is, and how much it omits: the writer's thinking about religion, monarchy, government, and education, to name only the most obvious areas. Quoting a range of authorities from Horace to Erasmus and More, she also makes the crucial point that the modern dichotomy

10

[handwritten marginalia: a thing belongs in an earlier time]

between laughter and seriousness is anachronistic; a false dichotomy, in fact.

Bowen divides Rabelaisian laughter into three distinct sections. The first is the portrayal of laughter among the characters, where the giants and Frère Jean only occasionally use expressions of mirth such as "Ha ha ha" or the verb "to laugh," although the minor characters regularly laugh. Moreover, such laughter is not unequivocally humorous from the modern standpoint. Panurge's laughter at the humiliation of the Parisian lady is a notorious instance of divergence between our understanding of comedy and its Rabelaisian counterpart. The wedding feast at Basché, in *Book 4*, is another such illustration. As Bowen agrees, laughter is ambivalent, usually revealing something of the laugh-er, for better or for worse. Comedy of situation, however, abounds and supplies most of the humor for the reader. In some cases, the incongruity is exploited for its own sake, in others to make a parodic or satirical point. Alongside situation comedy is the linguistic inventiveness for which Rabelais is renowned. Distortions of ancient learned languages, especially Latin, mongrel composite languages, and invented languages are all striking features of Rabelaisian humor. So is extensive punning, often difficult to translate, the hardest being the tongue-twisting portmanteau words.

Comedy of situation and comedy of language might be said to have a therapeutic effect, even though this notion overtly occurs in Rabelais on only one occasion. At any rate, they contribute to the result that Bowen identifies as a – indeed in her view *the* – key theme in Rabelais's humor: joy. Joy and its cognates define both the attitude to be adopted and the effect of viewing things from the standpoint of Pantagruelism. In other words, laughter in Rabelais does not just cover the techniques of humor, but expands to cover the very *concept* of humor; and both the technique and the concept give full exemplification of the Aristotelian adage that prefaces *Gargantua*: "Laughter is specific to humankind" ("Le rire est le propre de l'homme"). And as his work unfolds his laughter, the effect is moreover that of a skilled rhetorician, able to provoke particular reactions in his audience, or an orator capable of producing an ethical effect on his public. Bowen reminds us, indeed, that Cicero had written a mini-treatise on jokes, which Rabelais mentions in *Book 4*.

Bowen starts her chapter by stating, "Rabelais must surely be one of history's most misunderstood authors." Richard Cooper examines the story of that misunderstanding. His very first word – "incomprehensible," cited from the seventeenth-century writer La Bruyère – sets the tone for what follows. Things did not start that way. In the sixteenth century, the owners of Rabelais's works about whom we have firm evidence were largely lawyers

[handwritten marginalia, right margin: laughter ~ reveals something about the laugh-er; language; JOY = key theme; Joy the humor]

and booksellers (and their wives). But if we also take into account some evidence that Renaissance fiction was read aloud, Rabelais may well have reached a wider audience still – in which case, it is the dramatic, theatrical quality of some of his writing that would have been uppermost. In his lifetime, Rabelais faced various criticisms. It was common in some quarters to call him Lucianic or Epicurean (a mocker or an atheist). But it was after his death that the legend of a writer of monstrous appetites covering an irreverent attitude began to take shape. Condemned as an apostle of free-thinking by seventeenth-century Catholic apologists, Rabelais was also now perceived as obscure; obscurity and obscenity were thought to be the twin hallmarks of his writing, with the result that scholarly editions were brought out to explain his by now barely understood allusions and language, even as his scurrility never ceased to be deplored.

Celebration of our author continued alongside condemnation of his lewdness. Bowdlerized versions of Rabelais were produced in pre-Revolutionary days at the same time as there were attempts to turn him into a preacher of anti-clericalism. The nineteenth century showed greater enthusiasm for our author, but it was the twentieth that saw the most vigorous expansion in Rabelais scholarship and criticism. At its core lay questions fundamental to (mis)understanding him: topicality, politics, religion, subversion, bawdiness, sign systems, the search for allegorical meanings. These issues reveal a remarkable consistency across the centuries, with each succeeding generation interpreting Rabelais according to its own emphases. In this light, it is important to state that the contributions to this volume themselves come with their own emphases, but that, while maintaining a sense of interpretive diversity and plurality, they are complementary, not contradictory. To say, for example, that the literary sign is reinterpretable or potentially inexhaustible is not to say that no specific interpretation – of a passage, an episode, a character, a theme – is possible. On the contrary, determinant readings are crucial to our understanding of Rabelais, inasmuch as they restore to us part of the dialogue that his texts have with their own time. Careful historicizing and patient archive work can supply us with some of that dialectical exchange, even though some will remain lost and the text remain opaque. In general, Rabelais's work offers more for our sense-making than we can currently make sense of. Therein lies its challenge: attentive to the past and the historical contexts in which Rabelais operated, we must also be open to the future; the text lies ahead of us and not just behind us. This is a salutory reminder that this *Cambridge Companion* itself is inevitably caught up in the same hermeneutic quest that has characterized Rabelais's admirers and detractors over the past five hundred years. In that respect, it is also a reminder that literary texts such as Rabelais's invite decoding and yet always retain their ability to evade full capture, and so stimulate the wonder, chase, and ambiguity of which Montaigne speaks in the chapter "Of Experience" in his *Essays*. The final word can be left with Cooper, whose superb formulation about *Books* 4 and 5 would be susceptible of wider application: "we are shown . . . a whole series of clues, mysterious names and parables, to which no key is given: the companions debate but rarely resolve, and the signs remain enigmatic."

2

FLOYD GRAY

Reading the works of Rabelais

Reading Rabelais is no easy matter. His language constitutes an initial obstacle. Replete with clerical, medical, legal, philosophical, scholastic terms and terminology, various classical, foreign, or invented tongues, provincial dialects and urban slang, poems, anagrams, abbreviations, sounds, names, and quotations, his writing displays one of the most varied and extensive lexical ranges of any world author.[1] Intertextuality is rampant, usually displaced by willful distortion. And more is suggested than said, making every word even more polyvalent. Equally disturbing is his recounting the story of a family of giants in a learned, highly literary language. Ultimate meaning, frequently glimpsed but forever elusive, is another. So much so that there are almost as many readings of his works as readers, a positive sign of their successful resistance to any definitive interpretation and a sure criterion of their literariness. At times a single word presents a problem, at times a sentence or a paragraph; but usually it is the determinative intention of a word, an allusion, a chapter or a book, which remains problematic. The weightiest subjects are presented lightly, and trivial matters with great care. Ever-renewable, Rabelais's text is ever-rereadable, inasmuch as it is grounded on differences, sometimes within proximate interpretations, sometimes with alternative possibilities, sometimes both.

While the promotion of differences and alternative ways of reading encourages discursive complexity and interpretive proliferation, it tends as well to impede syntactic necessity and semantic coherence. Narrative progression is regularly postponed or retarded by digressive intrusions of words and things, variously altered, quoted, misquoted, named or misnamed. Prominent intellectual currents marking the advent of Renaissance humanism are recast in such a way as to make them seem ambiguous or incongruous.[2] More than simply a display of learning, Rabelais's topical allusions and immense range of erudition afford a pretext for a distorted rewriting of the past, frequently in conjunction with reference to the present.

Strands of contemporary personal, historical, political, and religious concerns are integrated into his narrative, but in such a way as to render them more immediately obvious than readily extricable. Moreover, since much of his book combines multiple levels of reference, it is difficult to circumscribe underlying philosophies and religious tendencies, whether stoic, epicurean, pagan, rationalist, evangelist, reformist, or orthodox. Thus, comic and serious affirm and negate one another, leaving the reader with the pleasant task of deciding which is what.

It has been suggested that sixteenth-century authors were influenced in their choice of subject matter by the commercial instincts of printers whose financial interest it was to remain responsive to the emerging and evolving demands of an ever-expanding reading public. It would be useful to know more precisely to what extent and in what ways Rabelais's writing actually reflects this new publishing reality, but many aspects of his life continue to confuse or elude us. Do we know, for example, all we need to know about the date of his birth or death, his years as a monk, the extent of his medical studies and practice, his literary career, the women in his life, and the children they bore him? And can we locate the voice of the "real" Rabelais in the world and words of his book? As a doctor, one might expect him to express his medical opinion through his characters. If this is so, it is difficult to distinguish his views on woman from the mass of antifeminist literature and anti-Galenic commonplaces of the day. And are we able now to read the "vulgar" Rabelais in the same way as his sixteenth-century public, to appreciate the degree of humor which seems to preside over his choice of religious, misogynist, coarse, or obscene material, to savor him when he is most "Rabelaisian"? Is there not a whole dimension of his work which, because of cultural changes or changes in taste, no longer amuses or even interests us today, and which requires, on the part of commentators, both lengthy explication and elaborate justification? Moreover, judging from often fierce disagreement on the way his work means and should be read, it would seem safe to conclude that his writing is carefully, artfully structured to avoid transparency and encourage multiple and often conflicting interpretations.

There is a tendency, however, especially in contextual or cultural criticism, to read literally, to equate words with things, instead of dealing with the problematic relation between the two, a relation which Rabelais exploits to great comic advantage. Numerous instances of object-words occur in his writing – words, that is, which are meant to be looked at and, perhaps, pronounced, but which remain resolutely incomprehensible. This is the case with legal abbreviations in *Book 3* or the "frozen words" of *Book 4*. There are sign-words in the Thaumaste episode, nonsense-words or parodies of words in the chapter on the "palaver of the potted" (F15–18/H17–20). There are invented words and bilingual words, Janotus de Bragmardo's pig-latin and the Limousin student's interchange of French and Latin. There are portmanteau words, monster or monstrous words (some in excess of fifty letters), words that puzzle or irritate, obscene or scatological words, all of which raise the larger question of which are comic and which are not. Do we laugh today at the same time and at the same things as Rabelais and his contemporaries? Moreover, to what extent can we be sure about such matters? When our reading remains within the lexical, synchronic, grammatical parameters of the text, we have a chance of coming out right, but when we venture into cultural, political, religious, historical matters, we are more likely to find ourselves on less stable ground.

Rabelais's particular, sometimes peculiar, sense of comedy adds an extra obstacle to an untroubled reading of his work. Humorous, even hilarious at times, his book is never truly witty or even particularly funny, unless one is readily amused by verbal incongruity, textual absurdity, mock epic, satire, slapstick, or scatology. Rather, it is comic in its treatment of serious matters facetiously and facetious matters seriously. Play and thought blend and combine disproportionately in his text, the one completing, even contradicting, the other, but only rarely does one materialize without the other. Nothing is sacred and no one is spared. Churchmen, schoolmen, lawyers, judges, and monks are frequent targets, along with peasants, townsmen, and women. But so too are historical figures and happenings, folklore, mythology, conventional literary or popular discourses, fixed expressions, and levels of style. While contemporary readers might have understood and appreciated some or most of his learned allusions or linguistic distortions, this is not always easy for readers today. Without a similar literary background and cultural frame of reference, we are less likely to know what is being mocked or why, making it necessary to transpose his writing into a less abstruse and idiosyncratic idiom.

If, in turn, we look to instances of metacommentary for reliable guidance, we are confronted with the problem of deciding when and where Rabelais actually intervenes, in unmediated fashion, in the presentation and conduct of his work. Where, for instance, in the sequence of prefatory and dedicatory material does paratext end and fiction begin? The programmatic voice of the prologue of the first two books is not immediately Rabelais's. Rather it is the voice of Alcofribas, an unreliable spokesman whose language, culture, character, and implied audience are his own. Thus, ignoring etymology, the prologues of *Pantagruel* and *Gargantua* are already integral parts of the world of the text. The introductory material of the remaining books is equally complex. *Book 3* presents an opening poem to the Spirit of Marguerite de

Navarre, two royal privileges, and a prologue, which, although under the name of "Master François Rabelais," exemplifies, through Diogenes, the question of comic writing and its right reception, making it difficult once again to separate program from performance. And *Book 4*, with its Old Prologue, Liminary Epistle, and New Prologue, all under the name of Master Rabelais, and all in dramatic reaction to the detractors of his previous writing, blurs even further the line between the two. When and where does Rabelais's prologue cease being self-reflexive? And when does it stop being writing and begin to be presence, expressive, that is, of the author beside or outside his words? It seems clear finally that questions of fact and fiction are not just liminary or preliminary problems for Rabelais. On the contrary, they form part of a complex narrative design that conflates them with deliberate and joyous purpose.

Surely, the real Rabelais did not expect the real readers of *Pantagruel* to believe in the therapeutic value or practical application Alcofribas claims for his work (*F133–4/H213–14*). Or readers of *Gargantua* to identify with the "illustrious topers" or "most precious poxies" of his dedication (*F3/H5*). While readers of *Pantagruel* would have experienced little difficulty in suspecting the reliability of the narrator's emphatic reference to various illustrious predecessors and insistent claim to the truthfulness of his every word, they would have found the prologue to *Gargantua* more problematic. No longer content with a simple claim to veracity, Alcofribas now pretends that his tale, along with "others of his creating", such as "*Tosspint, On the dignity of codpieces, On peas and bacon cum commento*, etc." (*F3/H6*), has a deeper, hidden meaning, "a substantific marrow" (*F4/H7*) which the reader is enjoined to take the time to discover.[3] But then, as if in retraction, he pretends to have dashed it off in impromptu fashion: "For in the composition of this lordly book, I neither wasted nor ever employed any more or other time than that which was established for taking my bodily refection, that is to say eating and drinking" (*F5/H7*). Are claim and disclaimer mutually exclusive, or are they to be taken together as components of the right way of reading? And if reading and writing are designated as correlative phenomena, the one participating in the fulfillment and determinacy of the other, is not meaning relegated to the eye and mind of the reader? This is the crucial question raised by Rabelais, the answer to which remains open and purposely undecidable, compounding thereby the interpretative difficulties of successive commentators.[4]

Must we conclude that the way the work means depends ultimately on our particular experience with it? Are we given license to read whatever and any way we want? Is it permissible to pretend, for example, that it operates only on the level of comic entertainment or, contrariwise, that it is exclusively the conveyor of a serious message? Obviously, both dimensions obtain – and are so conjoined that the one functions in close conjunction with the other. To attempt to rewrite Rabelais so that only one or the other prevails is wrong reading in pursuit of right meaning. And any "right" meaning becomes additionally subjective when we remember that the "real" Rabelais is conspicuously absent from the text, and that the mask he calls Alcofribas is difficult to penetrate or ignore. However, even when and if Rabelais seems to speak in his own name, does his voice differ significantly from the one assigned to Alcofribas? And how can we be sure that locating the real Rabelais can lead us to the right reading of his text, especially since we have so little of that Rabelais to go on? Moreover, any attempt to arrive at a definitive reading of a literary text is a misguided and, eventually, counterproductive enterprise inasmuch as it merely serves to limit its linguistic resonance and potential range of meaning.

The prologues, once again, should provide at least an echo of Rabelais's voice and an indication of the way he expects us to hear it. Yet they are filled with reminders of classical *topoi* articulated in a somewhat distorted and self-conscious manner. When, for example, Alcofribas refers to books and different ways of reading them, the pleasure and profit they can bring, his remarks constitute a kind of commentary on his own literary aspirations and apprehensions. Closer to Rabelais perhaps is the prototype of the active and anxious author in the prologue to *Book 3*, eager to please with another draught from his "inexhaustible barrel and real cornucopia of joyfulness and jesting" (*F259/H352*), sure of his intentions, yet uncertain of their reception, confident however, despite having inadvertently offended readers in the past, in his present recognition of their Pantagruelism, "on condition of which they never take in bad part things they know issue from a good, free, and honest heart" (*F258/H351*). From this reassuring prospect, semantic recuperation and critical fulfillment become products of complicit reading, which, once again, has the authority to impart authorial intention and interpretive parameters to still-born words.

Book 4, the last complete book attributed to Rabelais with certainty, appeared in 1552, shortly before the traditional date of the author's death in 1554. But a partial prepublication of some eleven of the first twenty-five chapters dates from 1548. Each had its own prologue, the first denouncing calumniators of the author and his previous books; the second, more restrained, celebrating moderation and good health, with Zacchaeus (*F427/H525*) and Couillatris (*F427/H526*) affording prototypical examples of properly receptive readers. Yet Dr. Rabelais's desire for a healthy reception of his works is most fully and clearly expressed in the Liminary Epistle to Cardinal de Chastillon:

> You are duly notified, most illustrious Prince, by how many great personages I have been and am daily asked, requested, and importuned for the continuation of the Pantagruelic mythologies, on the grounds that many languishing, ill, or otherwise vexed and heart-sick people had, in the reading thereof, beguiled their troubles, passed time joyously, and received new blitheness and consolation. To whom it is my custom to reply that, in composing these for sport, I aspired to no glory or praise; I had intended and regard only to give in writing what little relief I could to the absent sufferers and sick, which gladly, when there is need, I give to those who take help from my craft and service. (F421/H517)

These are undoubtedly Rabelais's final prefatory words as well as the most complete reassessment of his reasons for writing as he does, not for gain or glory, but for the pleasure of giving pleasure to those who derive pleasure from reading him in good faith.

When we turn from the prologues to the works themselves, we discover that the first two books were written, so to speak, backwards. *Pantagruel* (1532), in fact, recounts the son's story before the father's, affording chronological justification for reading *Gargantua* (1534) first. Although each recapitulates the story of the birth, education, and deeds of its respective hero, the second in date seems less schematic in structure and more focused in intent. Although this has been taken to mean that *Gargantua* is a better written and a more mature work, it can just as easily mean that, in order to assure renewal and obviate repetition, it attempts to realize alternate aspects of the same theme. Where, for instance, the first book develops at length the "origin and antiquity of the great Pantagruel," the second deals only briefly with "the genealogy and antiquity of Gargantua." What is especially distinctive in both books is the proliferation of occasional or episodic characters. As memorable as we may find Janotus de Bragmardo, the Limousin scholar, or Thaumaste, their participation is fortuitous as well as curiously momentary. Continuity of characters is provided by the eponymous giants and their respective companions, Frère Jean des Entommeures and Panurge. They confront and confound the experts consulted in *Book 3* and the inhabitants of the numerous islands in *Book 4*. Whereas thematic coherence as well as a semblance of sustained narrative impetus is provided essentially by the travel motif prevailing in all five books (thus Pantagruel and Gargantua proceed from their rural place of birth and childhood through various university cities to education in Paris and exploits beyond), variation is provided in *Book 3* by Panurge's marital plans and, in the final two books, by the sea voyage in search of an answer to his matrimonial doubts. Variously detained at ports of call and by adventures of the deep, our joyous crew finally arrive at their projected destination. Causal closure is not assured until the very end of *Book 5*, but problematically so, since there are solid arguments (presented by Glauser and Huchon) against the authenticity of this posthumous publication.[5]

One final obstacle to an easy reading of Rabelais is the way in which his words tend obstinately to remain words. In episodes like the "Antidoted Frigglefraggles" (*F9–12/H11–14*) or the controversy between Lords Kissass and Sniffshit (*F167–78/H250–60*), they seem to signify only in conjunction with one another, synchronically that is, without any evident relation to a prior, diachronic meaning. Whatever sense they manage to convey is reduced to the expression of the author's intention to *represent* or *imitate* meaning. These are episodes whose ultimate reading remains uncertain, giving rise to diverse but generally unverifiable interpretations. Without being unreadable, they need to be read otherwise, not as discourse, but as texts to be admired and savored, but with discriminate recognition of their inherent exegetical problems and possibilities. Interrupted by repeated intrusions of trivia or excursions into the marginal or peripheral, narrative continuity and stylistic uniformity are short-lived, even illusory. His work, here and elsewhere, seems to expand and contract at will, with episodes beginning and ending according to a logic of chance. Themes appear only to disappear; ideas form, then fade away; learned languages dissolve into gibberish or jabberwocky. What plot there is – and it is reduced to a minimum – serves as a tenuous reminder of fictional prerogative and structural order. This is another way of saying that refusal or reversal of the principle of narrative authority subverts the idea that discourse organizes or explains the form that meaning finally assumes. On the contrary, Rabelais's writing privileges discontinuity, the narrative's other, as a force so compelling at times as to be virtually autonomous in space and scope.

Plot founded on suspension and displacement has the advantage of being uniquely flexible in syntax and structure. It allows for the introduction of a practically limitless number of characters and situations, providing substantive tangential compensation for any lack of discursive sophistication or depth. Thus, each episode opens up new intellectual and linguistic horizons, expanding in digressive fashion its initial point of departure. By digression is meant, as etymology dictates, a stepping aside, a swerving from the main subject or trajectory, a procedure which, in classical terminology, contrary to a more modern, usually derogatory usage, is a recognized, even positive technique of amplification. Digression in the present instance refers to deviations from the narrative norm, a characteristic that is one of the outstanding tendencies of Rabelais's prose. Encouraging intermittent interruptions of plot and concomitant prioritizing of moments of extraneous development, digression could be construed as the textual equivalent of thematic giantism in that it results in the unrestrained piling up of words and things in flagrant violation of the fundamental logic of discursive linearity.

Compulsively digressive, Rabelais's text seems to be in no great hurry to get where it is going. If, that is, it is actually going somewhere. It lingers and dallies, stopping to dwell with extravagant profusion on seemingly incidental details. Thus the telling of Pantagruel's visit to the Library of St. Victor (F152–8/H235–41) is interrupted at great length by an extensive catalogue of the books it supposedly housed, opening a parenthetical space the limits of which are determined less by narrative exigencies than enumerative and imaginative energy. Whereas traditional rhetoric is especially designed to direct the reader's attention towards the author's intended meaning, Rabelaisian rhetoric leaves us in doubt as to what those intentions really are. On the one hand, his work demonstrates sufficient narrative impulse to make us suspect it sustains a determining direction and goal. This is one way, perhaps the ordinary way of structuring narration, but it is a way the intrusion of Rabelais's digressions thwarts at every turn, generating so many detours and excrescences that the very primacy of narrative is brought into question. And when this primacy is questioned, the reader is confronted with the problem of what is actually essential and what is merely incidental in the tale it tells.

Sudden departures from the straight and narrow inherent in the concept of *prorsa oratio* ("straight speech," the origin of "prose") may lose and amuse us – amuse us *because* and *when* they lose us – which is a predictable, maybe even a self-defensive reaction to disorientation or surprise. Whatever "substantific marrow" finally materializes is so fragmented by the discontinuous manner of its transmission as to be no longer recognizable or immediately recoverable as such. Surfacing tangentially in the interstices of theme and superabundance of words, it requires patient extracting and subtle decoding in order to endow it with some kind of relevant coherence. When and if we accept to play Rabelais's game of hide-and-seek with meaning, we become willing participators in a mode of interpretation which the text is specifically designed both to encourage and prevent. Enticed by the promise of concealed marrow, we are sidetracked by massive displays of collateral erudition which ultimately command much of our readerly attention and most of our critical commentary. Do we exit laughing – or does he?

When we turn to Rabelais's text in its more serious configurations, we are faced with an equally difficult problem of right reading. While, for example, there are numerous episodes where his work shows an affinity with the tenets of Erasmian ideas on such questions as education, monasticism, pilgrimages, warfare, they are written in a way which makes their

interpretation ambiguous or problematic. Thus a positive view of humanist renewal seems to emerge from Gargantua's letter to Pantagruel (*F158–
62/H241–6*):

> Now all branches of learning are reestablished, languages restored: Greek,
> without which it is shameful for a man to call himself learned; Hebrew,
> Chaldean, Latin; truly elegant and correct printings are now customary . . . The
> whole world is full of erudites, of very learned teachers, of very ample libraries;
> and, in my judgment, neither in Plato's time, nor Cicero's, nor Papinian's, were
> there such facilities for study as we see now . . . (*F160/H243–4*)

Many critics read this as a straightforward hymn to Renaissance ideals, but
overstatement and the inclusion of Papinian – a distinguished jurist, but in
no way comparable to Plato or Cicero – are troublesome. Dissonance, here
and elsewhere, is characteristic of the way in which Rabelais deflates or casts
into doubt the seriousness of a given proposition. Moreover, moments of
unrestrained flights of rhetoric, together with the unrealized – and unrealiz-
able – program of encyclopedic education devised for Pantagruel, may tell us
more about Gargantua's somewhat muddled views of the world of learning
than about Rabelais's own ideas on pedagogical reform.

His reactions to war and peace seem much less ambiguous. More precise in matters of location and military action than Pantagruel's campaign
against the Dipsodes (*F209–29/H298–320*), Gargantua's war against Picrochole (*F62–116/H75–137*) is set within the easily recognizable countryside
around Rabelais's Chinonais birthplace.[6] But war in Rabelais, as education,
is double-edged. His opposition to aggression seems clear, but his pleasure in transforming the "real" of an insignificant scuffle among shepherds
over some *fouaces* into the "reality" of war is equally clear. Thus, both the
measured tones of Grandgousier's letter of Christian love and peace (*F71–
2/H84–5*) and Ulrich Gallet's conciliatory remonstrance to the invaders
(*F73–5/H86–8*) readily give way to a resounding and energetic translation of
the clash and din of battle. Display of irenic ideology is quickly displaced by
the joy of vigorous writing or, at best, survives merely as a contrasting motive
in a war structured on the play of conflicting styles and belligerent reactions
or individual deeds. Similarly, the Abbey of Thélème (*F116–27/H137–50*),
and the *do as you will* rule which regulates the life and dress of the men
and women who live there, afford, on a superficial level, a criticism of, as
well as a correction for, the constraints and drabness of a medieval abbey.
But this easy dialectic is subsumed, even obscured, by a detailed description of the architecture of the building, the layout of the grounds, and the
sumptuous clothing of its inhabitants. Moreover, even if the principles on

which Thélème is founded reflect contemporary reformist views on monasticism, free will, and Christian charity, the *prophetic riddle* of the closing chapter (F127–30/H150–3) – borrowed perhaps from a contemporary poet – is disruptive in form and ambiguous in meaning. Emblematic as well as enigmatic, it affords a final lesson in the art of twofold writing which, in retrospect, is appropriate to Rabelais's work as a whole.

Between the publication of *Gargantua* (1535) and *Book 3* (1546), there is an 11 year interval, a period of Rabelais's life which brought travel to Italy, practice as a doctor, fatherhood, a revised edition of the first two books, and a newfound narrative model for the remainder. Thus, time and space are indefinite in *Book 3*, and fictional structure is projected from within rather than imposed from without. The work begins as a sequel to *Pantagruel*, but moves quickly from the outmoded giant motif to Panurge's matrimonial project and doubts. From the rakish, confident Parisian student he was, he now becomes a victim of indecision and fear. Paradoxically, the book opens with a praise of debt (F267–75/H360–9) and closes with an equally paradoxical praise of the herb named Pantagruelion (F401–12/H500–13), whereas the central section is given over to a search for an answer to the question whether or not Panurge should marry, and, collaterally, whether he would be beaten and cuckolded by his hypothetical wife. These same simple questions are asked over and over again, eliciting convoluted answers in redundant and learned profusion from a bewildering variety of sources. Two of the authorities consulted – for instance, Hippothadée the theologian and Rondibilis the medical doctor – foreground themselves and their science over Panurge's more pressing concerns. Throughout, our putative hero remains something of a pretext, whereas a series of professions and their specialized languages become the focus of representation and ridicule. Thus, while the subject is not actually changed, it is renewed and displaced by ponderous intrusions of irrelevant learning and advice, especially on the question of the lascivious nature of women.

Whatever is humorous or reprehensible in the antifeminist rhetoric of *Book 3* may not coincide with the perception or reception of Rabelais's contemporaries, making it necessary for us to reconcile our present-day prejudices with the cultural and deliberative practices of another age. Viewed by most modern commentators as Rabelais's misogynistic contribution to the "Querelles des Femmes,"[7] *Book 3* is concerned more directly perhaps with matters pertaining to life, learning, and the will – or lack of – to decide. For all the help proffered by a bewildering array of props and experts – Homeric and Virgilian lots (F284–92/H379–88), dreams (F293–300/H388–96), a sibyl (F305–10/H397–408), a mute (F311–16/H408–15), a poet (F317–24/H415–24), an astrologer (F327–31/H427–31), a theologian

(F349–50/H445–8), a doctor (F351–60/H448–62), a philosopher (F362–8/H461–7), a judge (F375–90/H474–87), and finally and most appropriately, a fool (F392–5/H490–4) – Panurge remains indefinitely perplexed. Satire and comedy prevail in all of these consultations, but in conjunction with the serious theme of the folly of wisdom and the wisdom of folly in the conduct of human affairs. Finally, it is Panurge's *philautia* (self-love) that provides the axis on which the book revolves. Extravagant he may be, but his extravagance has all the qualities of art.

Equally disjunctive in structure, *Book 4* deals with the voyage to the oracle of the Holy Bottle which, as a concluding sequel to the now discarded and rejected consultations theme, is supposed at last to supply the definitive answer to Panurge's matrimonial quest. Sailing from one fantastic island to another, our Pantagruelists confront a number of strange, frequently monstrous figures, are plunged into a violent and almost fatal storm, and find themselves at the end of the book still far short of their projected destination. Rabelais, it has been suggested, drew on the popularity of contemporary travel literature to shape the sea voyage of his travelers, but aside from the Dindenault (F447–54/H548–56), tempest (F477–90/H581–97), Physeter (F508–11/H616–20), and unfrozen words (F556–9/H667–71) sections, focus is fixed more on the customs, characters, and allegorical creatures of the islands visited on the way. It is not always easy to determine the location or intention of these episodes. The first landfall, for instance, is the island of Medamothi (F439–46/H540–7), "nowhere" in Greek, where purchases include paintings representing the Ideas of Plato and the Atoms of Epicurus, as well as a motley collection of mythical animals. The theme may be marine or mercantile, but the intent, aside from the obvious introduction of the strange and exotic, is not evident. More direct is the satire of the legal profession in the chapters on the Shysteroos of Procuration Island (F462–74/H564–78), and of disputes between Protestants and Catholics in the Fastilent of Coverup Island (F498–507/H606–15), the Chitterlings of Wild Island (F511–29/H620–37), the Island of the Popefigs (F533–9/H642–8) and the Papimaniacs (F540–4/H649–54). Attacks on various aspects of contemporary political life, the extremes of religious practices and philosophical positions are clear, but other episodes – for instance, the solemn reflections on the death of heroes and the demise of the late Lord of Langey in the Macraeons chapters (F492–8/H599–605) – seem somewhat incongruous.[8] While comic and serious alternatives continue to prevail, the work, at times, assumes a new and somewhat darker hue in its mixture of the strange and familiar. The proliferation of nightmarish figures and the amalgam of so many somber words so unexpectedly and lucidly connected are disconcerting. An epic voyage gone astray or amok, it comes to a perplexing end with a chapter on how Panurge beshat himself in panic fear (F589–92/H697–701). An ending perhaps, but not a conclusion, because the anticipated oracle remains beyond the horizon and in pressing need of a new departure.

Book 5, however, is both posthumous and mostly, perhaps entirely, inauthentic. Nevertheless, it takes up where Book 4 leaves off, and concludes with the arrival at the sanctuary of the Oracle of the "divine Bottle." Its long-awaited pronouncement consists, not unexpectedly perhaps given the prominence accorded to wine and drinking throughout the earlier books, of a single polyvalent word: *Trinch*! When Panurge asks for an explication, he is told that it means that he himself must be the interpreter of his own undertaking (F710/H834), an answer which simply begs the question. Whether by Rabelais or not, the concluding scene of Book 5 brings Panurge's quest to a fitting, but somewhat anticlimatic, close, since we are never apprised of his matrimonial fate or future. Overall, Book 5 is turgid and more ponderous than the first four. The chapters dealing with Queen Quintessence of Entelechy (F649–65/H766–85) and her chess pageant, Satinland and Lanternland (F678–85/H799–807), the arrival at the island of the Bottle (F685–716/H808–40), are laboriously detailed and descriptive. And the birds of Ringing Island (F615–30/H729–46) or the Furred Cats and Semiquaver Friars do little to alleviate the overall lassitude the reader is obliged to overcome in order to reach the long projected, and probably spurious, word of the Bottle.[9]

Reading Rabelais, consequently, *all* of Rabelais, is hard work. So much so that many, if not most, readers skip over or skim through the lists and enumerations which, because of their paradigmatic and tautological structure, seem hopelessly peripheral and redundant. Yet if Rabelais took the time and trouble to write them, he undoubtedly meant for us to read them, to take the time and find the patience to decipher, for example, each and every title in the repertory of books in the St. Victor library, each and every article of Fastilent's anatomy (F500–6/H608–15). Are we not right in suspecting that the new flexibility afforded by the spatial economy of the printed page is partially responsible for the development of this phenomenon? In any event, close reading of even these mini-texts is indispensable if we are to evaluate the degree of intention and the property of invention invested in their production. But close reading encourages myopic interpretation, a consequence which Rabelais's writing clearly anticipates and renders more or less inevitable. As a result, we are more likely to arrive at a fuller understanding of discrete passages or episodes than of a complete book or the work as a whole.

Finally, can we explain laughter in Rabelais theoretically and methodically? Do Joubert, Bergson, Bahktin, or Baudelaire work in his case?[10]

Readers have not always shared Panurge's laughter in the great lady of Paris (F203–9/H291–7) or the Dindenault episodes (F448–54/H550–6). And not everyone is amused by the new way of building the walls of Paris (F182–6/H267–72), the antics of the Panzoult sibyl (F305–7/H402–4), or the chapters on the Decretals (F542–54/H651–5). The advent of feminism has made it increasingly difficult to laugh today at certain things which may have seemed amusing before, even to women readers. Does comedy lie in words or things, or in the eyes and ears of the reader? Increasingly, laughter has come to be viewed as a cultural matter, requiring analysis of the reasons for Pantagruel's or Panurge's amused reactions, reasons that seem at times to differ radically from our own. Whatever the case, comic and serious tend to combine in Rabelais, the one providing the other with a contrasting context and meaning. This double perspective explains why, when we attempt to separate them, each loses its integrity, and why readings influenced primarily by cultural or historical concerns have produced most of the confusion and controversy characteristic of contemporary Rabelais scholarship.

While Rabelais's miscellaneous writings are not numerous, they are not lacking in importance or interest. They include two letters in Latin, one to Guillaume Budé, the other to Erasmus; three in French from Rome to Geoffroy d'Estissac, Bishop of Maillezais; several facetious and/or satiric prognostications and almanacs, also in French; four dedicatory epistles in Latin prefacing Latin works; and, finally, the *Shadow Battle* in French, copied in great part from an Italian original. The letter to Budé (F735–7/H993–7), the foremost Hellenist of the day, affords the earliest known example of Rabelais's prose. It is noteworthy in that it demonstrates the young Franciscan's interest and proficiency in Greek, a language both suspect and little studied at the time, as well as a desire to enter into contact with the intellectual world beyond his monastery walls. In addition, it displays a marked predilection for learned banter and linguistic manipulation. Thus, when he qualifies – in Greek – his letter as "deficient in both ability and any knowledge of fine languages" (F735/H993–4), the sustained allusion to Plutus, the god of riches, in emphatic reference to Budé's work on Roman coinage, playfully underscores the contrary. Significantly, this is already Rabelais – even Alcofribas – in Latin and Greek.

The Roman letters (F762–77/H1000–17) are the most informative and stylistically straightforward of these non-fictional works. As such, they provide a convincing model for measuring the difference between Rabelais's ordinary and his "Rabelaisian" French. Both personal and official in nature, they include details of recurrent monetary difficulties, his successful petition to the pope for absolution from apostasy and authorization to continue medical practice, botanical observations and descriptions of packets of seeds for his protector in France, together with pertinent information on politics of the papal and various European courts. Still, there is very little of an intimate nature in these occasional writings, and Rabelais the man remains essentially the elusive author of a fabulous book.

In the final analysis, what makes his fiction so fascinating is less *what* he writes than the *way* he writes. His prose is dynamic, full of life and color, overflowing with many more words than things. This is not to say that writing in Rabelais is ultimately language play or play on language. His books are filled with allusions to the most pressing religious and political questions of the day. They refer as well to places and persons from his own life. What makes them both easy and difficult to read is their admixture of comic and serious, rendering one inseparable from the other. Even passages which appear only serious or comic are not always as unambiguous as they seem. Fact and fiction, play and ideology are so closely integrated into the very fabric of his writing as to form a new, displaced fictional reality, making it difficult to abstract his ideas on education, religion, society, or politics without disqualifying the very linguistic structure that promotes and validates them. To limit the interest of his book to a search for "substantific marrow" is as reductive as presenting it as words without end. Laughter allows Rabelais to achieve a kind of complex equilibrium between the two, resulting in a text in which the fictitious unfolds in relation to a vast array of literary, ideological, and cultural contexts. Carefully structured and deliberately written, his work is fragmented into a multitude of disparate themes and episodes, all of which seem to revolve in one way or other around the problematic relation between words and interpretation.

Thus, Rabelais's writing is designed to please as well as instruct, but never the one without the other. Readers are expected to realize that allusion to deeper meaning and ultimate utility are common *topoi* of comic fiction. Fiction purporting to be fact is another, and claims to veracity are developed with such pointed emphasis that they discredit themselves. Finally, the inclusion of titles, quotations, random samples of erudition, which are the ordinary accoutrements of learned treatises, tends to generate an intertextual discourse in which the techniques of authority are mediated and mocked. Many references are false, luring us into believing momentarily that our attention is being directed outside the book, whereas, in fact, they open onto perspectives which work only within its parameters. In alluding to literary precedent and suggesting thereby an interpretative mode for reading his works, Rabelais means not so much to establish an example of prior authority as to replace it with a superior one, that generated by his own substantial writing on the workings of his world. The fact that there are more words *on* Rabelais's book than *in* it is a clear and positive sign of its cornucopian promise. It implies as well that whatever we have to say or write about his writing is ultimately digressive, that his work, despite our questions and answers, remains resolutely intact in all its mysterious, seductive potential, forever open to old and new readings, each of which has the privilege of adding its particular line or layer of interpretation to the meaning and history of the text.

NOTES

1 For a comprehensive survey, see Lazare Sainéan's *La Langue de Rabelais*, 2 vols. (Paris: Boccard, 1922–3); also J. E. G. Dixon and and John L. Dawson, *Concordance des Œuvres de François Rabelais* (Geneva: Droz, 1992).

2 Rabelais's works have generated over the years so many studies that it would take a small library to house them all. However, they tend to fall into two distinct categories, namely those concerned with his ideas and those which try to account for his art. A selective representation of both tendencies might include Jean Plattard, *François Rabelais* (Paris: Boivin, 1932); Lucien Febvre, *Le Problème de l'incroyance au XVIe siècle: La religion de Rabelais* (Paris: Albin Michel, 1942); Abel Lefranc, *Rabelais: Études sur Gargantua, Pantagruel, le Tiers Livre* (Paris: Albin Michel, 1953); François Rigolot, *Les Langages de Rabelais* (Geneva: Droz, 1972; reprint 1996); Alfred Glauser, *Rabelais créateur* (Paris: Nizet, 1966) and *Fonctions du nombre chez Rabelais* (Paris: Nizet, 1982); Mikhail Bakhtin, *Rabelais and his World*, H. Iswolsky, trans. (Boston: MIT Press, 1968); Donald Frame, *François Rabelais: A Study* (New York: Harcourt Brace Jovanovich, 1977); Michael A. Screech, *Rabelais* (London: Duckworth, 1979); Floyd Gray, *Rabelais et l'écriture* (Paris: Nizet, 1974) and *Rabelais et le comique du discontinu* (Paris: Champion, 1994); Guy Demerson, *L'Esthétique de Rabelais* (Paris: SEDES, 1996); Edwin M. Duval's trilogy, *The Design of Rabelais's "Pantagruel"* (New Haven: Yale University Press, 1991), *The Design of Rabelais's "Tiers Livre de Pantagruel"* (Geneva: Droz, 1997), and *The Design of Rabelais's "Quart Livre de Pantagruel"* (Geneva: Droz, 1998). The Pléiade Rabelais, *Œuvres complètes*, Mireille Huchon and François Moreau, eds. (Paris: Gallimard, 1994) provides an authoritative and exhaustive commentary on Rabelais's life and works. From what we know about both, it is clear that Rabelais the man has become "Rabelaisian" through contamination with his works.

3 It seems strange that many, maybe even most, readers of Rabelais tend to take his "substantific" claim at face value, overlooking the fact that he applies it as well to fictitious books he pretends to have written.

4 There are a number of excellent studies on Rabelais's prologues. In chronological order, the following are among the most significant: Floyd Gray, "Ambiguity and Point of View in the Prologue to *Gargantua*," *Romanic Review*, 56 (1965), pp. 12–21; Leo Spitzer, "Ancora sul prologo al primo libro del *Gargantua* di Rabelais," *Studi Francesi*, 9 (1965), pp. 423–34; Jean Paris, *Rabelais au futur* (Paris: Seuil, 1970), pp. 11–47; Gérard Defaux, "Rabelais et son masque comique: *Sophista loquitur*," *Études Rabelaisiennes*, 11 (1974), pp. 89–135; Raymond La Charité, "Lecteurs et lectures dans le prologue du *Gargantua*,"

Études Rabelaisiennes, 21 (1988), pp. 285–92; Richard Regosin, "Opening Discourse," *François Rabelais. Critical Assessments* (Baltimore and London: Johns Hopkins University Press, 1995), pp. 133–47.

5 Further evidence is considered in Franco Giacone, ed., *Actes du colloque international de Rome: Rabelais, le "Cinquiesme Livre"* (Geneva: Droz, 2001).

6 We owe this piece of topographic discovery to Abel Lefranc's search for examples of reality in Rabelais's work. See his introduction to the critical edition of *Gargantua* (Paris: Champion, 1912), pp. lxxii–lxxxvii.

7 A significant increase in feminist and antifeminist literature occurred during the first half of the sixteenth century, and Rabelais's book dramatizes, in comic fashion, many of its themes.

8 For a detailed reading, see Paul Smith, *Voyage et écriture: Étude sur le "Quart Livre" de Rabelais* (Geneva: Droz, 1987).

9 Alternative endings are provided by the final chapter of *The Ringing Island* (published in 1562) and the supplementary chapter of the BN manuscript, appended in Frame's translation as chapters A16 and A 32 (pp. 716–32).

10 All of whom have written on the mechanics of laughter: Laurent Joubert, *Traité du ris* (1579); Henri Bergson, *Le Rire* (1924); Mikhail Bakhtin, "Rabelais and the History of Laughter", *Rabelais and his World* (Boston: MIT Press, 1968); Charles Baudelaire, "De l'essence du rire et du comique," *Curiosités esthétiques* (1868).

3

BARBARA C. BOWEN

Laughing in Rabelais, laughing with Rabelais

Rabelais must surely be one of history's most misunderstood authors. The seventh edition of the *Oxford Advanced Learner's Dictionary*, published in 2005, gives for "Rabelaisian": "dealing with sex and the human body in a rude but humorous way," completely ignoring the by-now undisputed facts about Rabelais: that he was a dedicated Erasmian evangelical (in the sixteenth-century meaning of that term) Christian, whose often-hilarious "chronicles" convey serious messages about religion, good government, good education, the conduct of the Ideal Prince, and the importance of friendship. Moderns may tend to assume that writers must be either serious or comic, but the Renaissance knew better; following the Roman poet Horace's celebrated adage "What's to prevent speaking the truth while laughing?" (*Satires* 1.1.24), Rabelais, like his mentors Erasmus and Thomas More (who made a joke on the scaffold moments before his execution), was a master at the melding of serious and laughable. This chapter will first provide some Renaissance background on humor, and then examine laughter, laughers, and the laughable in Rabelais's four books.

Background

Three important contexts shaped Renaissance views on laughter: the philosophical, the medical, and the rhetorical. The short poem "To The Readers" at the beginning of *Gargantua* (*Book 1* in all collective editions, but in fact the second book written), quotes a Latin tag which can be traced back to Aristotle (F2/H3). Frame's "For it is laughter that becomes man best" is actually a misleading translation of "risus proprium hominis," which means something like "laughter is specific to man" (as, for instance, neighing is specific to the horse). While in all historical periods there have been authorities who disapprove of laughter, Rabelais's view was shared by many Renaissance writers. Petrarch listed God's gifts to man as reason, speech, tears, and laughter;[1] nearer in time to Rabelais, Heinrich Bebel, in the preface to the second book of his *Facetiae* (*Jokes*, 1508–12) stated: "I am a man, I sometimes laugh";[2] and Paolo Cortesi's 1510 treatise on the cardinal claimed: "nothing is so akin to human nature as humor sprinkled with sophistication of speech, and nothing so characteristic of a man as to delight in a repertoire of witticism" (*De cardinalatu*, Book 2, chapter 9, "De sermone" ["Of Speech"]). Like Erasmus's *Praise of Folly* or Thomas More's *Utopia* (which is more amusing in the original Latin than in the English translation), Rabelais's "chronicles" are both hilarious and fundamentally serious.

Rabelais was a practicing doctor, and medical specialists – again since Aristotle – had often argued about laughter; where in the body does it originate? In the heart, the brain, the spleen, or the diaphragm (for gladiators, it was said, died laughing if their diaphragm were pierced)? Laurent Joubert, author of an entire medical treatise on laughter, opted for the heart (*Traité du ris*, 1579), while Rabelais apparently agreed with those who favored the brain, if we go by his description of Janotus de Bragmardo, Ponocrates, and Eudémon laughing so hard "that tears came to their eyes through the violent concussion of the substance of the brain, at which were squeezed out these lachrymal humidities and made to flow next to the optic nerves" (*F46/H53*).

We might have expected Dr. Rabelais to provide some examples of therapeutic laughter, especially as there are several in contemporary joke collections (for instance, a sick man is cured by laughing at the antics of a pet monkey), but he does not do so. He did, in the prologue to the first version of *Book 4* (1548; *F419/H719*), stress that the doctor's face should be "joyous, serene, pleasant, laughing, open," but the passage quoted above about Janotus is the only example of "medical" laughter in the four books.

Like all Renaissance humanists, Rabelais was thoroughly grounded in the Ciceronian rhetorical tradition, and critics have often noted that rhetoric is important in the world of his giants; for instance, Panurge in *Book 3* is among other things a dishonest rhetorician. Cicero's mini-treatise on jokes (*facetiae*) in Book 2 of the *De oratore* was revived by Petrarch and nourished numerous Renaissance works including Castiglione's *Book of the Courtier* (Book 2). Rabelais refers in his *Book 4* to "Cicero's facetious and joyous responses" (*F520/H630*), but perhaps surprisingly makes little use of the numerous joke collections he must have known; we feel that a skilfully placed *facetia* might have enlivened Ulrich Gallet's exhortation to Picrochole, for instance (*Book 1*, chapter 31), or Gargantua's speech to the vanquished after the battle (*Book 1*, chapter 50). Joking, for Cicero, was essential to the successful lawyer, but for the Renaissance it often characterized the Ideal Prince (at whom Castiglione's work is certainly aimed), as well as the congenial, witty humanists we meet in Erasmus's colloquy "The Fabulous Feast." I shall have more to say about rhetoric later in this chapter.

Laughter in Rabelais

Even if Victor Hugo had not described Rabelais as "one enormous roar of laughter," and even if numerous critics had not claimed that laughter is omnipresent in his "chronicles," we would expect it to be so, since he quotes "laughter is proper to man," knew about medical theories on laughter and was familiar with the rhetorical joke tradition. But is laughter omnipresent? In the first book written, *Pantagruel (Book 2)*, our hero laughs only twice, in chapters 15 and 26 (although in the latter we are told that "good old Pantagruel laughed at everything," F218/H307), and his father Gargantua only once, very heartily ("like a calf," F143/H225), when his son is born (*Book 2*, chapter 3). Panurge laughs a number of times (*Book 2*, chapters 14, 16, 17, 22), as do assorted anonymous characters, "those present" (F178/H263) and chambermaids (F208/H297).

We might expect more laughter in later books, but in fact there is less, and we may also note that the exclamations which seem to us to signal laughter do not always do so. In the first book Gargantua's "Ho ho ho!" is definitely laughter with delight at the birth of his son (F143/H227), and Pantagruel's "Ho ho, ha ha ha" expresses amusement at Panurge's suggested construction of the walls of Paris (F184/H269), while his "Ha, ha ha" is laughter at Panurge's boasting about his sexual prowess (F217/H307). But, and this supports Screech's contention that "laughter for its own sake needs no excuse in *Pantagruel*, though it does later,"[3] these exclamations will not always be so clear. In *Gargantua*, if Janotus de Bragmardo's "Ha, ha, ha" (F45/H52) indicates a grin of fatuous self-satisfaction, the archer's "Ha" (which Frame translates "Ah") in chapter 44 (F101/H110) is obviously a pleading syllable – he is begging for his life. Similar examples could be adduced from the third and fourth books.

In *Gargantua*, Grandgousier, the giant's father, is described as laughing (Frame translates "kidding") during the birth of his son (F21/H23), and Gargantua himself laughs only once, as a small child (F30/H34). Even more surprising is that the light-hearted, devil-may-care Frère Jean is only once depicted "chuckling" (F90/H107). Again, assorted minor or anonymous characters laugh: most strikingly, as already mentioned, Janotus and two of Gargantua's companions in *Book 1*, chapter 20, but also peasants in chapter 3, visiting servants in chapter 12, and shepherds in chapter 25. And in *Book 3* the only laughers are Carpalim, at Dr. Rondibilis's consolatory story about cuckoldry (F359/H458), Epistemon recalling his merriment at the performance of a farce in which Rabelais was one of the actors (F361/H460), and an otherwise unknown character named Tielman Picquet (F379/H478); in *Book 3*, chapter 19, Pantagruel, now a very different personality, refuses to laugh at a genuinely funny story.

Book 3 is the only one without action, concentrating on intellectual discussion. *Book 4*, to the reader's relief, returns to the epic adventure ambiance, and to at least a little laughter. Pantagruel, it is true, laughs only at the very end (chapter 67), but when listening to the ridiculous reasoning of the Potentate on the island of Ennasin he "nearly broke up" (F457/H559). Once more, a number of minor characters laugh: in a story by Frère Jean, the ladies who have played a trick on the lord of Guyercharois (chapter 10); Breton Villandry (chapter 11); several of Basché's servants during the trick played on the Shysteroos (chapters 12, 14, 15); Philemon and Zeuxis the painter who both died laughing (chapter 17); the monster Fastilent (chapter 32); Grosbeak, bishop of the Papimaniacs (chapters 52–3) and Messere Pantolfe (chapter 67).

So the cliché about laughter in Rabelais turns out, like so many clichés, to be a myth, and we are left wondering why his heroes laugh so little, and why they do not use laughter as a rhetorical weapon. But these are not the only relevant questions.

Functions of Laughter

Laughter, for most of us, is probably by definition good. "Laughter is the best medicine," we say, unconsciously echoing Renaissance physicians, or "Laugh and the world laughs with you," or "laughter is the universal language" – a fine example of wishful thinking. Rabelais leaves us in no doubt on this subject. In his first book, Panurge makes the ladies laugh by farting (F189/H276), hoots with nasty laughter himself at the discomfiture of the "fat puffed-out councillor," and laughs even harder when the councillor's page is unjustly beaten (F193/H280); sufficient indications that Panurge is not, despite Pantagruel's inexplicable fondness for him, an admirable character. A few chapters later, he also laughs nastily at the success of his stratagem to humiliate the Parisian lady (F208/H297), whereas Pantagruel merely finds the spectacle of dogs peeing all over the lady "very fine and novel."

Another kind of "bad" laughter is illustrated in *Book 1* à propos of Gargantua's childhood. Chapter 11, to explain the animal nature of the small child, consists mainly of a long series of clichés – children do not yet act according to the dictates of reason. Among these clichés are "he bit while laughing, laughed while biting" ("to bite while laughing" meant to deliver a reproach in a humorous manner) and "he tickled himself to make himself laugh" (F30/H34); two examples among many of pointless childhood activity. However, once Gargantua's humanist education has made a man of him, he need not renounce laughter; his one day a month of relaxation in the countryside includes a number of lighthearted activities including mocking and jesting (F61/H72).

Book 4 provides more detailed information about "bad" laughter. It can be an aid to hypocrisy, as in the Shysteroo episode, where the Lord of Basché instructs his servants (chapter 12) to laugh while beating the legal representatives arriving with a summons (ostensibly a ritual exchange of "pretend" blows after a wedding, but actually a real drubbing); this works so well the first time that when the second Shysteroo arrives they all laugh in anticipation (chapter 14), and in the climactic episode the "new bride," pretending to be wounded by Shysteroo, "was crying as she laughed, laughing as she cried" (F471/H574). The grotesque monster Fastilent is described in a variety of surrealistic ways, including a series of clichés reminiscent of those of the child Gargantua, one of which is "He laughed as he bit, bit as he laughed" (F506/H614); and Grosbeak, bishop of the Papimaniacs (who think the Pope is literally God on earth) concludes his lyrical praise of the Decretals in chapter 53 by bursting out laughing – but his laughter is presented in a decidedly animal context: "Here Grosbeak began to burp, fart, laugh, drool, and sweat . . . " (F553/H664).

So laughter, in Rabelais, is ambivalent. It can be hearty and healthy, but it can also betray an animal nature (Gargantua as a child, and Grosbeak), or signal a malicious character (Panurge), a hypocrite (Fastilent) or a strategic maneuver (the Lord of Basché's servants). But in either case, Rabelais's fictional characters laugh much less than we would assume, so the question is: Why were we expecting constant fictional laughter?

Laughing at Rabelais

The answer is simple enough: since the reader (I mean, of course, the instructed and alert reader who is well informed about the Renaissance and attuned to Rabelais's thought processes) laughs constantly, she or he misleadingly projects laughter on to the giants, their friends and their grotesque adventures. Even in English translation there is much rib-tickling material in the "chronicles," and we can see that our laughter has a variety of functions. Perhaps most obviously, we laugh at larger-than-life characters, some satirized and some merely amusing: the trickster Panurge (whose intentions are sometimes good and sometimes, as noted above, malicious), Picrochole the stupid ruler with his grandiose dreams of world conquest (Book 1, chapter 33), the Vergil-inspired Sibyl of Panzoust (*Book 3*, chapter 17) who adds picturesque and erudite color to Panurge's marriage quest, the giant Bringuenarilles who eats cooking-pots and windmills (*Book 4*, chapter 17), and many others.

It is usually clear how much satirical intent underlies the comedy, but not, I think, always. Janotus de Bragmardo, in the first edition of *Book 1*, was not a sophist but a Sorbonne theologian – and the Sorbonne was a powerful institution which could ban books and condemn authors to be burned at the stake. Was Rabelais hoping that laughter could be strong enough to disarm enemies, and did he later lose that hope? An even more doubtful case is the judge Bridoye, to whom Rabelais devotes four chapters (*Book 3*, chapters 39–42); are they a protracted joke aimed at fellow legal specialists, or a serious criticism of legal procedure? Critics disagree.

As well as outrageously comic characters, Rabelais loves the apparently straightforward description of an impossible event or situation: Pantagruel's emergence from his mother's womb preceded by sixty-eight salt-vendors with their mules, nine dromedaries loaded with hams and tongues, seven camels with eels, and twenty-five cartloads of leeks, garlic, onions, and chives (*Book 2*, chapter 2; *F142/H224*); anything so precisely enumerated, we think, must be factual. All readers surely laugh at this, as at the pilgrims swallowed by Gargantua and subsequently stranded in his garden by a flood of his urine (*Book 1*, chapter 38); the "conversation" between Panurge and Trouillogan the Pyrrhonian philosopher who refuses to give a straight answer to any question (*Book 3*, chapter 36); the battle pitting Pantagruel, Frère Jean, and a squadron of cooks against the Chitterlings (*Book 4*, chapter 41 – "sausages" would be a more exact translation), and many, many more.

There is no shortage of such ludicrous characters and situations, nor of surrealist descriptions (Fastilent's "notions" are "like snails crawling out of strawberries," *F502/H610*), amusing narrative surprises (the narrator's first encounter, in the impressive New World inside his giant master, is with a very ordinary peasant planting cabbages, *F239/H331*), and brusque changes of tone: Panurge's lyrical outburst to the lady of Paris – "O celestial gods and goddesses, how happy will be the man to whom you grant that boon to embrace this lady, to kiss her, and to rub his bacon with her" (*Book 2*, chapter 21; *F204/H292–3*) – is comic in English, though more so in the original. And of course we are intended to laugh at the obscenity – which is much rarer than many readers think: the child Gargantua's search for the perfect "ass-wipe" (*Book 1*, chapter 13; after his humanist education there will be no more mention of excrement); the involuntary defecation of the Limousin scholar (*Book 2*, chapter 6), the Englishman Thaumaste

(*Book* 2, chapter 19), and Panurge from fear of a cat he has taken for a devil (*Book* 4, chapter 67).

We laugh, too, at Rabelais's incorrigible irreverence, as he makes hilarious fun of medicine (in *Book* 2, chapter 33, Pantagruel swallows workmen in copper globes, who clean up the fecal matter accumulated in his stomach), law (the lawsuit between Kissass and Sniffshit is a light-hearted parody, *Book* 2, chapters 10–13), and, more seriously but at the same time comically, theology (in the long Papimania episode Rabelais is siding with his king who resents the all-powerful Catholic Church and its financial demands on France, *Book* 4, chapters 48–54). He also flaunts a host of other dislikes, including old-fashioned education (*Book* 1, chapter 14), church music (*Book* 1, chapter 27), intellectual snobs who speak Latinized French (*Book* 2, chapter 6), tall tales of the New World (*Book* 2, chapter 32), and believers in assorted methods of divination (*Book* 3, chapter 25).

Some of these episodes may strike us as light-hearted slapstick, but we need to be very careful here. During the *Book* 4 sea voyage, the companions land on the island of Ruach (*Book* 4, chapters 43–4), whose inhabitants live on wind and die farting; just an excuse for some farting jokes, we thought. But Florence Weinberg claims convincingly that this is satire specifically aimed at Dutch Protestants.[4] And we are not surprised that comedy can cover up serious satirical intent, as I believe it does in the Janotus de Bragmardo episode (which, as already noted, is received with the heartiest fictional laughter of all).

Linguistic comedy

So readers with no French can find much to enjoy in Rabelais, but in the original there is so much more, although even French readers today require a critical edition with copious footnotes. Rabelais's supreme gift was for a stunning linguistic inventiveness, in French and also in other languages, which is necessarily lost in translation.

Rabelais's intended reader was of course fluent in Latin, so that the jokes in the catalogue of the St. Victor library (*Book* 2, chapter 7) would be immediately obvious. Take, for instance, the Latin title *Maneries ramonandi fournellos*, which Frame translated as "The way to sweep out flues" (*F*156/*H*239), but an unfortunate misprint in the book replaced "flues" with "glues," which makes no sense. The author Eccius, or Eckius, was a well-known Catholic theologian, and Rabelais is thinking of a sexual metaphor, exemplified in a farce called *The Chimney-Sweep* in which an old man laments that he can no longer do his job with the vigor of his youth...[5] Chimneys also suggest fires, and as we have seen Catholic theologians were too often associated with the burning of heretics. Most of the titles in this library are asking for this kind of decoding, so that in translation a great deal is lost.

Rabelais loved to play with different varieties of Latin (the horrendous Latinized French of the scholar from Limoges [*Book 2*, chapter 6], the poor Latin spoken by ignorant Sorbonne theologians [*Book 1*, chapter 19]), and also with other languages: Greek, occasionally Arabic, and Hebrew (the Ruach mentioned above is the Hebrew word for "the spirit of God" at the beginning of Genesis). He enjoyed creating imaginary languages: Panurge, when asked by Pantagruel on their first meeting (*Book 2*, chapter 9) who he is, replies in thirteen different languages, of which three are invented; they are identified as "a language of the Antipodes" (*F*164/*H*247), Lanternese (the language of the country they will visit in *Book 5*), and the language of Pantagruel's own country, Utopia.

But it is Rabelais's inventiveness in French which is the most astonishing, and poses the greatest problems for translators; I can give only a few examples here. Onomatopoeia is difficult to transfer from one language to another, and Frame tends to stick quite closely to the original. During the *Book 4* voyage the companions encounter frozen words (*Book 4*, chapters 55–6) which unfreeze on the deck of the ship (*F*559/*H*670); Frame leaves intact *hin*, *brededin*, *brededac*, *bou*, *tracc*, *trr*, and *trrrrr*, and only slightly modifies *ticque*, *torche* and *lorgne*. Similarly, Frame leaves a Latin-French composite word like "circumbilivaginer" as it is: "circumbili-vaginating" (*F*349/*H*446), although part of the joke is lost; in French the Latin word *cum*, "with," is pronounced like *con*, "cunt."

Puns are also notoriously difficult to translate. In *Book 1*, chapter 27, Frère Jean celebrates his first appearance in the narrative with the first of many puns: to the prior's reproach that he is disturbing divine service ("le service divin") he responds with a crack about "le service du vin" (the wine service, *F*66/*H*78); Frame again has to resort to an explanation in parentheses. Earlier in the same book, Gargantua had taken refuge from importunate Parisian crowds on the top of Notre-Dame, whence he "bathed" with his urine those below "par rys" – "for a laugh" (*F*42/*H*48), which incident explains the name of the city, according to our narrator.

Translating names is another problem; Frame leaves many names in the original, which is not necessarily the ideal solution. In chapter 7 of *Book 1* we are told how Gargantua got his name: his father Grandgousier ("great gullet" in French), on hearing the noise made by the baby, exclaimed "Que grand tu as!" meaning "What a huge (gullet) you have!" Frame is obliged to give the non-reader of French an explanation in square brackets (*F*21/*H*23). And even when he does translate, something in the original can be lost, as in the case of an author/title in the St. Victor library: "Tartaretus *de modo cacandi*" (F154/H237). Frame renders this "Craparetus, *On the Methodology of Shitting*" which is correct as far as it goes (*tarter* did mean "to shit"), but ignores the dig at a certain theology professor Tartaret or Tateret of the Sorbonne (see *H1263*, note 8).

And what is a translator to do with an imaginary noun like "morderegrippipiotabirofreluchamburelurecoquelurintimpanemens" (F470/H574)? This is one of several such portmanteau words conveying violence in the Shysteroo episode; one of the Lord of Basché's grooms uses it to convey the beatings ostensibly suffered by himself and his fellows. The seventeenth-century translator of Rabelais, Thomas Urquhart, whose version often conveys the gusto of Rabelais's language quite well, hardly changes this at all: "morderegrippippiatabirofreluchamburelurecaquelurintimpaniments," which is quite effective; Cohen, author of the standard paperback edition of Rabelais, tries something different – "deathanddamnation-slashdashandpulverizing us on the shins" – which I think Rabelais would have liked; Raffel's solution is "beatthebloodyhelland-damnation into us," and Frame for once is quite inventive: "snatchatchadoodahodgepodgehumdrummings." Any one of these can make a reader smile, but not one can convey the precise flavor of Rabelais's French.

Conclusions?

So although Rabelais only once illustrates the therapeutic laughter which, as a doctor, he might be expected to approve, and although his fictional characters laugh less than we would expect, his readers find no shortage of hilarious characters, events, descriptions, and dazzling linguistic fireworks to chortle over. Sometimes their laughter is simply pleasurable, as at the description of Pantagruel's birth in *Book 2*, chapter 7, but frequently it is accompanied by appreciation of the satirical point being made, as with Janotus de Bragmardo and Grosbeak. We may ask, however, a final question: if "laughter" and cognates are not key terms in Rabelais's text, are there any such key terms? The somewhat surprising answer is yes: a key term is "joie," "joy." Pantagruel is characterized, at the end of *Book 3*, as "the ideal and exemplar of all joyous perfection" (F407/H506), and while none of the four definitions of "Pantagruelism" in the "chronicles" (*Book 1*, chapter 1; *Book 2*, chapter 34; prologues to *Books 3* and *4*) mentions laughter, the one in *Book 2* specifies that good Pantagruelists "live in peace, joy, and health, always having a good time" (F245/H337).

The word joy and related terms (gaiety, delight, and so on) are much more frequent in the text than those related to laughter. To give just a few examples: baby Gargantua is described as joyful (*Book 1*, chapter 7) and later he and his companions travel joyfully (chapters 16 and 42), while his education includes "joyfully" debating the properties of the food on the table (chapter 23). The *Book 3* prologue describes Diogenes as "joyous" (*F254/H346*), promises not just a "gallant" third book but a "merry" (*joyeux*) fourth (*F257–8/H350*) and a "real cornucopia of joyfulness and jesting" (*F259/H352*); Panurge's imagined Golden Age includes not laughter, but joy (*Book 3*, chapter 4). In *Book 4* the word occurs frequently, in the context of the arrival of Gargantua's messenger (chapter 3), the meeting with the ship full of merchants (chapter 5), and a number of other episodes full of "cheery remarks" ("joyeux propos," *F587/H695*). We might also note that the *Book 5* Prologue refers to "the joyous fruitful books of Pantagruelism" (*F611/H725*). For Rabelais it is the joy of the good Christian which should be the *proprium hominis*[6] – a joy which may very readily include laughter, but need not by definition do so.

Finally, I suggest that there are two basic reasons for the happy hilarity of Rabelais's readers (he claims explicitly that they laugh, in *Book 4*, chapter 38: "Now you're laughing at me, topers," *F518/H628*). First, he was a doctor, and in both the Old Prologue and the Liminary Epistle to *Book 4* he stresses that the doctor must "cheer up" his patient in order to cure him; Hippocrates compared the practice of medicine to "a combat and farce" (*F421/H518*), we are told. Secondly, as this quotation already suggests, Rabelais was a Renaissance humanist for whom rhetoric was of crucial importance both in literature and in life. So the doctor, like the orator, is to some extent a man of the theater; and whereas the doctor can certainly smile and look joyful to help his patients' morale, the orator may produce more comic effect by keeping a straight face, as strongly recommended by Quintilian (*Education of the Orator*, VI.3.26).

Laughter, then, while not frequently presented in the text of the "chronicles," is certainly the desired reader reaction; and so far from being "pure" laughter without ideological content, it is very often contributing to some satirical, or serious, end. The Dindenault episode (*Book 4*, chapters 5–8), in which Panurge takes an oratorical revenge on the merchant who postpones bargaining for his sheep in favor of florid oratory, is mainly light hearted (and a tribute to its source in the *Baldus* by Teofilo Folengo, a macaronic poem written in a mixture of Latin and Italian),[7] but the Limousin scholar's outrageously Latinate French (*Book 2*, chapter 6) makes pointed fun of intellectual snobs who want to "improve" the French language by importing Latin terms into it. Rabelais the rhetorician wants language properly used, as Rabelais the doctor wants to cure his France of the ills caused by ambitious rulers, bigoted theologians – and dishonest rhetoricians. It is our good fortune that his sense of humor, if properly understood, has traveled intact across the centuries.

NOTES

1 Quoted in Charles Trinkaus, *In Our Image and Likeness: Humanity and Divinity in Italian Humanist Thought*, 2 vols. (London: Constable, 1970), vol. 1, p. 400, note 35.

2 See Gustav Bebermeyer, ed., *Heinrich Bebels Facetien: Drei Bücher* (Leipzig: Hiersemann, 1931), p. 46.

3 Michael Screech, *Rabelais* (London: Duckworth, 1979), pp. 62–3.

4 Florence Weinberg, "Rabelais's Isle de Ruach (*Quart Livre*, 43–44)," *Romance Languages Annual*, 6 (1994), pp. 203–7; reprinted in *Rabelais et les leçons du rire: Paraboles évangéliques et néoplatoniciennes* (Orléans: Paradigme, 2000), pp. 195–205.

5 *Le Ramoneur de cheminées*, in *Recueil de farces (1450–1550)*, André Tissier, ed., 13 vols. (Geneva: Droz, 1989), vol. 4, pp. 111–66.

6 Barbara C. Bowen, "Rire est le propre de l'homme," in Jean Céard and Jean-Claude Margolin, eds., *Rabelais en son demi-millénaire: Actes du Colloque International de Tours (24–29 septembre 1984)*, Études Rabelaisiennes, 21 (Geneva: Droz, 1988), pp. 185–90.

7 See most recently the edition by Emilio Faccioli (Turin: Einaudi, 1989), although this is not the version of the *Baldus* which Rabelais knew.

4

FRANÇOIS CORNILLIAT

Interpretation in Rabelais, interpretation of Rabelais

Few works of fiction in the canon of French literature have been subjected to so many – and so widely divergent[1] – interpretations as Rabelais's *Gargantua* and *Pantagruel* chronicles; and few, beyond the great allegorical narratives of the Middle Ages, appear to give so central a role to interpretation itself, either as a premise or as a theme – by requesting it of actual or implied readers, or by showing fictional characters engaged in hermeneutic tasks, with effects ranging from the perplexing to the hilarious. The first book of *Pantagruel*, for example, offers a series of episodes in which what is said or signified defies comprehension. In one of the most amusing, Panurge and a philosopher named Thaumaste ("Admirable") hold a debate in which, at the latter's demand, only signs are used in lieu of the spoken word. The dispute is supposed to deal with the sulfurous secrets of geomancy and the Cabbala (F194/H282), or so Thaumaste believes: he proclaims himself convinced by Panurge's elaborate gestures, in which others might recognize common obscene signs instead of cabbalistic significations.[2]

Gargantua, for its part, begins with an Author's Prologue dedicated to the issue of interpretation, quickly followed by an opaque piece of verse, the *Antidoted Frigglefraggles* (F9–12/H11–14). Symmetrically, the book ends with a "prophetic riddle," also in verse, found on a bronze plate in the foundations of the newly built Abbey of Thélème. This "énigme" (composed for the most part by the poet Mellin de Saint-Gelais) announces the coming of a new "kind of men," who will spread strife among mortals, wreak havoc with the "round machine," and cost innocent animals their "bowels," before the "elect" get "refreshed at last." This prophecy saddens Gargantua, who takes it to mean "the continuance and upholding of divine truth" in the face of persecution; but Frère Jean, who gets the last word, rejects such "allegories and interpretations" for being too "ponderous," and claims that the riddle (whose author he identifies) is only the description of a "game of tennis" hidden under "obscure words": "the racket strings are made of lamb or goat guts; the round machine is the pelota or ball"; and "after the game, the players refresh themselves" (*F*130/*H*153).

Our present purpose is not to summarize interpretations of Rabelais, let alone to synthetize a "new" one. Other contributions will ponder the subjects – such as religion, or "ethics" in the general sense (the art of governing self, family, and society) – which the "Author"[3] of *Gargantua* claims are discussed in his books under the appearance of "derision and jest" (*F*4/*H*6). Our task is not to explore specific meanings attached to any one of these domains, but to convey a sense of the pervasiveness and ambiguity of interpretation, as an activity, a theme, or a problem in Rabelais's books.

Let us start with *Gargantua*'s beginning and ending: their symmetry may have had a clarifying purpose, if we accept Edwin Duval's suggestion[4] that in this second volume Rabelais rewrote not only the popular *Chroniques gargantuines*, but also his own *Pantagruel*, in an attempt to dispel misunderstandings triggered by the first book. Accordingly, the Author claims that it was not enough for readers to laugh at the earlier works' "mockeries, tomfooleries, and merry falsehoods": he warns us that the books' comical exterior may have been as misleading as that of the "Sileni" (little boxes painted with grotesque or frivolous pictures, but containing "fine drugs" or "precious stones") to which Alcibiades, in Plato's *Symposium*, compared his beloved Socrates – ugly, ridiculous, and "always gibbering" on the outside, yet supremely wise and virtuous within (*F*3/*H*5). Just as we should not judge Socrates on his appearance, we have to "interpret in a higher sense" what we presumed "was said casually."

Like "a dog coming upon some marrow bone," the prologue urges the reader,

> ...it behooves you to be wise enough to sniff out and assess these exquisite books...; then by careful reading...break the bone and suck out the substantific marrow – that is to say what I mean by these Pythagorean symbols, in the certain hope of being made more astute and brave by the said reading; for in this you will find quite a different taste and more abstruse doctrine, which will reveal to you some very lofty sacraments and horrific mysteries, concerning [our religion as well as] our political state and our domestic life.
>
> (*F*4/*H*7; translation corrected)

This passage suggests, quite explicitly, what possible content could be extracted from the book's "mockeries": high matters indeed, though not *too* high, not the kind that Thaumaste was after. At the same time, the Author uses mock-heroic language to make this very claim, so that we might wonder to what extent it should be taken seriously and thus itself receive the treatment that it advocates.

Just like that of the "Sileni" (which came from Plato via Erasmus),[5] the imagery that is recycled here is of the highest pedigree. While the epithet "substantific" belongs to the mock-heroic register, the metaphor of the marrow is borrowed from the tradition of biblical exegesis: from Saint Jerome on, it referred to the higher meaning hidden behind the "letter" of the Scriptures, from which it can be deduced by a method known as allegory (according to *H1064*, note 3, this "marrow," however, was vegetable in nature: the transposition of the metaphor to the animal kingdom gives it a different flavor). The Author then explains the signification of his own images: by calling them "Pythagorean symbols," he playfully invokes a prestigious esoteric tradition (via Erasmus again)[6] even as he proceeds to clarify the meaning of the bone metaphor, which is fairly obvious at this point. The message is that we, the readers, have to look for a *higher* meaning (*altior sensus*, another phrase borrowed from allegorical exegesis), which is supposed to make wiser people out of casual consumers looking for quick entertainment. Yet this lesson on the proper handling of "tomfooleries" is itself riddled with foolish-sounding claims regarding interpretation and its purported results: this "Author" will not remove his "comic mask" (as Gérard Defaux put it)[7] so as to instruct us on the best way to be properly instructed by his jokes.

Our predicament deepens as the prologue continues:

> Do you believe in all good faith that Homer, writing the *Iliad* and *Odyssey*, ever thought of all the allegories with which he has been calked by Plutarch, Heraclides Ponticus, Eustathius, Cornutus...?
>
> If you believe it, you come nowhere near my opinion..., which affirms that these were as little thought of by Homer as were the sacraments of the Gospel by Ovid in his *Metamorphoses*, as a certain Friar Booby [Frère Lubin], a real bacon-snatcher, has tried to demonstrate... (F4–5/H7)

This refers to another kind of allegory, concerning poetry and what we call "mythology." The "fables" involving gods and heroes, as deployed in poetic narratives, had long been interpreted so as to expose the moral, spiritual, or historical lessons that they were supposed to "veil." Common throughout antiquity, this practice took a different turn in the Middle Ages: attempts were made to extract Gospel-inspired meaning from pagan stories. In the fourteenth century, the gigantic *Ovide moralisé* poem did this with the *Metamorphoses*; adaptations ensued at the hands of other commentators, including one Pierre Lavin who may be Rabelais's "Lubin" here. But "humanist" writers and scholars, who developed a new respect for the cultural integrity of both Christian and pagan texts, typically rejected this type of allegory: for them it was still appropriate to mine a poet's fictions for

45

"serious" content, but it was no longer acceptable to mix up such lessons with the evangelical message – unless one did so in a humorous way.

The question, then, seems to be whether Homer ever thought up the meanings – whether pertinent or silly – that commentators bestowed upon his work:

> If you don't believe that,[8] on what grounds will you not do so with these merry new chronicles, although, while dictating them, I had no more thought of it than you...
>
> $\qquad\qquad\qquad\qquad\qquad\qquad\qquad\qquad\qquad\qquad$ (F5/H7)

As a method of reading, allegory does not consider itself bound by the author's "intention," which may be considered part of the "literal" sense. Here, the very fact that the author did not envision such higher meanings becomes the best reason to look for them, and the contrast between this position (no matter how sound methodologically) and his own previous hints produces a teasing effect. Thus we may be encouraged to presume that the real Rabelais, behind the "mask," knew exactly what he wanted to say about religion or politics.

Yet the Author proceeds to tell us that he only wrote this book while he was "eating and drinking," which is in fact "the right time for writing these lofty matters" without thinking about them at all:

> To me is due honor and glory to be called and reputed a good fellow and jolly companion, and in that name I am welcome in all good companies of Pantagruelists.
>
> ...Therefore interpret all my deeds and words in the most perfect sense; hold in reverence the cheese-shaped brain that is stuffing you with these fine idiocies, and, as best you can, always keep merry. $\qquad\qquad\qquad$ (F5/H7)

By appearing to abdicate all responsibility over the content of his text, Rabelais taunts the hated theologians of the Sorbonne, openly lambasted in *Pantagruel* and *Gargantua*, who did in fact find, and with good reason, subversive substance behind the farcical appearance of the books. But the Author, as Defaux has shown, is also asking for our sympathy:[9] to "interpret" is not just to discover a higher meaning inside his "idiocies," but to appreciate him and take his work "in the most perfect" way. At the beginning of *Book 3*, something similar will be said of Pantagruel's wisdom: "All things he took in good part, all actions he interpreted for the good; never did he torment himself, never did he take offense..." (F264/H357). And the prologue to the same book will define "Pantagruelists" as people who "never take in bad part things they know issue from a good, free, and honest heart" (F258/H351).

A "perfect" interpretation should not be satisfied with the simple act of opening the box or breaking the bone in order to savor their content. Socrates cannot be thus "opened": genuine wisdom has to be enjoyed *together* with the vulgar, funny exterior that protects and enables it by attracting our sympathy (as well as the malevolence of curmudgeons and fanatics). Therefore the Author-as-drunkard fulfills his promise, despite all appearances to the contrary: there may be another meaning there, which he may in fact have put there; but it will not do to break the charm, stop "drinking," and get serious in order to discover it. We have to find it while – or, rather, *by* – keeping merry and well disposed, which is easier said than done. This paradoxical undertaking becomes our responsibility as readers of goodwill – and it entails a measure of risk, as some readings are in fact stupider than others.

Let us now return to the riddle which closes *Gargantua*. We note that the giant does not have to "interpret" it to find a "higher sense": such a meaning (bolstered by the last ten lines, which were added by Rabelais and filled with evangelical references) speaks directly to his heavy heart. Frère Jean is the one who builds a carefree "allegory" (which happens to correspond to Saint-Gelais's original intention): thus the "round machine," which could refer to our planet or cosmos, now shrinks to the size of a tennis ball; and the gravest of spiritual and political problems is left to coexist, in our imagination, with an innocuous game in which conflict is resolved with a good drink by the fireside. This is a pedagogical example of what Mireille Huchon calls "steganographic art" (from the Greek *steganos*, "covered," "opaque"); she borrowed this notion from the late sixteenth-century writer Béroalde de Verville, who defined it as the art of concealing certain subjects under a pleasant appearance, so that some viewers or readers may be happy with the latter, while enlightened others access a higher order of signification.[10]

In a regular allegorical composition (with "allegory" now understood as a method of writing, by developing strings of metaphors), a material object – even a trivial one – could become the symbol of a higher, even divine, reality: a pair of glasses could be made to signify the cardinal virtues, and horse-riding gear the theological ones. In such cases (which Rabelais ridicules) there is nothing covert about the process of interpretation, which is guided by the text. But here the concrete and the divine enter into a dialogue in which they compete for our attention,[11] and they end up *discriminating* among hermeneuts instead of taking everyone for the same mandatory ride. In this new system, one is satisfied according to one's own lights. Interpretation then becomes a matter of opinion; and while all opinions are not equal (some readings are "higher" than others), we should remember that Frère Jean's explanation is not absurd. Moreover, the giant and the monk are the merriest of friends – and indispensable to one another. Sometimes a lowly, entertaining interpretation can serve as foil to one that is high minded and morally urgent; or a severe, lofty interpretation finds itself undermined by a trivial and cheerful one (as happened in the Thaumaste episode of *Pantagruel*). Yet here, both views are left for the reader to compare, without another word of guidance; both meanings dance in front of our eyes in a kind of anamorphosis.

So the "company" that Gargantua and Frère Jean keep together could be construed as a *type* of what the Author had in mind when he invited us to drink to his health while reading his book. Yet if Socrates embodies the cohabitation between low form and high content, laughter and serious matter, here this dialectic is realized in a less compact fashion: although they are friends, and although one *could* interpret their interpretations "in good part" so as to reconcile them, there is no denying that the monk and the giant disagree. To get a larger sense of what is at stake here, let us jump to a famous episode of *Book 4*, in which the navigators are startled by "voices and sounds . . . of men, women, children, and horses" (F556/H667) that come from nowhere.[12] Panurge is terrified, and Pantagruel wonders: could these disembodied sounds come from another world? Or from the severed head of Orpheus? Perhaps they were frozen by winter and are thawing out only now – a phenomenon which Antiphanes, one of Plato's friends, compared to the philosopher's teaching remaining stuck in the brains of children until they have grown old, at which point they begin to understand it. Thus the mystery may allegorize the very problem of interpreting an "abstruse doctrine."

The skipper confirms that these sounds, produced by a battle between the "Arimaspians" (one-eyed people)[13] and the "Nephelibates" (cloud-walkers), were indeed frozen by the Arctic winter and are now beginning to thaw. Now reassured, Panurge wishes to *see* the frozen words. Pantagruel obliges by grabbing some; the companions are dazzled by their brilliant colors, less so by the sounds (horrible cries and combat noises) that they release as they melt. Panurge wants to see more; for his part, the narrator would like to preserve some "motz de gueule": "red" words, in heraldic terms. In each case Pantagruel objects: it is improper to give, sell, and above all keep words, especially "motz de gueule" (which also means "bons mots," witticisms that please both brain and mouth: "lusty jests" in Frame, F558/H669), as though they were material things, when in fact "you never lack" them and always have them "in hand," at least "among all joyous Pantagruelists" (F559/H671). Thus the problem of the frozen words' meaning and origin transforms into the seemingly different issue of what to *do* with words, no longer understood as mysterious signs or utterances, but as the kind of spontaneous discourse that circulates between friends. Users are being both indulged about and warned against their *lust* for words; they may or may not notice that this verbal candy originated in a merciless battle between two nations, one of which is half-blind while the other walks on clouds. Pantagruelian friendship, within which language and meaning are exchanged while remaining perpetually fresh, is thus cast as an alternative to a world in which some people are at each other's throats while others, from the safe distance that words seem to provide, enjoy what they "see" – but in fact misunderstand.

How are we to interpret this shift from the problem of interpreting to the art of fraternizing? The episode suggests that these practices are not incompatible, and may share a common enemy: to stash beautiful words for one's own private use is to compromise their integrity. But this does not clarify the desired relation between hard-earned individual insight and harmless collective delight: should we consider the latter an alternative, a complement, a pathway to the former? Should this relation even be defined according to one hermeneutic model? We also note that it is Pantagruel's friends (Panurge and the narrator) who misconstrue what to do with words: the enemy is among "us." There is a discrepancy between theoretical Pantagruelism, in which different things may be understood, but all "in good part," and practical Pantagruelism, which is exposed to actual misunderstandings[14] and has to include, in Panurge, someone who cannot share the company's ethos.[15]

The "frozen words" episode triangulates the issue of high vs. low, serious vs. frivolous: there are good and bad ways to indulge one's sense of fun. But triangulation is theoretical: in reality, the same people can be involved in good and bad play; the elite of the "elect" is not – contrary to the truly utopian Thélème – immune from the woes of the world. Some Pantagruelists dream of selling or hoarding words in the middle of the very "company" that should teach them otherwise. We – characters, readers, and writers alike – make the mistake of taking our pleasure in the wrong place, about the wrong object, while Pantagruel gently towers over us all. One could read in this light the many passages in which the books' unreliable narrator oversells his own interpretations – whether or not he may be "right": thus in *Gargantua* on the meaning of colors, or at the end of *Book 3* on the enigmatic plant known as "Pantagruelion."[16]

To what extent, then, can the Pantagruelian "company," *as* a company, be true to its dual nature as though it were a kind of collective Socrates? The closing of *Gargantua* does provide a possible model. We have seen that the "higher" comprehension of the riddle was both immediate and painful to the giant – while the monk offered an elaborate joke. Thus the pleasant side did not function as a mere "bone" to be "broken": even though Gargantua's torment is profound, he might also find solace in the idea of a "game" – if shared among true Pantagruelists. Steganography can feed the most arrogant elitism, as an exercise in which the enlightened alone understand the stakes, while lesser minds play with trifles. There is a great deal of tension between this cultural conceit and the inclusive ideal of *caritas* (charity) commanding what Edwin Duval calls "*moral* interpretation":[17] not only would the latter wrap high meaning in joyful play, but it might prefer a wrong-headed yet good-hearted reading to an accurate yet hostile one. Frère Jean in fact shows us that an earthy but friendly explanation can *also* be valid at its own level; behind the monk, however, lurks the much tougher case of Panurge, whose moral delinquency worsens as he returns in *Book 3*.

At the end of the so-called *Book 5*,[18] after Pantagruel, Panurge and their companions finally hear the word of the Divine Bottle ("Trinch," "Drink" in German), "the noble pontiff" Bacbuc "interprets" it thus:

> If you have noted what is written in Ionic letters over the door into the temple, you have been able to understand that in wine truth is hidden. The divine Bottle sends you to it; you yourselves be the interpreters of your own undertaking. (*F710/H834*)

The inscription stated that "In wine [is] truth" (Erasmus, *Adages*, I. vii.17). After Panurge hears the word, he drinks from a flask full of wine, and inquires (not without irony) if this was "all that was meant to be conveyed by the word of the greatest of great bottles." Bacbuc's response is a hymn to the powers of wine, which heralds the revelation brought forth by absorbing this holy substance. The oracle said it literally – one has to "drink" in order to find truth – while saying nothing whatever about the truth in question.

The word requires an interpretation; but in fact the meaning is obvious[19] (assuming minimal knowledge of Germanic languages): there is no obscurity at the literal level. Bacbuc, however, will not explore figurative levels of meaning. Instead of an opaque word requiring a competent hermeneut, we have a transparent one that delays and displaces interpretation: "you" will have to do it by "yourselves." Could this mean "drinking" in the literal sense, as though from a magic potion? When Bacbuc admonishes the pilgrims to become the "interpreters" of their own "undertaking," she points to a different kind of revelation: by being sent back to "drinking," the truth-seekers are in fact left to their own devices. They will have to interpret whatever insight this "drinking" gives them, including what it consists of in the first place.

The power of wine may be understood in all kinds of substantial and metaphorical ways (see, for instance, what Weinberg and Naya make of this motif).[20] In *Gargantua*, Frère Jean distinguishes between "service du vin," "wine service," and "service divin," "divine service" (*F66/H78*), in order to rebuke his fellow monks' ill-timed devotion to the latter, and to buttress his own right to defend the monastery's vineyard against invaders.[21] In *Book 5*, Bacbuc insists that "de vin divin on devient," "from wine we incline to the divine" (*F710/H834*): the pun that Frère Jean had used in order to separate now serves to reunite, and should be understood in Platonic terms (as an allusion to "Bacchic enthusiasm," one of four kinds of God-inspired "furies" described by the philosopher Marsilio Ficino),[22] or in Christian terms (as an allusion to a host of biblical and evangelical symbols). These versions of the wine/divine relationship are neither incompatible nor identical: timing and intention determine each case's degree of appropriateness. Bacbuc tacitly acknowledges this when she extols the mystic virtues of wine but places the burden of interpretation back on the drinkers' shoulders: revelation will not suspend but *activate* a duty to understand – not just the revelation itself, but what we sought in it and intend to make of it. Not only the word of the Bottle, but any meaning we assign to it, is only the beginning: interpretation is not a last "word," but an undertaking in search of its own understanding.

Pantagruel warmly approves; as he reminds Panurge, "I said as much to you the first time you spoke to me about it. So *Trinch*; what does your heart tell you when roused by Bacchic enthusiasm?" (*ibid.*). Again such "enthusiasm" could be merely channeled by the truth-seeker. Here, on the contrary, it confirms a moral set-up that the giant had established at the beginning of *Book 3* (most of the pseudo-*Book 5* may have been *Book 3*'s primitive sequel).[23] When Panurge first asks his master whether he should get married, Pantagruel gives a series of contradictory answers ("get married then"/"then don't get married"), responding each time to a new argument (drummed up by Panurge) for or against matrimony. Unaware of his own wavering, Panurge criticizes his master's "contrary repetitions," to which Pantagruel replies: "Aren't you certain of your will? The main point lies there; all the rest is fortuitous and dependent on the fated dispositions of heaven" (*F284/H379–80*). The giant sees nothing logically wrong or semantically obscure with his responses: they merely send Panurge back to the conflicting impulses of his own "will."

This paradoxical advice is repeated further in *Book 3*, when Panurge comes back to Pantagruel with a poem written by the dying poet Ramina-grobis, whom he was sent to consult on the matter of his marriage under the rationale that poets are divinely inspired (poetry being another kind of "fury" according to Platonic theory), especially when they approach death. As adapted by Rabelais from an original generally attributed to the poet Guillaume Cretin, the poem features the refrain "Take the lady, take her not" (*F318/H417*), from which Panurge concludes that the old man is a "sophist," answering in "disjunctives" (mutually exclusive alternatives) so as to be right in all cases. Pantagruel's reaction is very different:

> I haven't yet seen a reply that I like better. He means, in sum, that in the undertaking of marriage each man must be the arbiter of his own thoughts and take counsel of himself. Such has always been my opinion, and I told you as much the first time you spoke to me about it. (F347/H443-4)

The giant goes on to diagnose his friend's moral illness, previously described by Plato and Erasmus:[24] it is his "philautia," his "self-love," which blinds Panurge[25] and prevents him from making up his mind, as well as from interpreting messages that are confusing in appearance only. Raminagrobis's poem is indeed ambiguous from a logical standpoint; yet such ambiguity only remains obscure as long as one does not refer it back to the diversity of human behavior – for which it is equally right to marry or not to marry. Interpretation in this case dispels obscurity not by clarifying the internal meaning of the poet's sentences, but by emphasizing their external relevance to different individuals, who are expected to be their own "arbiters."

The reader, however, is left with another problem: what are we to make of the giant's initial exposé on the value of prophesying at the point of death? This is the argument that persuaded Panurge to go hear the poet's song, in the hope that "Apollo" himself would resolve his doubt. The poem's wit is anything but prophetic, and Raminagrobis's own attitude ("joyful bearing, open face, and luminous glance," F318/H417) is a model of self-consciousness, on the part of a good Christian preparing to meet his Maker. Further, when the time comes to interpret, Pantagruel seems to forget all that he has said about divine inspiration. He praises a non-committal opinion that was already his, regarding the human dimension of our choices: we should remain aware of our limits, and do as best we can. Far from hearing a god who solemnly tells us what will happen or what to do, we read a man who insists, in a whimsical way, that it is up to us.

This is why Duval concludes that Pantagruel could not mean what he said about the divine origin of the poet's swan song.[26] Indeed the entire set-up of *Book 3* becomes troubling: after declaring that Panurge should take advice from himself, Pantagruel proceeds to organize a series of divinatory consultations about what will happen to him. Each such consultation (using verses read at random, the patient's own dream, a decrepit pseudo-Sibyl, a mute, and a fool) requires some preliminary persuasion, and a subsequent interpretation: one oracle after the other is shown by the giant to "predict" that the *philaute* (self-lover) will be cuckolded, beaten, and robbed by his wife (Raminagrobis's contribution is exceptional in that the poet does not forecast Panurge's fate, but instead sends him back to his own choosing).

The oracles "speak" in a fairly clear fashion, which Panurge alone insists on reading "the other way around," spending treasures of sophistic invention in the process. When he dreams that his wife will plant "two pretty little horns over [his] forehead," Pantagruel has no trouble deducing that he will be cuckolded, but Panurge counters that Diana and other gods wore horns innocently, and that his own will be "horns of abundance" (F298/H395). It is doubtful that Rabelais, in episodes such as these, meant to imply that all interpretations are acceptable and should peacefully coexist. Let us assume that Pantagruel is right, and that Panurge, blinded by self-concern, is wrong; the trickster's denials are a far cry from Frère Jean's playful rebuttal of Gargantua. Yet that is only the first of the questions raised here.

Why is Pantagruel doing this? Given the distance between his lectures on prophecy and the crassness of the supposed oracles, are we to conclude that his words are spurious? If the giant means to educate Panurge by showing him that any attempt at foreseeing the future will only stir up images of his fears, why does he fail so spectacularly? Other troubling problems arise on Panurge's side: is he someone with whom we should sympathize because he is "one of us" – or just a target for enlightened readers to laugh at? There is no denying the charm of Panurge's rhetorical skills, especially when his cause is hopeless. That he can touch us against all odds is sufficiently proved by the many critics who take his side and refuse to give themselves over to the giant's enigmatic charity (Tournon, for example, offers a subtle "defense" of Panurge).

Pantagruel, the perfect prince, does love Panurge, and manages to size him up without condemning him;[27] but can real readers, struggling to figure out their strange relationship, be at once so magnanimous and so lucid? What if their determination to take Panurge "in good part" leads them to deny his problem? What if they have to deny his appeal in order to understand the wrong in him? The notion that charitable embrace should prevail over cold deciphering may well define ethics *in* Rabelais,[28] but in truth readers *of* Rabelais, imperfect Pantagruelists all, will often be torn between the two modes, because they love what they read yet cannot afford *not* to understand it, in the manner of "Friar Booby." Panurge is the touchstone of this dilemma. Such is the human dimension of Rabelaisian comedy: appreciation and interpretation contaminate each other, and *involve* us in a manner that cannot be reduced to "the terms of the debate" – for *we* are the terms of the debate. What remains true is that no interpretation should fail to interpret itself just like any other "undertaking": again, easier said than done.

Panurge's *philautia* is both an obvious target and a troubling experience that also taints us; Pantagruel's wisdom is both an ideal to be pursued and something that we are unable to share in. It is Pantagruel who, at the end of *Book 3*, agrees to follow Panurge in his quest for the oracle of the Divine Bottle: the giant has to know that the hunt will lead nowhere, but his "prognosis" is that "along the way we won't breed melancholy" (*F397/H495*). As a result, the community of the "elect," while sailing through the monstrous, war-torn world of *Book 4*, also has to deal with Panurge's cowardice and assorted flaws. He is the grotesque face of Socrates trying to function on its own; the "Silenus" that will not quietly "open" to let some essence shine through. Panurge makes the undertaking necessary, but unable to interpret itself; for if it did, it would recognize its own vanity. Pantagruel, on the other hand, is by definition able to interpret the undertaking, but that is because he finds it useless – and yet, somehow, worthwhile.

Without Panurge, it would be *easier* for a Pantagruelian undertaking (and for our reading of it) to merrily keep interpreting itself; and for the art of steganography to assume a kind of irenic harmony between its "high" and "low" levels, as happens between Frère Jean and Gargantua. But the jolly monk marks the limit beyond which Pantagruelism, as a universal moral project, gets *disturbed* by the stubborn carnality of bodies and signs – which it insists on treating charitably. Pantagruel himself may remain serene, but his company hurtles from trouble to trouble, and it is a measure of Rabelais's "comic courage" (as Thomas Greene puts it) that it welcomes such a disturbance. With Panurge, "shit happens," as he demonstrates by soiling himself at the end of *Book 4* – which certainly does not "breed melancholy," but does not attest to moral progress either: before a final call to "drink",[29] the wretch ends up claiming, with typical bravura, that his fear-induced excrement is nothing but "Hibernian saffron" (*F592/H701*). Thus human interpretation remains both indispensable and chronically flawed: for it is not just a matter of "seeing through a glass darkly,"[30] but also of trying (or pretending) to see through a blind spot.

NOTES

1 The problem is not new: see Marcel de Grève, *L'Interprétation de Rabelais au XVIe siècle* (Geneva: Droz, 1961). For a sample of conflicting modern views, see François Rigolot, *Les Langages de Rabelais* (Geneva: Droz, 1972; reprint 1996); Gérard Defaux, *Pantagruel et les sophistes: Contribution à l'histoire de l'humanisme chrétien au XVIème siècle* (The Hague: Nijhoff, 1973); Terence Cave, *The Cornucopian Text: Problems of Writing in the French Renaissance* (Oxford: Clarendon Press, 1979); Michael Screech, *Rabelais* (London: Duckworth, 1979); Jerome Schwartz, *Irony and Ideology in Rabelais* (Cambridge:

Cambridge University Press, 1990); Carla Freccero, *Father Figures: Genealogy and Narrative Structures in Rabelais* (Ithaca and London: Cornell University Press, 1991); Edwin Duval, *The Design of Rabelais's "Pantagruel"* (New Haven: Yale University Press, 1991); Michel Jeanneret, *Le Défi des signes: Rabelais et la crise de l'interprétation à la Renaissance* (Orléans: Paradigme, 1994); André Tournon, *"En Sens agile": Les acrobaties de l'esprit selon Rabelais* (Paris: Champion, 1995); Guy Demerson, *L'Esthétique de Rabelais* (Paris: SEDES, 1996); Gérard Defaux, *Rabelais agonistes: Du rieur au prophète. Études sur "Pantagruel," "Gargantua," "Le Quart Livre,"* Études Rabelaisiennes 32 (Geneva: Droz, 1997).

2 For a full reading of this episode, see Duval, *Design of Rabelais's "Pantagruel,"* pp. 75–84.

3 He is not called "Alcofribas" as in *Pantagruel,* but will recover this name after 1542.

4 Duval, *Design of Rabelais's "Pantagruel,"* pp. 148–9.

5 Erasmus, *Adages*, III.iii.1 (*Sileni Alcibiadis*); see also *Enchiridion Militis Christiani* (*Handbook of the Christian Soldier*), XIII, and *Praise of Folly*, XXIX. Jesus is the ultimate "Silenus"; hypocrites are *inverted* "Sileni."

6 Erasmus, *Adages*, I.i.2; see James Helgeson, "'Ce que j'entends par ces symboles pythagoricques': Rabelais on Meaning and Intention," *Études Rabelaisiennes*, 42 (2003), pp. 75–100.

7 Defaux, "Rabelais et son masque comique," in *Rabelais agonistes*, pp. 407–53.

8 For a clarification of this clause (and of the whole prologue), see Edwin Duval, "Interpretation and the 'Doctrine absconse' of Rabelais's Prologue to *Gargantua*," *Études Rabelaisiennes*, 18 (1985), pp. 1–17.

9 See Gérard Defaux's seminal reading in *Marot, Rabelais, Montaigne: L'écriture comme présence* (Paris: Champion, 1987), pp. 101–24.

10 Huchon, introduction to *Gargantua*, in Rabelais, *Œuvres complètes*, p. 1042.

11 See Véronique Zaercher, *Le Dialogue rabelaisien. Le "Tiers Livre" exemplaire* (Geneva: Droz, 2000).

12 See Schwartz, *Irony and Ideology*, pp. 192–4; Defaux, *Marot, Rabelais, Montaigne*, pp. 124–42, and *Rabelais agonistes*, pp. 517–36; Edwin Duval, *The Design of Rabelais's "Quart Livre de Pantagruel"* (Geneva: Droz, 1998), pp. 37–9.

13 The text prints "Arismapiens," which may be a mistake – or not; see Marie-Luce Demonet, *Les Voix du signe: Nature et origine du langage à la Renaissance, 1480–1580* (Paris: Champion, 1992), p. 380.

14 See Jan Miernowski, "Literature and Metaphysics: Rabelais and the Poetics of Misunderstanding," *Études Rabelaisiennes*, 35 (1998), pp. 131–51.

15 Apart from one or two exceptional moments (see *Book 4*, chapter 65).

16 See *Gargantua*, chapter 10 (cf. Defaux, *Rabelais agonistes*, pp. 432–7); *Book 3*, chapters 49–52.

17 Edwin Duval, *The Design of Rabelais's "Tiers Livre de Pantagruel"* (Geneva: Droz, 1997), pp. 188–91, quotes from Erasmus's paraphrases of the Gospels, regarding the Christian duty to "interpret in the best part."

18 The posthumous *Book 5* was probably concocted from discarded drafts found in Rabelais's papers; see Huchon's notice in Rabelais, *Oeuvres complètes*, pp. 1595–1607.

19 Not that this "universal" word is devoid of resonance; see Demonet, *Les Voix du signe*, pp. 567–72.

20 Florence Weinberg, *Rabelais et les leçons du rire: Paraboles évangéliques et néoplatoniciennes* (Orléans: Paradigme, 2000); Emmanuel Naya, *Rabelais: Une anthropologie humaniste des passions* (Paris: Presses Universitaires de France, 1998).

21 See Guy Demerson, *Humanisme et facétie: Quinze études sur Rabelais* (Orléans: Paradigme, 1994), pp. 171–89; and François Rigolot, "'Service divin, service du vin': L'équivoque dionysiaque," in M. Bideaux, ed., *Rabelais-Dionysos* (Montpellier: Laffitte, 1997), pp. 15–28.

22 See Marsilio Ficino, *Commentary on Plato's Symposium*, VII.xiv, Sears R. Jayne, ed. and trans., reprint (Putnam, CT, and New York: Spring Publications, 2000).

23 The Bottle episode was the original ending conceived before the creation of the current *Book 4*. See Huchon's notice, pp. 1603–4; and Edwin Duval, "De la Dive Bouteille à la quête du *Tiers Livre*," in Michel Simonin, ed., *Rabelais pour le XXIe siècle* (Geneva: Droz, 1998), pp. 265–78.

24 Erasmus, *Praise of Folly*, L; and *Adages*, I.iii.92; Plato calls *philautia* the source of all ills (*Laws*, V, 731d).

25 Another source is Horace, *Carmina*, I.xviii.14: "caecus amor sui," "blind love of self."

26 See Duval, *The Design of Rabelais's "Tiers Livre de Pantagruel,"* pp. 99–102; Raminagrobis may even be an actor playing a dying man.

27 See Ullrich Langer, *Perfect Friendship: Studies in Literature and Moral Philosophy from Boccaccio to Corneille* (Geneva: Droz, 1994), pp. 91–114.

28 Thus, for Duval, interpretation in *Book 3* is "never primarily a question of hermeneutics... but always essentially a question of moral judgment – of forgiving and forbearing, as opposed to judging and condemning" (*The Design of Rabelais's "Tiers Livre de Pantagruel,"* p. 196).

29 The last word of *Book 4* ("Beuvons!") reprises, in a "more subtle" manner (Huchon, p. 1607), the "Trinch" that Rabelais had first attributed to the Bottle.

30 See Saint Paul, 1 Cor. 13: 12. The whole chapter (on charity, prophecy, and imperfect vision) is relevant.

5

NEIL KENNY

Making sense of intertextuality

Rabelais's writing bristles with visible, subtle, or fictitious[1] traces of other texts. Most obviously, like much sixteenth-century writing, it is saturated by the ancient texts, especially Greek and Roman, which humanists cherished. Yet the case of Rabelais is also specific. Even by his period's standards, the range of what he rewrites is extremely eclectic. He incorporates alien texts into narrative fiction in imaginative ways which constantly push the reader to confront self-consciously problems of interpretation.

Some pre-existing texts are incorporated virtually verbatim or in the form of a translation, but without a quotation being signalled. Some are quoted, cited, paraphrased, parodied, satirized, alluded to. Some are clearly identified within Rabelais's text, others are not. Some provide him with motifs, narrative structures, styles, and specific terms, which he reworks. Many of these modes are vernacular variations on practices of imitation which were now taught in France in humanist colleges. Boys were trained to rewrite an ancient text in various ways, on a sliding scale of increasing distance from it, from translation (*translatio*) to paraphrase (*paraphrasis*) to imitation of its style and/or themes (*imitatio* in a narrow sense) to allusion (*allusio*).[2] A single composition could rework several texts. This technique, known as *contaminatio*, is at work throughout Rabelais's chronicles.

Pupils were trained not only to rewrite individual texts, but also to enrich their own written or spoken Latin with choice excerpts from the full range of their classical reading. The best-selling rhetoric textbook by the great humanist Desiderius Erasmus, *De duplici copia rerum ac verborum* (*On the Twofold Abundance of Words and Things*), first published in 1512, was widely used in northern Europe, in and after Rabelais's time, to teach students how to extract and recycle in this way.[3] Erasmus's textbook advised students how to enter excerpts from their reading under general headings in their own notebook, for future reapplication in their compositions. He called many of those excerpts commonplaces (*loci communes*). They and other fragments taken from ancient texts were also listed in printed reference books.[4] Like other writers, Rabelais drew some of his materials from such ready-made humanist research tools rather than directly from the ancient texts themselves.

He and his contemporaries would not have dignified their use of such recent intermediaries by calling it imitation. Indeed, where he imitates an ancient via a modern reference book, he sometimes mentions the former but rarely the latter. Yet the fact that reference books were used is important: it determined the fragmentary form in which he read and rewrote some ancient texts. That is one reason why the modern term "intertextuality" encapsulates better than the period term "imitation" the full range of relationships between his texts and others. If we use "intertextuality" (coined by Julia Kristeva in the late 1960s) in the general sense of a relationship between texts that may be of any kind, then the term can keep open – or simply pose – the question of what exactly that relationship is in any particular instance, rather than prejudging it, as do terms such as "source", "influence", "borrowing", or "authority," which designate particular modes of intertextuality.[5] The latter term keeps similarly open the question of the emotional tenor of the relationship between a text and (what I am calling) its subtexts. The relationship could range from respect to rivalry, from adulation to aggression, from acceptance to rejection.[6]

"Intertextuality" describes reading as well as writing, but not in the same way as "imitation" does. "Intertextuality" designates not only, say, how Rabelais wove into his writing numerous subtexts which he had read, but also how readers have always inevitably interpreted his texts by applying other texts *they* have read, including ones from after Rabelais's lifetime.[7] Even if one focuses – as the present chapter seeks to – only on those texts which Rabelais himself read and reworked, it is still impossible to draw up a definitive list of them. The inclusion of some depends on one's interpretive methods.

Rabelais's subtexts

Ancient

The Bible, Old Testament and New, is a pervasive subtext in Rabelais's chronicles, quoted, cited, paraphrased, and imitated in numerous ways.[8] Among ancient "pagans,"[9] the authors reworked in the most prominent or sustained fashion are predominantly Greek rather than Roman: the philosopher Plato, the medical writers Hippocrates and Galen (see Antonioli), the satirist Lucian of Samosata,[10] and Plutarch the writer on history, customs, and morals.[11] These ancient Greeks had a paradoxical aura of novelty in

Rabelais's time. Some (Lucian and Plutarch) had only become known to the West thanks to humanist rediscovery of them. Although others (Plato, Hippocrates, Galen) had been known in the Middle Ages, new works by them had been recovered by humanists. And even the previously known works had been renewed by being made available by humanists in the original Greek rather than the familiar Latin translation. Rabelais read some of them at least partly in Greek. Perhaps the only Roman author to be woven into Rabelais's chronicles as much as these Greek ones is Pliny the Elder, whose *Historia naturalis* (*Natural History*) is a huge collection of supposed facts about the natural world.

Rabelais's subtexts include not only discrete works, but broader discursive traditions. Let us take the example of Cicero and Aristotle, associated perhaps more than any other ancients with, respectively, the new humanism and (what humanists portrayed as) the old scholasticism. First, the Roman orator and politician Cicero is mentioned relatively often in the chronicles, which also seem to draw on some of his works for specific details – for example, concerning divination in *Book 3*. Yet at those striking moments when Rabelais gives the narrator or a protagonist French that imitates the elegant, balanced structure and rhythm of Cicero's periods (groups of sentences),[12] the imitation is not of any particular work but of Ciceronian style as practiced by numerous humanists as well as by Cicero himself. Similarly, the representation in *Gargantua* of deliberative political rhetoric as a tool for avoiding violence – an ineffective one in the case of the Picrocholine War – reworks in a general way not only speeches by Cicero himself but also the Ciceronian civic humanism that in more recent times had spread (changing as it went) from Italy to France. In the case of Aristotle, although several specific works by him are explicitly cited – whether seriously or playfully or both – for their authoritative verdicts on a wide range of matters,[13] it is the late medieval discursive tradition of scholasticism, grounded in a Latin Aristotle but going well beyond him, which permeates the writing even more (e.g., when the narrator defines Pantagruelism, *F258/H351*), and not just when there is humanist anti-scholastic propaganda.[14]

The more rarified a philosophical tradition was, the clearer it is that Rabelais reworked specific texts within it. Pyrrhonism, the most radical variety of ancient Skepticism, was certainly rarified in 1546, when Panurge's consultation with the philosopher Trouillogan in *Book 3* (*F362-8/H461-7*) sprang on a largely unsuspecting reading public the first searching French-language exploration of it. Trouillogan's attitude is that there is no more reason to affirm that Panurge should get married than to affirm that he should not. As Emmanuel Naya has demonstrated, what enabled Rabelais to provide a sophisticated version of this pyrrhonist "no more" (*ou mallon*) argument (i.e., that one argument is "no more" valid than the other) was the fact that he had just read the account of it contained in the fourth-century *Praeparatio evangelica* (*Preparation for the Gospel*) by Eusebius of Cae-sarea, the full text of which had just been printed for the first time, and in the original Greek, in 1544. This provided more detail than did the three other texts upon which Rabelais seems to have drawn here, Diogenes Laertius's life of Pyrrho, Cicero's *Academica*, and Lucian's *Vitarum auctio* (*Auction of Lives*), the first two of which were the standard sources of knowledge about pyrrhonism at this date, prior to the 1562 publication of a Latin translation of Sextus Empiricus's *Hypotyposes* (*Outlines of Pyrrhonism*).[15]

At the other end of the spectrum is Stoicism, which was so widely dif-fused in Rabelais's time – through the works of various ancients (such as Epictetus, Seneca, Marcus Aurelius, Cicero, and Plutarch) and more recent intermediaries – that it is difficult to argue that Rabelais drew on any particular work when he wove Stoic themes and terminology into cer-tain parts of the chronicles.[16] In the case of Plato – whom the first four books of the chronicles mention considerably more than any other ancient[17] – although Rabelais reworked and/or cited particular works by him, it is sometimes difficult to disentangle that reworking from Rabelais's engage-ment with the tradition of neo-Platonism which originated in late antiquity and was further developed and Christianized in late fifteenth-century Italy, notably by Marsilio Ficino, some of whose writings Rabelais probably knew directly.[18]

In other words, even in Rabelais's time, when humanist veneration of some ancients made so much discourse and knowledge coalesce around key authors, there was also a strong counter-tendency for such an author's works to merge into a surrounding intertextual swamp. Even when Rabelais and his contemporaries read an ancient work directly rather than as excerpts in reference books, they read not just the work itself but also the humanist paraphernalia that accompanied it, especially commentaries and annota-tions. For example, as Screech has shown, the 1548 version of the *Book 4* prologue (*F415/H715*) reworks not only the Roman poet Ovid's poem on the Roman calendar (*Fasti*), but also the fifteenth-century commentaries on it by Antonius Constantius Fanensius and Pietro Marsi.[19]

By contrast, in other cases, commentaries are highlighted parodically or satirically, as hopeless deviations from an original source. That is one way of reading some of Rabelais's numerous citations of real and imaginary scholas-tic legal glosses – for example, in the Judge Bridlegoose episode of *Book 3*. Rabelais can be read here as broadly sympathizing with Andrea Alciati and other humanist advocates of the "French way of teaching law" (*mos gallicus iuris docendi*), for whom understanding the *Corpus iuris civilis* (the texts of Roman law collected together by order of Justinian in the sixth century) in their historical contexts was an indispensable preliminary to reapplying them in the modern world.[20] In his efforts to advise Panurge about his marriage question, Bridlegoose draws on contemporary reference books such as the *Brocardia iuris* (*Brocards of the Law*) to cite a bewildering range of "brocards" or juridical maxims, many derived from the glossators. The example of the *Corpus iuris civilis* shows that authoritative originary texts are not necessarily associated with a single author. Here they are glimpsed at the bottom of the intertextual morass of interpretative accretions, which Bridlegoose further thickens with his own eccentric glosses.

In other cases, parody rather than commentary constitutes the intertextual network into which even prestigious authors merge, making it difficult to disentangle Rabelais's subtexts from one another. He alludes to and reworks on several levels the ancient Greek and Roman epic poets Homer and Vergil.[21] However, his subtexts include not only classical epic but also parodies of it, both ancient (Lucian) and modern: the 1517 mock epic *Baldus*, written by Teofilo Folengo in macaronic verse (interspersing Latin with varieties of Italian), is, like Vergil's *Aeneid* which it parodies, imitated by Rabelais on many levels.[22]

In other words, if the meanings of Rabelais's work are generated by its relationship to other texts, then so are the meanings of those other texts. That is particularly self-evident in the case of an ancient Roman compilation or miscellany from which Rabelais quotes and borrows, Aulus Gellius's *Noctes atticae* (*Attic Nights*).[23] It is also flagrantly true of Plutarch, who wove into his own writing in late Greek antiquity numerous pre-existing materials (e.g., Platonic and Stoic). Indeed, that probably explains why Rabelais mentions Plutarch much less than he uses him.[24]

Modern

If some ancients, such as Plutarch and Pliny, are used more than they are mentioned, the same is even truer of many of his modern subtexts, even the most crucial of all, Erasmus's vast *Adages*, published from 1500 onwards. It is a repertory of ancient proverbs and sayings to which Erasmus added, in his commentaries on them, abundant information and reflections. Rabelais does not mention Erasmus in the chronicles but makes numerous borrowings from the *Adages*.[25] His rewriting, in the opening lines of *Gargantua*, of the adage *Sileni Alcibiadis* (*The Sileni of Alcibiades*) – which he turns into an image for the text of *Gargantua* – is only the most celebrated instance (F3/H5–6). It involves no explicit mention of the *Adages*, only of Plato's *Symposium*. While Erasmus's compilation is exceptional in the extent to which he makes the stone-like ancient fragments gather thick layers of inter-textual moss that are permeated by his own personal reflections, it belongs to the same set of genres as the other modern anthologies of ancient excerpts upon which Rabelais draws.[26]

Rabelais's chronicles make many other intertextual forays into human-ist writing. From the leading French humanist of the 1520s and 1530s, Guillaume Budé, Rabelais drew not only general inspiration, as we can deduce from their correspondence, but also some of his striking, Greek-based names and terms, such as "Encyclopedie," a recent French neologism of Budé's.[27] Rabelais's reworking in *Book 3* of elements drawn from a controversial 1530 treatise on occult philosophy by the German Heinrich Cornelius Agrippa von Nettesheim culminates in the irruption into the die-gesis of a Her Trippa, an expert in what Rabelais here represents as the least respectable forms of divination (*F*327–31/*H*427–31). Recent or contempo-rary Italian authors reworked by Rabelais range from the neo-Latin scholar Celio Calcagnini,[28] to the celebrated vernacular writers Folengo, Francesco Colonna,[29] and Baldassare Castiglione.[30]

However, Rabelais's secular subtexts stretch beyond humanism. Follow-ing the 1545 publication in French of an account of Jacques Cartier's second (1535–6) voyage to Canada, Rabelais wove elements of that text – or possi-bly of hearsay about Cartier – into the voyage of his *Book 4*.[31] Other non-learned subtexts are certainly at least partly oral in nature, such as dialects and certain genres (riddles, farce). Indeed, some of Rabelais's most crucial printed subtexts – the *Chroniques gargantuines* (*Gargantuan Chronicles*) – probably derive from oral story-telling in what one might call "popular" culture (though the latter's imbrication within social elites, for example in court circles, has long been established). On the other hand, caught in a rich intertextual web of their own, the *Chroniques gargantuines* also par-ody chivalric romances, which were still much printed in Rabelais's day and which he in turn parodies, and probably satirizes, both directly via his own reading of romances and indirectly via the *Chroniques gargantuines*.[32] Let us briefly consider the latter.

If *Gargantua* opens under the sign of Plato and (more tacitly) Eras-mus, *Pantagruel* opens under that of one of the *Chroniques gargantu-ines*, the *Grandes et inestimables cronicques: Du grant et enorme geant Gargantua* (*H*213–15). This short narrative had recounted how Merlin, in King Arthur's time, used magic to create the giants Grant Gosier and Galemelle, who then engendered Gargantua. Rabelais's narrator, Alcofribas Nasier, presents *Pantagruel* as a continuation, devoted now to Gargantua's son. Extending his intertextual web further into folkloric culture, Rabelais jokingly chooses for his new giant the name of a dwarf-devil (Panthagruel) well known from mystery plays. The opening chapters of *Pantagruel* rework many details from the *Grandes et inestimables cronicques*. And, following the success of *Pantagruel* (1532), Rabelais returned to the giant Gargantua, from whom his fiction had engendered Pantagruel. *Gargantua* (1535) revivifies and respells the hero's parents as Grandgousier and Gargamelle, as well as making Rabelais's version of the hero steal and return the bells of Notre Dame, as his eponymous predecessor had done in fewer words (F42–8/H48–55, 161–2).

The case of the *Chroniques gargantuines* shows how an intertextual perspective whittles away any absolute autonomy that one might wish to ascribe not only to the authors whom Rabelais reworked but also to Rabelais himself as author. It is difficult to draw a hard and fast distinction between text and subtext, between what he authored and what he did not. The *Grandes et inestimables cronicques* were printed in 1532 (possibly not for the first time). They were followed in the 1530s not only by *Pantagruel* but also by other anonymous versions of the Gargantua narrative. It is even faintly possible, as Mireille Huchon has speculated, that Rabelais himself had some limited hand in these folkloric Gargantua narratives. But even if he did not, they in turn were soon influenced by *his* Pantagruel narrative – they turned Gargantua into a king and started mentioning Pantagruel. And they were lumped together with it in readers' minds thanks to printers and booksellers, such as François Juste, the first printer of *Pantagruel* in 1532, who then reprinted it in 1533 in the same volume as the *Cronicques du roy Gargantua*, which, as "king" in the title shows, had already been influenced by *Pantagruel*.[33] Intertextuality is shaped by material conditions of book circulation as well as by the meanings of words on the page.

This was only the first episode in the history of what John Lewis has called "the intertwining of the Rabelaisian and the para-Rabelaisian."[34] Other works that exploited the saleability of Rabelais's chronicles, which they used as subtexts, were then themselves reworked by Rabelais as subtexts. Thus, Rabelais's *Book 4* reconfigured elements drawn from the anonymous narrative of island-hopping *Le Disciple de Pantagruel* (*Disciple of Pantagruel*, 1538 or earlier), as did *Book 5*. Aspects of François Habert's serious-toned *Songe de Pantagruel* (*Dream of Pantagruel*, 1542) may have been more remotely reconfigured in Rabelais's *Book 3*.[35] And, most spectacularly of all, the exact dividing line in *Book 5* between Rabelais's hand and others is still unclear, despite advances made by scholarship (as represented most recently by Giacone's colloquium proceedings). *Book 5* is part continuation, part interpretation of *Book 4*, with which it has a compelling intertextual relationship regardless of the extent of Rabelais's involvement in its composition.[36] The perspective of intertextuality reminds us that questions of authorship, while they do make a difference to interpretation, are not its be-all and end-all.

Reading Rabelais's intertextuality

Approaches

In the above survey of many of Rabelais's main subtexts, I have been reticent in interpreting their role. Broadly speaking, two critical approaches to Rabelais's intertextuality have been developed in recent years.

The first views certain subtexts as keys to the correct interpretation of the chronicles. This approach extrapolates from Rabelais's local, particular, intensive reworkings of a subtext outwards to the whole of one of his books. Thus, for M. A. Screech, Pantagruel's one-off Erasmian rebuke of Panurge for his "philautie" (self-love) indicates how to view Panurge throughout *Book 3*.[37] For Edwin Duval, the echoes of the New Testament and Vergil's *Aeneid* in *Pantagruel* suggest that this whole book should be read as an evangelical epic.[38] This approach certainly does not diminish the extraordinary range of Rabelais's subtexts. Indeed, it has led to many of them being identified. But it does involve establishing a firm hierarchy among them. Some are argued to be particularly decisive in shaping a work's overall meaning.

The second approach locates Rabelais's meanings in the tensions *between* subtexts. These tensions arise from the ways in which he has woven the subtexts into his narrative in any given passage. The subtexts do serve to shape and delimit the potential range of the passage's meanings, but they do not arrange themselves in a definitive hierarchy which privileges some subtexts over others. Such hierarchies might emerge, but they are provisional, constantly challenged by discrepant textual details. This approach involves greater reluctance to extrapolate from selected intertextual encounters to a work's overall meaning, one that can be formulated in abstract terms. For André Tournon, prestigious subtextual fragments – such as the *Sileni Alcibiadis*, Saint Paul paraphrases, or the quasi-Ciceronian formulations of Christianized Stoic wisdom – are landmarks which do broadly guide interpretation, for example in evangelical directions, but without being universally applicable keys.[39] Tournon does propose an intertextual hierarchy in that he makes one subtext especially decisive: Menippean satire as practiced by Lucian. Yet it operates as a self-negating kind of model, providing not a set of precepts or even a precise way of writing but a precedent for staging clashes between sets of precepts and different kinds of writing (cf. Tournon, "Le Paradoxe"). In similar vein, Terence Cave argues that straightforward allegorical readings of Gaster's abode (*F560–2/H671–3*) are evoked inter-textually – most obviously through allusion to the Greek poet Hesiod's Rock of Virtue – only to be disrupted by competition from other intertextually evoked possible interpretations, by an unsettling narrative (that of Gaster, the hungry belly, who has usurped the Rock), and by a digressive, copious style.[40]

Both approaches have been practiced in a variety of ways. And the contrast between them is often less sharp in practice than this summary indicates. Yet it is perhaps rooted in two conflicting tendencies which, as John O'Brien has pointed out, were already present in Renaissance theories of intertextuality, "reading as integration and reading as fragmentation."[41] Both approaches have produced indispensable studies, though personally I find the second matches better the experience of reading the chronicles. Let us explore possible intertextual readings of one episode.

The death of Pan

In *Book 4*, Pantagruel and friends stop at the islands of the Macraeons. There they discuss the death of "heroes" – a slippery term designating demigods in an ancient context but also exceptional humans in a modern one. Frère Jean asks Pantagruel whether he agrees with their island guide, the old Macrobe, that demigods and heroes die. "Not all of them," answers Pantagruel, whose reply includes the reported opinion of some ancients, based on Hesiod's calculations, that the sum total of the life-span of all such intermediate beings is 9,720 years. Pantagruel then cites as his source a Plutarch treatise (Book 10), which does indeed include that information:

> " . . . See Plutarch in his book *On the cessation of oracles*."
>
> "That," said Frère Jean, "is not a breviary matter. I don't believe a word of it except what you'd like me to."
>
> "I believe," said Pantagruel, "that all intellective souls are exempt from the scissors of Atropos. All are immortal: angels, daemons, and human souls. However, in this connection, I'll tell you a very strange story, but one written and attested by many scholarly learned theologians."

28
How Pantagruel relates a piteous story concerning the decease of heroes.

> "As Epitherses, father of Aemilian the rhetorician, was sailing from Greece to Italy . . . " (*F496–7/H603–4*)

Pantagruel here recounts how those on board Epitherses's ship were terrified to hear a voice calling "Thamoun" from the island of Paxos. Thamous was their pilot's name, which the voice called twice more. Thamous asked what it wanted. It instructed him to spread the news, upon reaching Palodes, that Pan was dead. When Thamous later obeyed, unison sighs and lamentations were heard. The news reached Rome. The emperor, Tiberius Caesar, summoned Thamous, believed his account, and commissioned scholarly advice, which concluded that the Pan in question was the son of Mercury and Penelope. Pantagruel then adds (accurately) that Herodotus and Cicero confirm this parentage. He continues: "[However], I would interpret it to be about that great Savior of the faithful, Who was ignominiously slain in Judaea by the iniquity of the pontiffs, doctors, priests, and monks of the Mosaic Law. And the interpretation does not seem preposterous to me . . . " (*F498/H605*), since "Pan" means "all" in Greek and Christ is our all, whose death was indeed accompanied by universal sighs and cries. Pantagruel adds that the chronology fits too: "The time concurs with this interpretation of mine . . ." The chapter then ends:

> Pantagruel, on finishing this statement, remained in silence and profound contemplation. Shortly after, we saw the tears flow down his cheeks, big as ostrich eggs. God take me if by one single word I'm lying about it.   (*F498/H605*)

Many subtexts are in play. The whole of the Thamous/Pan story, taking up the first two thirds or so of chapter 28, is an unacknowledged, mostly close translation from a little further on in the same Plutarch treatise (Book 17). (Rabelais's use of the accusative form "Thamoun" suggests he worked directly from Plutarch's Greek rather than from an intermediate source.) Both reworkings of the treatise are uttered by Pantagruel. His statement of belief in the immortality of all intellective souls seems to act as a bridge between them. But the relation between those three segments is cloudy. First, Pantagruel's speech starting "Not all of them" initially implies that some demigods, heroes, and so on *do* die. It is contradicted by his ensuing statement about the immortality of all intellective souls. There is a further twist in his line of reasoning when he introduces the Thamous/Pan story with the conjunction "However" ("toutes foys"): no sooner has Pantagruel announced his general rule than he recounts at length what he introduces as an exception to it. But the "toutes foys" turns out to be specious. It is cancelled out by a second "Toutesfoys"[42] when Pantagruel interprets Pan as Christ.

How are we to interpret this sequence? In an illuminatingly intertextual reading, Screech interprets Pantagruel as a mouthpiece here for Rabelais's syncretism, his Christianizing correction of those pagan writers to whom some partial revelation was granted.[43] But another reading, while deeply indebted to Screech's, might bring out how Rabelais incorporates these

Plutarch subtexts in such a way as to highlight and problematize the process of interpreting ancient texts. Pantagruel's assertion of the immortality of all intellective souls could be read as one of Tournon's "landmarks," with its forthright, sententious parataxis and its categorical repetition of "all." It is uttered as if to provide an orthodox counter-weight to the bewildering yet fascinating possibility of calculating the total life-spans of certain heroes, daemons, and others. Pantagruel's landmark thus has the same structural function as Frère Jean's colloquial version – "not breviary matter." Rabelais could have had Pantagruel dissociate himself more clearly from the hetero-dox possibility. He prefers to create a certain distance between Pantagruel and it by inserting the explicit reference to Plutarch as its source. So, while the landmark, taken on its own, is unequivocal, its relationship to the sur-rounding text is not.

The next borrowing from *On the Cessation of Oracles*, the Thamous/Pan story, is represented as corresponding to a deeper belief on Pantagruel's part than the first. Not only does Rabelais grant it pride of place at the start of a new chapter, but by being less specific about its provenance, by not acknowledging that it comes from the source Pantagruel has just mentioned, Rabelais perhaps represents it as having been digested more by Pantagruel (to use a metaphor common in the period's imitation theory). Similarly, Pantagruel's subsequent interpretation of the story is represented as a highly *personal* act. Rabelais could have had Pantagruel say "This Pan was really Christ," or something similar. That would have occluded both the act of interpreting and the interpreter. Instead, within a few lines, Pantagruel mentions the act three times, and twice as a first-person one: "[However], I would interpret it to be about the great Savior . . . And the interpretation does not seem preposterous to me . . . The time concurs with this interpretation of mine . . ." (*F498/H605*). This echoes the more extreme exchange between Pantagruel and Frère Jean at the end of the previous chapter (quoted above), in which Frère Jean comically puts the first- or even second-person dimension of belief above third-person Truth ("I don't believe a word of it except what you'd like me to," *ibid.*).

On the one hand, the personal nature of Pantagruel's interpretation of Pan, which culminates in tears, and has evangelical overtones, contributes to what Screech has identified as the passage's moving quality. On the other hand, it means Pantagruel's interpretation does not have an aura of dogmatic certainty. Introduced via the conditional tense ("I would interpret it"), it is represented as a personal choice from among the various interpretations which Screech and others have shown were available when Rabelais wrote this.[44] Intertextuality can take the form of evoking some subtexts implicitly, in order to exclude them.

The characteristically abrupt Rabelaisian switch of register in the episode's closing lines (quoted above) further deprives Pantagruel's interpretation of any aura of dogmatic certainty. The comparison of his tears to ostrich eggs – whether or not it bears a serious meaning via intertextual echoes[45] – combined with the narrator's Lucianesque[46] affirmation of the truthfulness of this tall tale about a giant, reminds us that we are reading a fiction, not a theological treatise. Whatever Rabelais believed himself, he has represented not "what Plutarch's story means" but "what one might imagine Plutarch's story to mean to someone."

Moreover, here as often elsewhere, Rabelais handles intertextuality in a way that seems designed to make his readers aware of problems of interpretation that they too face. His incorporation of Plutarch's story intensifies the riddle-like qualities that the subtext already possessed. Although Rabelais revises Plutarch on at least one point to fit in with Pantagruel's interpretation,[47] he makes that interpretation follow rather than precede the story, which, because of the introductory "However," has an unclear relation to Pantagruel's overall line of argument during his narration of it. Indeed, the two mutually canceling instances of this conjunction serve as a strained verbal frame for this enigmatic intertextual fragment, this "very strange story." The two "Howevers" are examples of the markers of intertextuality that Michel Riffaterre calls "agrammaticalities."[48]

Even Pantagruel's eventual proposed solution to the riddle has gaps which the reader must fill. The solution is itself phrased like another riddle, albeit an easy one: Christ is not mentioned directly, only alluded to through periphrasis over several lines. The solution does restore clarity to Pantagruel's overall line of argument: the Pan story turns out *not* after all to be an exception to the general rule about intellective souls. Yet the reason – Christ's resurrection – is not mentioned directly either. It emerges only indirectly, through the striking shift from the preterite ("Who was ignominiously slain") to the present tense ("He is our All"). It requires active readerly interpretation to keep the resurrection in sight given that the explicit emphasis is so much on Christ's death, for which Pantagruel weeps.

So, rather than smoothly incorporating these two passages from Plutarch's treatise into his own narrative, Rabelais pushes his reader to meditate on the extent to which it is possible to do so. Throughout his chronicles, he draws his readers' attention to both the excitement and the disturbances that intertextuality generates. To what extent can a text domesticate subtexts and draw energy or inspiration from them without being overrun or swamped by them? The question was especially acute in Rabelais's time because of humanism, but the extraordinary range of his own intertextuality also poses it in contexts beyond humanism. He offers no definitive answer.

Intertextuality pervades his chronicles as both a centripetal and a centrifugal force.

NOTES

1 E.g., the spoof titles held in the Library of St. Victor (*F*152–8/*H*236–41).

2 On these exercises and their permutations in some vernacular writing, see Thomas Greene, *The Light in Troy: Imitation and Discovery in Renaissance Poetry* (New Haven and London: Yale University Press, 1982), especially p. 51.

3 Terence Cave has demonstrated how Rabelais, Ronsard, and Montaigne explore Erasmian "abundance" (*copia*) of expression and subject matter: an ideal of achieving a plenitude of meaning is haunted by an anxiety that copious words are empty ones. (See *The Cornucopian Text: Problems of Writing in the French Renaissance* (Oxford: Clarendon Press, 1979), I.2 on Erasmian imitation and II.2 on Rabelais.)

4 See Ann Moss, *Printed Commonplace-Books and the Structuring of Renaissance Thought* (Oxford: Clarendon Press, 1996).

5 On intertextuality in Renaissance writing, see Gisèle Mathieu-Castellani and François Cornilliat, "Intertexte phénix?", *Littérature*, 55 (1984), pp. 5–9; John O'Brien, "Introduction: The Time of Theory," in John O'Brien and Malcolm Quainton, eds., *Distant Voices Still Heard: Contemporary Readings of French Renaissance Literature* (Liverpool: Liverpool University Press, 2000), pp. 11–14. On the relation between intertextuality and imitation, see Cave, *Cornucopian Text*, pp. 76–7.

6 See Mathieu-Castellani and Cornilliat, "Intertexte phénix?", p. 6; Greene, *Light in Troy*.

7 See Michael Worton and Judith Still, eds., "Introduction" (especially pp. 1–2) in *Intertextuality: Theories and Practices* (Manchester and New York: Manchester University Press, 1990).

8 See Edwin Duval, *The Design of Rabelais's "Pantagruel"* (New Haven: Yale University Press, 1991), chapter 1; A. J. Krailsheimer, *Rabelais and the Franciscans* (Oxford: Clarendon Press, 1963), pp. 283–7; Michael Screech, "Index of Biblical Passages," in *Rabelais* (London: Duckworth, 1979), pp. 482–3.

9 For an overview, see Jean Plattard, *L'Œuvre de Rabelais: Sources, invention et composition* (Paris: Champion, 1910), chapter 6.

10 See Christiane Lauvergnat-Gagnière, *Lucien de Samosate et le lucianisme en France au XVIe siècle* (Geneva: Droz, 1988), chapter 7; André Tournon, "Le Paradoxe ménippéen dans l'œuvre de Rabelais," in Jean Céard and J.-C. Margolin, eds., *Rabelais en son demi-millénaire: Actes du Colloque International de Tours (24–29 septembre 1984)*, Études Rabelaisiennes, 21 (Geneva: Droz, 1988), pp. 309–17.

11 See Screech, *Rabelais*, index, pp. 491–2.

12 E.g., *F*158–62, 278/*H*241–5, 372.

13 Examples are listed in Peter Sharratt, "Aristotle," in Elizabeth Chesney Zegura, ed., *The Rabelais Encyclopedia* (Westport, CT, and London: Greenwood Press, 2004).

14 See Krailsheimer, *Rabelais and the Franciscans*, pp. 212–15.

15 Emmanuel Naya, "'Ne scepticque, ne dogmatique, et tous les deux ensemble': Rabelais 'on phrontistere et escholle des Pyrrhoniens'," *Études Rabelaisiennes*, 35 (1998), pp. 81–129.

16 E.g., *F278/H372*. See Michael Screech, "Some Stoic Elements in Rabelais's Religious Thought," *Études Rabelaisiennes*, 1 (1956), p. 78 n.

17 See Krailsheimer, *Rabelais and the Franciscans*, p. 268.

18 This uncertainty has produced differing verdicts among scholars. See G. Mallary Masters, *Rabelaisian Dialectic and the Platonic-Hermetic Tradition* (Albany, NY: State University of New York Press, 1969); Robert Marichal, "L'Attitude de Rabelais devant le néo-platonisme et l'italianisme," in *François Rabelais: Ouvrage publié pour le quatrième centenaire de sa mort (1553–1953)* (Geneva: Droz, 1953), pp. 181–209; Screech, *Rabelais*, pp. 226, 394, 417–19, 441, 442.

19 Screech, *Rabelais*, pp. 262 n., 299–301, 358–9.

20 See J. D. M. Derrett, "Rabelais's Legal Learning and the Trial of Bridoye," *Bibliothèque d'Humanisme et Renaissance*, 25 (1963), pp. 111–71; Michael Screech, "The Legal Comedy of Rabelais in the Trial of Bridoye in the *Tiers livre de Pantagruel*," *Études Rabelaisiennes*, 5 (1964), pp. 175–95.

21 See, for example, Terence Cave, "Panurge and Odysseus," in K. Aspley, D. Bellos, and P. Sharratt, eds., *Myth and Legend in French Literature: Essays in Honour of A. J. Steele* (London: MHRA, 1982), pp. 47–59; Gérard Defaux, *Le Curieux, le glorieux et la sagesse du monde dans la première moitié du XVIe siècle: L'exemple de Panurge (Ulysse, Démosthène, Empédocle)*, French Forum Monographs 34 (Lexington, KY: French Forum, 1982), pp. 20–38; Guy Demerson, "Paradigmes épiques chez Rabelais," in *Rabelais en son demi-millénaire*, pp. 225–36; Duval, *Design*, chapter 1.

22 See Barbara C. Bowen, "Rabelais and Folengo Once Again," in *Rabelais in Context* (Birmingham, AL: Summa, 1993), pp. 207–31; Michel Jeanneret, "'Ma patrie est une citrouille': Thèmes alimentaires dans Rabelais et Folengo," *Études de lettres*, 2 (1984), pp. 25–44.

23 See Plattard, *L'Œuvre*, pp. 181–3.

24 See Krailsheimer, *Rabelais and the Franciscans*, p. 270.

25 For a useful list, see Screech, *Rabelais*, index, p. 487. Rabelais's uses of Erasmus more generally are discussed throughout Screech's study. For an overview, see Michael Heath, "Erasmus," in *Rabelais Encyclopedia*.

26 E.g., Petrus Crinitus, *De honesta disciplina* (1500); Coelius Rhodiginus, *Antiquae lectiones* (1516); Alexander ab Alexandro, *Dies geniales* (1522). On commonplaces in Rabelais, see Terence Cave, "Thinking with Commonplaces: The Example of Rabelais," and Neil Kenny, "Plautus, Panurge, and 'les aventures des gens curieux'," both in G. Ferguson and C. Hampton, eds., *(Re)Inventing the Past: Essays on French Early Modern Culture, Literature and Thought in Honour of Ann Moss* (Durham: Durham Modern Languages Series, 2003), pp. 34–50 and 51–71.

27 *F201, 781/H290, 951*. See Barbara C. Bowen, "Budé," and Neil Kenny, "Encyclopedism," in *Rabelais Encyclopedia*.

28 The many reworkings of Calcagnini include the Physis and Antiphysis story of *Book 4*. See Michael Screech, "Celio Calcagnini and Rabelaisian Sympathy," in G. Castor and T. Cave, eds., *Neo-Latin and the Vernacular in Renaissance France* (Oxford: Oxford University Press, 1984), pp. 26–48.

29 Rabelais rewrites elements of Colonna's allegory of the quest for knowledge (*Hypnerotomachia Poliphili*, 1499) in his description of the Abbey of Thélème (*Gargantua*). The Rabelaisian *Book 5* includes lengthy translations and paraphrases of architectural and other descriptions from Colonna (especially F659–65, 692–3, 698–9/H778–85, 816–17, 821–3). They rework the original, not Jean Martin's 1546 French translation. See Richard Cooper, "L'Authenticité du *Cinquiesme livre*: État présent de la question," in Franco Giacone, ed., *Actes du colloque international de Rome: Rabelais, le "Cinquiesme Livre"* (Geneva: Droz, 2001), pp. 10–11; Gilles Polizzi, "Le Voyage vers l'oracle ou la dérive des intertextes dans le *Cinquième livre*," in *Rabelais, le "Cinquiesme Livre,"* pp. 577–96, and "Thélème ou l'éloge du don: Le texte rabelaisien à la lumière de l'*Hypnerotomachia Poliphili*," *Réforme, Humanisme, Renaissance*, 25 (1988), pp. 39–59.

30 Elements from Castiglione's manifesto for new ideals of courtly civility, *Il Cortegiano* (*The Courtier*), published in 1528, were probably reworked especially in Rabelais's description of the inhabitants of the Abbey of Thélème in *Gargantua*. See François Rouget, "Rabelais lecteur de Castiglione et de Machiavel à Thélème (*Gargantua*, chapitres 52–57)," *Études Rabelaisiennes*, 42 (2003), pp. 101–16. On Rabelais's Italian readings in general, see Richard Cooper, "Les Lectures italiennes de Rabelais: Une mise au point," *Études Rabelaisiennes*, 37 (1999), pp. 25–49.

31 See Lance Donaldson-Evans, "Cartier," in *Rabelais Encyclopedia*.

32 See Jean Céard, "Rabelais, lecteur et juge des romans de chevalerie," in *Rabelais en son demi-millénaire*, pp. 237–48.

33 See Christiane Lauvergnat-Gagnière and Guy Demerson, "Introduction," in Christiane Lauvergnat-Gagnière and Guy Demerson, eds., with the collaboration of R. Antonioli, C. Bonilauri, M. Huchon, J. Lewis, and B. Teyssot, *Les Chroniques gargantuines* (Paris: Nizet, 1988); François Cornilliat, "L'Autre géant: Les *Chroniques gargantuines* et leur intertexte," *Littérature*, 55 (1984), pp. 85–97; John Lewis, "Quelques aspects de la littérature para-rabelaisienne d'avant 1562," in *Rabelais en son demi-millénaire*, pp. 357–64.

34 Lewis, "Quelques aspects," p. 363.

35 See Guy Demerson and Christiane Lauvergnat-Gagnière, eds., *Le Disciple de Pantagruel (Les Navigations de Panurge)* (Paris: Nizet, 1982); John Lewis, "François Habert, Le Songe de Pantagruel," *Études Rabelaisiennes*, 18 (1985), pp. 103–62 (an edition of *Le Songe*), "Disciple of Pantagruel" and "Dream of Pantagruel," in *Rabelais Encyclopedia*, "Quelques aspects," pp. 360–3.

36 See Cooper, "L'Authenticité," p. 21.

37 F347/H444. Screech, *Rabelais*, pp. 235–8.

38 Duval, *Design*, chapter 1.

39 André Tournon, *"En Sens agile": Les acrobaties de l'esprit selon Rabelais* (Paris: Champion, 1995).

40 Terence Cave, "Reading Rabelais: Variations on the Rock of Virtue," in P. Parker and D. Quint, eds., *Literary Theory/Renaissance Texts* (Baltimore: Johns Hopkins University Press, 1986), pp. 78–95. Other leading practitioners of this approach include Michel Jeanneret and François Rigolot (e.g., Rigolot, "Rabelais, Misogyny, and Christian Charity: Biblical Intertexuality and the Renaissance Crisis of Exemplarity," *PMLA*, 109/2 (1994), pp. 225–37).

41 O'Brien, "Introduction: The Time of Theory," p. 14.

42 Frame, *The Complete Works of François Rabelais*, translates "Nevertheless" this time.

43 Screech, *Rabelais*, pp. 353–65.

44 Eusebius of Caesarea – whom Rabelais read, as we saw above – interpreted Plutarch's dead Pan as an evil devil cast out by Christ. Rabelais's contemporary Guillaume Bigot, who like Rabelais had links with the du Bellays, had recently interpreted the story as one of evil devils covertly spreading news of Christ's death (1549). The interpretation given by Pantagruel is also found in a gloss by Marsi in the edition of Ovid's *Fasti* mentioned above. See Screech, *Rabelais*, pp. 355, 358–9.

45 See Screech, *Rabelais*, p. 363.

46 Rabelais's narrators frequently present themselves as if they were one of the lying tellers of outlandish, pseudo-truthful tales whom Lucian satirizes in his *True History* (see esp. I.2–4).

47 Pantagruel adds "God" when he has the voices tell Thamous that "the great God Pan is dead" (Screech, *Rabelais*, p. 357).

48 For an application of Riffaterre's concept to Renaissance poetry, see Sarah Alyn-Stacey, "Intertextualité mythologique: Érosion et interprétants," in John O'Brien, ed., *(Ré)interprétations: Études sur le seizième siècle*, *Michigan Romance Studies*, 15 (1995), pp. 55–75 (especially 58, 71–2).

6

MARIE-LUCE DEMONET

Pantagrueline humanism and Rabelaisian fiction

Contextualizing humanism

Secularization

The current debate about the definition of humanism attempts to encompass the change that took place between the late Middle Ages and the Renaissance. It is as well to keep to a definition of humanism as the restoration of "humane letters" in contrast with theology which dominated the whole curriculum when Rabelais was a Franciscan monk (between about 1511 and 1524).[1] Its influence diminished considerably during his Benedictine period (up to 1536) and still further during the following years when he was a doctor and secular priest. From now on, the active life took precedence over the contemplative life in the context of "civic" humanism, and this was linked, in France, to the supreme political authority, the king.[2] From their acquaintance with classical philosophies, many French humanists aspired to become Royal Counselors, like Guillaume Budé, thus directly rivaling the traditional role of the regular (monastic) clergy. Secular (non-monastic) clergy were often Gallican and contributed to strengthening the monarchy. As the secretary and doctor of two intimates of the king (Guillaume and Jean du Bellay), Rabelais, after the publication of *Pantagruel* and *Gargantua*, found himself drawn into a political humanism whose militant character is clear from *Book 4*.

All the sects of classical philosophy were rediscovered, fueling the search for syntheses between the "philosophy of Christ" (Erasmus)[3] and Platonism, Stoicism, and even Epicureanism, Skepticism, and Cynicism. Likewise, the work of Aristotle was certainly criticized by humanists such as Petrarch and Lorenzo Valla, but was nonetheless edited, commented, and widely known. Far from being rejected wholesale, it remained basic to the study of logic (in a simplified version), rhetoric (as expanded by Cicero and Quintilian), metaphysics, ethics, and politics, while awaiting the rediscovery of poetics, indirectly known before 1550. Rabelais did not escape that grammar of philosophical thought, Renaissance Aristotelianism.[4]

Knowledge and curiosity

Thanks to the "academies" (the word was as yet rarely used in French) scattered throughout France and to the increasingly independent teaching of the new colleges and the Royal Readers, the medieval division of the liberal arts into the *trivium* (grammar, rhetoric, and dialectic or logic) and the *quadrivium* (arithmetic, geometry, astronomy, and music) was broken up to the advantage of the new disciplines favored by Rabelais's generation: philosophy (up until then subsumed under theology and logic), history and literature (which were part of grammar and rhetoric), politics (formerly linked to law), and the applied arts and sciences, which up to that point had been left to "rude mechanicals" or classed under philosophy on the theoretical side.

At the same time, a new pedantry developed, transferring to Cicero and the Elder Pliny the adulation once given to Aristotle. Rabelais mocks this fetishism of ancient writing by proposing his own fictions as being just as much worthy of belief. In *Book 3*, the novel of indiscreet curiosity about the future, Pantagruel asks, "What harm is there in always finding out and always learning, even if it's from a sot, a pot, a dipper, a mitten, or a slipper?" (*F303/H400*). Panurge's quest takes up facetiously medieval quarrels about future contingents, the Calvinist version of which was predestination, mentioned by the philosopher Trouillogan: "Have you ever been a cuckold?" Panurge asks. "No, unless it is predestined," replies the philosopher (*F367/H466*). The *Pantagrueline Prognostication* of 1533 is unambiguous on this point: God alone is the master of human destiny, something that the theologian Hippothadée wisely restates when setting aside the danger of cuckoldry "if God please" (*F349–50/H446–8*). The "Know Thyself" directed by Panurge at Her Trippa does not resolve the problem, for it also depends on that unknown other, the potential wife (*F329/H428*).

During his time with the Observantine Franciscans at Fontenay-le-Comte in Poitou, Rabelais frequented the humanist circle of the lawyer Tiraqueau, just as the new Latin and Greek studies were in full swing. He is said to have begun a translation of Herodotus in 1522 and undertaken one of Lucian, but his Greek books were confiscated (1523). He probably studied law in Poitiers or Paris, and then, when he was a Benedictine at Maillezais (in Saintonge), of which Seuillé was a dependency, he also moved in the cultivated circles of the abbeys of Ligugé and Fontaine-le-Comte near Poitiers and met the "Grand Rhétoriqueur," Jean Bouchet. This procurator, whose surname is used for his helmsman Xenomanes (*Book 3*, *F306/H495*, *F401/H500*; *Book 4*, *F437/H539*), published moralizing works (poetry and plays) and a substantial local and national history (the *Annales d'Aquitaine*) which dispensed with folklore and propaganda.[5] Just like philosophy going back to the ancient sources, history gained its independence. The fabulous histories told by Rabelais in his first two novels parody the hagiography and the excessively heroic "lives" of characters more at home in fiction than in educational curricula. That was also Lucian's point of view in "How To Write History."[6]

The temptation to encyclopedism

In the catalogue of the Library of St. Victor (*F152–8/H235–41*) are a large number of titles that caricature the Scholastic learning taught in monasteries and faculties of Theology: for example, *On peas with bacon, with commentary* (*Des poys au lart cum commento*, *F154/H237*), a play on words on the *Commentaries on the Sentences* of Peter Lombard (thirteenth century), the keystone of theology for three centuries. Mingled with this are obviously satirical authors, such as Pasquino, the legendary talking statue unearthed in Rome in the sixteenth century and the Italian cousin of the Pierre du Coignet mentioned in the prologue to *Book 4*. Contrasted with the indigestible mass of useless learning is humanist pedagogy, based on a new encyclopedism. Optimism about the progress of letters is expressed in Gargantua's famous letter to Pantagruel (*F158–62/H241–6*) in which individual learning is enriched by the cultural rise of the human race. Novelty is first of all marked by a stylistic change, for the king develops oratorical arguments in an elevated style, with well-turned maxims ("science without conscience is but ruin of the soul," *F162/H245*) and a grandiloquence far removed from the burlesque narrative that surrounds it. The letter sets out a detailed program of study: after noting the end of "the infelicity and calamity of the Goths" (*F160/H243*), the king exhorts his son to virtue and to "every liberal and praiseworthy branch of learning" (*F160/H243*) so as to become "an abyss of knowledge" (*F161/H245*). His rhetoric is so labored and the program so ambitious that it has been questioned whether we should take Rabelais seriously. Gargantua quotes Cicero and Plutarch, Athenaeus and Pausanias, but not Aristotle: he shows he is well read by recording progress in the liberal arts since the invention of printing. Although it no longer contains dialectic, the *trivium* is in no way reduced because it extends to history and cosmology, and to all the classical languages which could then be studied: Greek, Latin, Hebrew, Chaldean, and even Arabic. The imbibing of knowledge is envisaged as "the knowledge of nature's works"

(F161/H244), but it is first and foremost studied in books. Anatomical dissection (hardly tolerated at the time) is still accompanied by all the traditional medical books, including Hebrew. As for theology – and this is a huge innovation – it concentrates on Holy Writ, initially the New Testament, then the Old, and in the original languages.

The content of the letter remains an encyclopedism vastly expanded by printing and language learning, in which modern idiom has no place. Far from what the novel actually accomplishes, the program is still burdensome, utopian, fit only for a king. The letter is a *tour de force* without any great immediate effect, for the trip around the universities is more amusing than instructive: Pantagruel is hardly seen studying, except law at Bourges, which enables him to settle the lawsuit between Kissass and Sniffshit in a legally facetious way. One learns from a teacher, not from a university. Moreover, Rabelais pictures the ignorant young giant as possessing several innate forms of knowledge – the invention of the asswipe, the composition of the scatological ditty, the naming of the region of Beauce. These potentialities will be exploited by Ponocrates who takes Gargantua in hand, teaching him to become a prince after the Italian model, exercising himself in the new humanist disciplines of observation, experiment, the study of cases and examples, and nourishment properly proportioned to exercise. Even games of dice become useful for arithmetic and are made virtuous by the presence of cultivated company. Gargantua learns to form well-proportioned letters, to compose poetry, epigrams in Latin and *rondeaux* and *ballades* in French, but also to construct automata. These "self-moving" objects symbolize the ambition of this educational program: to shape a being capable of personal judgment and autonomy.

The Abbey of Thélème now looks like a collective version of humanist educational freedom, "do as you will" (empathetic, automatic, and uniform but without obligation) also being an evangelical precept, although the Thélémites do not have many religious duties: rather, they are engaged in worldly pursuits against the background of an academic castle. Whereas the abbey prides itself on the absence of rules, its construction, based on significant numbers, signifies order, harmony, proportion: an ideal clearly set out as utopian, constructed the opposite way around from a real monastery or college, but practicing explicit exclusions against hypocrites and sneaks. The anathema closes with a "prophetic enigma" (F127–30/H141–4), the counterpart of the "Antidoted Frigglefraggles" (F9–12/H11–14) which opened *Gargantua*: the threat hanging over those who preach the Gospel "live and true" ("en sens agile," F122/H143) is warded off by a pleasant real-tennis match, thus offering a message of twofold reading for the whole work.[7]

Humanism and polemic

If one distinguishes between the two periods of composition of Rabelais's works, the relationship with humanism has palpably changed. From 1532 to 1535, the publication dates of *Pantagruel* and *Gargantua*, the first prognostications and almanachs, and the editions of Hippocrates, Marliani, and Manardi's medical letters, and persecutions against the "Evangelicals" had hardly begun. The Royal College had been founded and the struggle was both literary, against the survival of medieval university methods, and politico-religious, against those (academics, in the main) who opposed any reform of the Church. Reformist leanings were particularly prevalent in Parisian humanist circles and in the central French provinces, where, however, the elites wavered between reform within a renewed Erasmian Catholicism (following the example of Marguerite de Navarre, sister of François I, and Guillaume Briçonnet, a native of Touraine) and the rise of a more radical reformist strain. In the first novels, the struggle against the Sorbonne is at once in the service of a renewed piety, often drawn from the religious orders themselves (e.g., the Benedictines of Chezal-Benoît in Berry, whose reforms were adopted by Briçonnet at St-Germain-des-Prés in Paris), and a political struggle to stabilize the Gallican principles of the separation of spiritual and temporal powers, and the submission of France to its king.

Between the two groups of novels, Rabelais published revised reprints of *Gargantua* and *Pantagruel*. Yet 10 years had now passed during which the humanist struggle diversified: thus, although Calvin was himself an heir of the renewal of letters, Rabelais was not a brother in arms for him and in 1550 he called him an "Epicurean." Calvinism then became one of Rabelais's targets in the revised *Book 4* of 1552, in which the "demoniacal Calvins, impostors of Geneva" (*F507/H615*) rub shoulders with other enemies such as Postel or Putherbe (Gabriel Dupuy Herbault, *ibid.*).[8] Rabelais's humanism, already polemical, became even more combative in *Book 3* and especially in the revived *Book 4*, which returns to favorite targets of Gallican circles: denunciation of the temporal power of Rome and its attempts to draw gold from France to Rome (*F552/H662*), and the massacres of Pope-figs behind which stand the Provençal Vaudois (Waldenses) of Mérindol and Cabrières (1545).[9]

Comic fiction

Imbibing antiquity

While literary practices were certainly renewed with the diffusion of humanism – editing sound texts according to philological methods, producing new commentaries free from university authorities and the Faculty of Theology, making the genres of classical antiquity better known – two literary forms met with real success: the sonnet, which owed nothing to antiquity (Rabelais calls it a "virgin's fart," F_{531}/H_{639}), and the novel, which seems to have owed it little. Though epic is undone by his parody, its frame is repeated from narrative to narrative, with a prologue that acts both as a justification to the audience and as a "prologus" in the sense of Latin comedy: this is the "fore-play" of the narrator who wears the double mask of the author and one of the characters in the narrative. The inserted poems convey Rabelais's admiration for poetic forms popularized by Clément Marot, the most important poet of the early sixteenth century (*rondeau, ballade, épître, épitaphe*) and for apothegms and precepts ("Know thyself," "Do as thou wilt"), while Erasmus's adages can be found in his work in all the forms of adaptation, allusion, and citation.[10] Learned discourse can often appear in caricatural form (Bridlegoose for the law), but not always: the theologian Hippothadée is nothing like Janotus and the dietary advice of Rondibilis – the doctor Rondelet – is not necessarily ironic. As for dialogue, it owes far more to Lucian and the theater than to Plato.

Humanist novels

Can we speak of the "humanist" novel, in respect of these narratives filled with doctrine and knowledge making use of classical texts as inexhaustible founts of myths, plots, fictional characters, and narrative models? By parodying the standard forms of the medieval adventure story, which had already been parodied in the *Grandes Chroniques* of Gargantua which he may have edited just before his *Pantagruel*, Rabelais demonstrates his mastery of the structure of the heroic tale, organized chronologically like a king's or saint's life, but rewriting a pre-existing popular vein in the humanist style. Rabelais's narratives are not perceived by his contemporaries as "novels," for, at the time, this title refers to the novel of love or knightly deeds. He himself defines the hybrid nature of his novels (a term he does not use) with the very vague "histories" or with the pleasant oxymoron "true tales" (F_{229}/H_{330}; translation modified).[11] Whereas the first two narratives have the loose framework of "heroic deeds and words," the fictional narrative imitated from Lucian is more at work in *Book 3* before imitating the sea quest in *Book 4* after the manner of the *Voyage of the Argo* and the anonymous *Disciple of Pantagruel* (1538) which itself imitated Lucian's *True History*. Between *Pantagruel* and *Book 4*, the effect of medley increases and the last narrative admits its debt to Menippean *satura* ("hotch-potch," "medley"). Classical and medieval models mingle together without questioning the more general principle of "fiction," whose field of interpretation stretches from traditional mythological figures and allegories (Messere Gaster) to the more general category of "mimesis" (representation) which, since the time of Aristotle, included the genres of *fabula*: not only fictional narrative, but also the theater. Rabelais knows Plautus and Terence well, but must also have been acquainted with the *commedia erudita* which had adapted Latin comedy to the Italian tradition. Besides his debt to comic theater when he alludes to his role in the farce of *The Man Who Married a Dumb Wife* at Montpellier (F361/H460), a direct source is possible with the recent discovery of a farce printed in Paris in 1521, the subject of which is the desire for marriage of a fogey who fears cuckoldry.[12] Theater and novel share the principle of fiction, but the second offers, along with a more or less evanescent narrator, the possibility of marking or masking the author's viewpoint, or broadcasting it. Rabelais's voice is scattered among the diffracted voices of his characters, now present in a discreet "I" ("I likewise...," F256/H348), now standing behind Pantagruel's speech lamenting the death of Guillaume du Bellay, now hidden under Panurge's apparent fear of the Decretals, or under Frère Jean's denunciation of the "culinary cabala" of monks (F302/H399). This dispersal, characteristic of the "dialogic novel" according to Mikhail Bakhtin, also explains its difficulties of interpretation, since no one character is the author's mouthpiece.[13]

Inspiration (wine)

Wine ("piot" in French, "vino" in English) holds an important place in Rabelais, and it is tempting to see in it the wine of the Eucharist or the wine of the symposiastic tradition.[14] However, it seems doubtful that its purpose is to recall principles which might be clearer in apologetic treatises or commentaries on Scripture. It is expressly connected with inspiration in Aristotle's *Problem* XXX, which was taken very seriously by Renaissance doctors who used it to explain the physiological nature of creativity; Bacchic "frenzy" was also the first step towards the *furor* of inspiration in Ficino. Rabelais links it to wine and the wine barrel, "[his] one real Helicon... [his] one and only enthusiasm" (F257/H349) – and it is an enthusiasm which, far from inspiring sublime poetry derived from the Greek poet Pindar or elsewhere (as with the Pléiade), dictates scatological verse and merry inventions. Wine in Rabelais is a fundamentally community phenomenon and accompanies get-togethers and banquets of reconciliation. The "abstractor of quintessence" Alcofribas (i.e., "the distiller of alcohol"; title-pages of *Gargantua* and *Pantagruel*) boasts of using more than oil (literary labor) in composing his books: and yet it has been claimed that a careful principle of structuring is at work.

Labor (oil)

Comparison between the different editions of Rabelais highlights a certain art of arrangement, but one that has nothing to do with poetry collections at the same period. Following the medieval prose romances, Rabelais begins by imagining the life of the son of a well-known father, but rewrites the life of the father by the introduction of Frère Jean, the repeated struggle against Scholastic education, and the anti-monastic utopia of Thélème. *Pantagruel* expands from within, since it increases by a good third in 1542, and it is a secondary character, Panurge, who sets another dynamic in motion, one that is foreign to war and doughty deeds, but directed towards an essential peace-time occupation – marriage: an "economic" perspective, as the prologue to *Gargantua* puts it. The journey by land and water of *Book 3* is a consultation of two sorts of expertise: divinatory for the first series (from the consultation of Vergilian lots to Her Trippa) and consultation of experts who, however, contain some failures: the Judge Bridlegoose episode ends abruptly, while Triboulet is "idiotic" to the extent that the emptiness of the bottle is interpreted as a promise of fullness. *Books 3* and *4* have the overall shape of a quest, but insisting on a concentric structure, for *Book 3* especially, can only be demonstrated by distorting and by focusing on centers that are too specific not to raise doubts.[15] Whereas the conciliatory position of the giants-kings limits their room for maneuver, the flexibility and inventivity of Panurge, Frère Jean, and their acolytes increase the unpredictability of the episodes in the first two books; then the inventory of knowledge and the wind play the role of dynamos for the author's whims. If the adventures are implausible and based on an ironic "merveilleux," Rabelais highlights the causal order of fiction which substitutes for the Fortune of medieval narrative, the Destiny of the Stoics, and Christian Providence.

The aesthetics of Rabelais's novels can be compared with the medieval grotesque and that "rustic" style that Ernst Kris understood as a component of Renaissance Mannerism.[16] Even though Rabelais borrows settings from the *Dream of Poliphile*[17] and the Abbey of Thélème is inspired by the architecture of the new *châteaux*, the typology of characters and the implausibility of the plot derive more from the burlesque, such as Poggio's *Facetiae* or Folengo's *Baldus*. Thus the massacre at Seuillé is made bearable by its burlesque parody of heroic exploits; Olympus will later be derided; while many episodes are generated by distention rather than by digression: bloating dominates the birth of Pantagruel, "the year of great medlars"

(F137/H217; translation modified) which make the body swell, in whole or in part. The resurrection of Epistémon is an outgrowth of an episode of war, Gargantua's double education an extension of an episode in a fairytale childhood. The story of the wedding at Basché (F462–71/H564–75) reveals the masochistic personality of the Shysteroos, and the misdeeds of the Decretals populate the island of the Papimaniacs. Novelistic adventures are pregnant with potential lists – the games and genealogy of Gargantua, the asswipes, the twofold *blason* of the bollock and the madman, the anatomy of Fastilent, and the proliferating list of plants accompanying "Pantagruelion" (F404–5/H503–5). Rabelais thus employs a popular and learned humanism, in a vernacular language which contains all others, drawing into his novels a good many folklore elements, the laughter of carnival, the festive calendar, and the burlesque, thus offering a savory and strongly sexualized humanism.

Gender

The future of man

The question of women seems to be concentrated in *Book 3*, where Panurge questions himself about his marriage:[18] the divinations give results interpreted pessimistically by Pantagruel and confirmed by what scholars say about the nature of woman. These views derive both from the fairly misogynist comic tradition well established in France in the Middle Ages and from a theological question about the compatibility between marriage and the demands of Christianity – the disadvantages of married life and the connection between flesh and sin were the principal obstacles to the contemplative life.

The ambiguity of the word "devoir" in French links the moral question to divination: on the one hand there is "devoir" as "must" ("Must Panurge get married?") which is axiological and normative, to which the wise ought to be able to reply, and on the other hand there is "devoir" as "to be about to" which bears on the future, of which prophets are the specialists. The end of the narrative proposes a sort of convergence since the philosopher Trouillogan puts everything in the hands of heaven (F364–8/H463–7), while Judge Bridlegoose with his tiny dice (F375–6/H474–6) and Triboullet with his empty bottle (F396/H494) equally refer to fate and the uncertainty of interpretation. The empty bottle could signify a drunken woman or a sober woman, and the indecisiveness about "the word of the Bottle" subsists right to the end of *Book 4*, where the narrative is suspended in an unfinished quest. The problem of the authenticity of the pseudo "final" book in which Panurge would at last joyously embark on a happy married future (an epilogue ultimately rejected by Rabelais) brings us back to uncertainty about the author's "antifeminism."

It is indeed difficult to know Rabelais's position about "the excellence of the feminine sex," a debate which was reopened in 1529 by Henry Cornelius Agrippa, after the preceding "Querelles des Femmes" (quarrels over women) in the time of Christine de Pisan and the "Querelles des Amies" (quarrels over lady-loves) contemporary with *Pantagruel* and *Gargantua*. The defenders of women had been outraged by the crude misogyny of the *Roman de la Rose* (*Romance of the Rose*) in the part written by Jean de Meung, whereas the adoration of "lady-loves" in the courtly and Petrarchist tradition was the subject of new collections of poetry from the Marotic and Lyons poets, then by members of the Pléiade whose beginnings Rabelais knew. Devotion to the Virgin and the praise of virtuous women in moral literature also privileged exceptional women. By contrast Rabelais's work may have seemed like a confirmation of the ontological inferiority of woman.

Commonplaces

At a time when the Protestant Reformation returned to the incompatibility between apostolic vocation and marriage in order to reject priestly celibacy, Rabelais sets out all the elements of the debate from the most well-worn *topoi* that sustained the literature of *fabliaux* and *nouvelles*, to the Apostle Paul's distrust of women and marriage (F364/H463). With the exception of the incomparable figure of Marguerite de Navarre, a real person, and the Sibyl of Panzoust, a creature of almost infernal fiction (F306/H402), the female characters present or alluded to in the narratives have walk-on parts or get only fleeting mentions. In *Pantagruel* and *Gargantua* women contribute to the parody of learned historiography which uses fiction without admitting to it: the female giants as wives and mothers of giants fulfil their gigantic destiny. Galemelle, created by Merlin like her husband Grandgousier, becomes Gargamelle in Rabelais who expands the previous model without mentioning her any further after the astounding birth of her son Gargantua (*Gargantua*, chapter 3, F12–13/H14–15). Badebec, who is likewise sexually well provided (*Pantagruel*, chapters 2–3, F140–4/H222–5), is invented by Rabelais to give Gargantua a wife and she dies at the birth of the giant Pantagruel. She is, above all, the inspiration for a lament *pro et contra* from her husband (F143/H225) and for a grotesque epitaph which portrays her with a "face as lean and as fair as any crow" (F144/H226). Just as circumstantial are the "Parisian Lady" wooed by Panurge and then the victim of his mean-spirited prank, and the enigmatic lover of Pantagruel in episodes which are the direct antithesis of the Petrarchism fashionable at the time. Rabelais pretends that Constant Love did not exist, and the gigantic obscenity of the first two novels is then principally taken over by Panurge who proposes to construct new indestructible walls for Paris by the commingling of genitalia.

Legal inferiority

If certain humanists granted woman an important place in the Christian household (Erasmus, Vives), encouraging a simple piety and a virtue compatible with social order, and if the renewed religious orders (Observantines, Minims, Béguines, Third Orders) saw emerging in their midst a female piety and the desire for a specific organization, they hardly objected to the return to Roman Law which was much less favorable to women than French customs in respect of inheritance and independence. The principle of woman's basic defectiveness which Rabelais seems to borrow from Vives (based on curiosity, superficiality, and disobedience) comes up again in her backward-looking legal status. Woman was a "relative" being and was only considered in her relationship with her parents, her husband, God, the go-between or the master. In 1524, a friend of Rabelais's at Fontenay-le-Comte, the lawyer André Tiraqueau, published an expanded version of his *De legibus connubialibus* (*On the Laws of Marriage*) in which he claimed to be following ancient Lombard or Gallic law but was rather Roman and canonical in inspiration, putting the married woman under the watchful eye of her husband without, however, restricting the rights of the spinster or the widow.[19] There is nothing to prove connivance between the two authors at the time of *Book 3*, and another friend of Rabelais, Amaury Bouchard, had refuted Tiraqueau (1522). Moreover, the opinions largely unfavorable to women expressed in the four novels are put in the mouths of fictional characters and can only with reservation be attributed to Rabelais. The Thélème episode which advocates equal education for young people (all beautiful) contains a statement of brutal reality: a woman who is neither beautiful nor good is only suitable for "putt[ing] in a convent" (Gargantua, F117/H138) or for "mak[ing] shirts" (Frère Jean, *ibid.*).

Comic targets

The heart of this misogyny is composed less of legal presuppositions than by the speech of Dr. Rondibilis about "muliebrity" (*Book 3*, chapters 31–4, F361–2/H448–61), which takes up Plato's theory – widespread at the time – that made woman a being dominated by the moon and by a "frenzied animal" (*F357/H455*) which directed all her appetites towards insatiable sexuality (chapter 32). This gave philosophical and medical support to the traditional image of the adulterous woman, because every woman naturally "lusts after" forbidden things, as farce and satirical literature already demonstrated. This time-honored comic mechanism of the talkative and cantankerous wife, beating her husband like a "wedding drum" (*Book 4*, *F470/H574*) if she is faithful, seems the only feminine image which is contrasted with the strumpet, another source of dread for men expressed by Panurge.

Since the Virgin is absent from this work except for a few exclamations by Panurge or the narrator bordering on disrespect, it is the flesh of women which is the focus for jokes, fears, and lechery. In examples quoted by the main characters are rapidly mentioned some goddesses, mothers, the wife of the jealous Hans Carvel (*Book 3*, chapter 28, *F346–7/H442–3*), young girls lusted after as they are encountered by Panurge and even Frère Jean (*Book 4*, chapter 10, *F458–9/H561–2*), a large number of prostitutes, nurses with limp breasts, midwives, widows, serving girls and chambermaids "sampled" by their masters (*Book 4*, *F538/H647*), picturesque nuns (Sister Bigass, *F313/H410–11*; the nuns of Thrustitindeep, *F360/H459*), and old women who teach lessons: involuntarily in the case of the "everlasting old woman" in Panurge's tale (*Pantagruel*, chapter 15, *F184/H269*) and the ploughman's wife in the risqué tale told by the narrator (*Book 4*, *F535–9/H642–7*), and intentionally in the case of the witch-cum-Sibyl of Panzoust, the only "real" female character, the harbinger woman of *Book 3*. If she fits in with the unflattering stereotype of the witch with dubious rituals, she seems as venerable as an ancient Sibyl. The final display of her "Sibyl's hole" does not exclude a positive interpretation of an archaic myth referring to the archetype of the fruitful power of a subterranean comic divinity, a Proserpine who is hideous but productive of children. The repulsive hag and the attractive young woman play their respective roles in the great cycle of cosmic renewal to which Rabelais the naturalist may not be insensible. It is the very mystery of a "whatsitsname" ("comment a nom," *F539/H648*) that has produced many offspring which puts the devil of Popefigland to flight (*Book 4*, chapter 47).

However, the allegorical characters put a question mark over the antagonism of the sexes: the warlike Chitterlings of *Book 4* (chapter 35) are shaped like the male member, as the Hebrew name of their queen Niphleseth ("male member") indicates, and are said to represent the effeminate enemies of the time (the English rather than the Genevans),[20] destined to be chopped to pieces if they persist in waging war. The political allusion seems to prevail here over the unlikelihood of a female target.

Book 3 was exploited by the *Louenge des femmes* (*Praise of Women*, 1551) attributed to Thomas Sébillet, who approvingly picks up Rondibilis's speech. It was attacked for the same reason by François de Billon in the *Fort inexpugnable de l'honneur du sexe féminin* (*The Impregnable Fort of the Honor of the Feminine Sex*, 1555), and modern criticism has attempted to extricate Rabelais from the apparently conservative position of the narrator and the fictional characters. Women are at the very least desired readers: the prologue to *Pantagruel* numbers among its audience "ladies and maidens," and *Book 3* is placed under the protection of the Queen of Navarre, this woman "drawn from the blood of France" whom the prologue praises unreservedly. Protection was indeed necessary since Rabelais's novels – heretical, obscene, and evangelical – could not be put into just anybody's hands, particularly those of women.

Sign manipulations

Ciphers

Rabelais's work displays a great variety of interpretive methods. Humanist dialectic and rhetoric seem to have scorned the very elaborate semiotics of the late Middle Ages, but it informs many episodes over the four books. Thus, in addition to the dispute by signs with Thaumaste and gesticulation with Goatsnose (Nazdecabre, *Book 3*, chapters 19–20), we also find the physiognomy of Panurge and Frère Jean, the divine sign of Tau, the gestures of Eudemon and Triboulet, the magical signs of Her Trippa, the story of Sister Bigass (*F*313/*H*410–1), and the rites of the Papimaniacs; the storm in *Book 4* is the sign and consequence of the death of a hero (who also happens to be Rabelais's protector). Their institutional and performative character highlights the relationship between belief and signs that are supposedly natural or divine, whereas there is no greater absolute truth in linguistic signs than there is in the rest. It is the shared nature of signs that is the basis of their efficacy and, like other humanists, Rabelais downplays the linguistic obstacle.

Rabelais remained a Hellenizing disciple of Budé, Erasmus, Hippocrates, and Galen. In medical practice, he belonged to the school of Galen, although he leant towards medical humanism: the practice of dissection, an interest in anatomical description, and the mechanisms that link body and soul in passions and desire.[21] He followed Hippocrates in his conception of the cure as a "farce with three characters" (the doctor, the patient, and the illness) and, taking fiction as therapy seriously, recommended reading Pantagrueline books as one prescribes psychotropic medication, able to chase away one's cares if not to cure toothache. His medicine remained a classic blend of the Arab and Greek traditions, and while he did not deny the influence of the stars on the body, he rejected the use of astrology in legal cases. From neo-Platonism, he takes the demonology set out in *Book 3* about some types of divination, dreams, and the dying poet, and in *Book 4* to explain the storm: the existence of intermediary spirits was often accepted at the time, although Rabelais makes limited use of them, and in this and in other areas his attitude seems at the very least ambivalent.[22] Thus the great magus Her Trippa, who caricatures two well-known figures – Henry Cornelius Agrippa, a neo-Platonic philosopher, and Johannes Trithemius, a Benedictine infatuated with cryptography – is ridiculed outright.

In addition to reading a large number of the Greek texts available at that time, Rabelais is also acquainted with biblical and rabbinic Hebrew. *Book 4* displays a notable use of the latter: the 1552 edition names the character Bacbuc (until then, merely "Dive Bouteille" [Divine Bottle]). Several of the islands have Hebrew-sounding names and Rabelais follows the example of the Jewish philosopher and Aristotle commentator Levi ben Gerson in reversing the letters of the name of the prophet *Habaquq* (Habakkuk) into "Ha-Baqbuq" ("The Bottle"), thus turning Bacbuc into a sublime prophetess who holds the key to all secrets.[23]

Languages

Rabelais's multilingualism had late medieval precedents such as Pathelin and his patter, Villon's "Ballade en jargon," farces, and mystery plays. But he turns this into a feature of Panurge, at once adroit and clownish, who, more so than his master Pantagruel, expresses the vitality of vernacular French.[24] Panurge's great skill in languages in the meeting episode might be a representation of the humanist ideal of Pentecostal glossolalia (as found in polyglot psalters), which obviates the curse of Babel by learning all languages.[25] And whereas the Limousin schoolboy finds out to his cost that he does not even know French, the national language, Panurge, by contrast, recenters his polyglossia on the French of Touraine, the "Garden of France," already considered the province where the best French was spoken because the monarchy had made it their residence. He thus proceeds the reverse way round from Folengo's macaronic burlesque (Latin mixed with Italian).[26] On the other hand, Panurge takes things to extremes: Basque, Lanternois, Scottish, and Danish are added to his languages after 1532 and Rabelais seems aware of the dangers of encyclopedism and humanism's hunger for texts and languages. In his parody, the *Brief Declaration*, he apes the qualities and failings of contemporary lexicography, throwing in, for example, irrelevant definitions ("tragœdies," *F595/H705*, and "période," *F594/H704*) as did plagiarizing lexicographers of his times. He imitates true lexicographers by glossing his own scatological neologisms ("pital" or "earthenware pot for a close-stool," *F606/H712*; "spyrathe" or "turd of a nannygoat," *F606/H713*) and his popular terminology ("marmes, merdigues," "turd of God," *F595/H705*), and provides a highly relevant definition of his own register: "Satyricque mocquerie [. . .] a way to speak ill of each and every one at will" (*F594/H704*). As part of his legacy, Rabelais's learned neologisms will themselves end up in Robert Estienne's *Dictionnaire français-latin* (1549), Nicot's *Trésor de la langue française* (1573–1606), and Cotgrave's *French and English Dictonnarie* (1611).

Pantagruelism or humanism of the middle way

Imitation of Lucian, the Greek rhetor, already appears in those episodes of *Pantagruel* situated in "another world" (the resurrection of Epistémon, the trip round Pantagruel's mouth). It is less marked in *Gargantua*, perhaps owing to the Greek author's increased reputation for impiety.[27] Lucian returns, however, in a more clearly philosophical form in *Books* 3 and 4 since he is linked to the figure of Diogenes. The prologue of *Book* 3, centered on Diogenes the Cynic, presents the author as powerless and penniless, like the philosopher, able only to reflect back to men their own image in enlarged form. Like the new leader of a philosophical sect, Rabelais founds "Pantagruelism." The term appears in the subtitle to *Gargantua* only in 1535,[28] and the verb "to pantagruelize" can be found in the first chapter, with the definition: "Pantagruelizing, that is to say . . . drinking your fill and reading the horrific deeds of Pantagruel" (*F8/H10*). "Pantagruelists" feature in the plural, in the epilogue to the *Pantagruel* of 1534, signifying those who "live in peace, joy, and health, always having a good time" (*F245/H337*), and the prologue to *Gargantua* speaks of "good companies of Pantagruelists" (*F5/H8*). The prologue to *Book* 3 makes the philosophical nature of Pantagruelism explicit: "a specific form and individual property that our ancestors called Pantagruelism, on condition of which they never take in bad part things they know to issue from a good, free, and honest heart" (*F258/H351*). We recognize here at one and the same time an evangelical precept, a Stoico-Epicurean attitude (*ataraxia*, imperturbability), and a legal expression, "not to take in bad part," "to take in good part" ("in meliorem partem"),[29] echoed in the description of Pantagruel: "All things he took in good part, all actions he interpreted for the good; never did he torment himself, never did he take offense; else he would have quite departed from out the deific manor of reason, if otherwise he had not let himself be affected" (F264/H357). Earlier, Pantagruel "took everything at pleasure" ("il prenoit tout à plaisir," F237/H329; translation changed), just as in *Book 4* he represents "the ideal and exemplar of all joyous perfection" (F407/H506). Rabelais suggests that the reader can imitate this character by a similar attitude, not only through Stoic *ataraxia*, but through what it shares with Epicureanism – an indifference encouraged by Diogenes and by the charity of the "fool in Christ."

The prologue to *Book 4* reinforces this philosophical dimension without forgetting that the Pantagruelist is a banqueter; thus the narrator defines himself as a Pantagruelist, ready to drink and practice "a certain gayety of spirit confected in disdain for fortuitous things" (F425/H523). The expression emphasizes detachment, a mix of gaiety and *ataraxia*, neither completely Epicurean nor Stoic, but closer to the scorn of the world affected by Diogenes, who was also a disciple of Socrates. The equivalence between Diogenic Cynicism and the Pantagruelic outlook is made in the prologue to *Book 3*: "[I am going to draw] a merry fourth, of Pantagruelic sayings; by me it will be licit to call them Diogenic" (F258/H350).[30]

In the prologue to *Gargantua*, the reader was invited to observe the rational attitude of the dog (already a symbol of Cynicism?) that provided the hermeneutic lesson. In *Book 3*, Diogenes operates in person: he is the only man in Corinth to "harry his barrel" (F256/H348), just as the author is the only one in France to write such Diogenic novels, apparently inoffensive simulacra of reality. Both proceed back-to-front and paradoxically, just as a modern Pantagruelist takes life "backwards way on" (F404/H503; translation changed) "in a way paradoxical to all philosophers" (*ibid.*). The paradoxical couples of Pantagruel and Panurge, Gargantua and Frère Jean (who imagine a back-to-front abbey) narrativize the small-scale model of philosophical fiction that is the Diogenic barrel, which is used as a house and then a weapon of war. Far from presenting Pantagruel as the only real "humanist" in his novels, Rabelais accepts all the members of the company, including the rebellious Panurge, who recalls the power of discourse and the importance of the reader. Panurge is the one who starts the quest going and his duo with Pantagruel is always looking forward to the next episode in the search for a solution that is never satisfying, as in an endless game of real-tennis. Pantagruelism is a humanism also because the lessons of classical rhetoric have been preserved and the reception of the text taken account of: "Pantagruelizing" implies reading.[31]

Translated by John O'Brien

NOTES

1 For further details about these aspects of Rabelais's biography, see Henri Busson, "Les Églises contre Rabelais," *Études Rabelaisiennes*, 7 (1967), pp. 1–81; Richard Cooper, *Rabelais et l'Italie*, Études Rabelaisiennes, 24 (Geneva: Droz, 1991); Jean Dupèbe, "Remarques critiques sur la date de la naissance de Rabelais," in Jean Lecointe, Catherine Magnien, Isabelle Pantin, and Marie-Claire Thomine, eds., *Devis d'amitié: Mélanges en l'honneur de Nicole Cazauran* (Paris: Champion, 2002), pp. 732–7; and Marie-Luce Demonet, "Trois vies de Rabelais: Franciscain, bénédictin, médecin," in Christian Tottmann and Frank La Brasca, eds., *Vie solitaire, vie civile* (Paris: Champion, forthcoming). For humanism in Rabelais's works, see Verdun-Louis Saulnier, *Rabelais dans son enquête*, 2 vols. (Paris: SEDES, 1982–3) and Michael Screech, *Rabelais* (London: Duckworth, 1979). For the definition of humanism as "humane letters," see Paul Oskar Kristeller, *Renaissance Thought, 1: The Classical, Scholastic, and Humanist Strains* (New York: Harper & Row, 1961), p. 9, for the "umanista" and his work as a teacher of the Greek and Latin Classics.
2 Diane Desrosiers-Bonin, *Rabelais et l'humanisme civil* (Geneva: Droz, 1992).
3 The "philosophy of Christ": the precepts of Scripture acting as humankind's moral standard. See Léon-E. Halkin, *Erasmus. A Critical Biography*, John Tonkin, trans. (Oxford: Blackwell, 1993).
4 See Charles Schmitt, Quentin Skinner and Eckhard Kessler, eds., *The Cambridge History of Renaissance Thought* (Cambridge: Cambridge University Press, 1988); and for the literary aspects of Aristotelianism, see Ullrich Langer, ed., *Beyond the "Poetics": Aristotle and Early Modern Literature* (Geneva: Droz, 2002).
5 The Poitiers connections have been studied in Marie-Luce Demonet and Stéphan Geonget, eds., *Les Grands Jours de Rabelais en Poitou* (Geneva: Droz, 2006).
6 Walter Stephens has analysed this criticism of historical material at length in *Giants in those Days: Folklore, Ancient History, and Nationalism* (Lincoln: University of Nebraska Press, 1989).
7 André Tournon develops this point in *"En Sens agile." Les acrobaties de l'esprit selon Rabelais* (Paris: Champion, 1995); on interpretation and "disturbance," see also Terence Cave, *Pré-histoires: Textes troublés au seuil de la modernité* (Geneva: Droz, 1999).
8 Dupuy Herbault's condemnation of Rabelais is not only based on the fact that he writes fictions, but also on the "lascivious" aspects of these works and the "false religion" expounded in Thélème: *Theotimus, sive de tollendis et expungendis malis libris* (Paris: Roigny, 1549).
9 This massacre of three thousand Waldenses in Provence represents the triumph of intransigent policy over the more conciliatory approach of Cardinal Jean du Bellay.
10 See Screech, *Rabelais*, *passim*; Margaret Mann Phillips, ed. and trans., *The "Adages" of Erasmus: A Study with Translations* (Cambridge: Cambridge University Press, 1964).
11 Pascale Mounier, *Le Roman humaniste* (Paris: Champion, 2007), argues in favor of a specific "humanist novel" with Rabelais and Barthélemy Aneau (*Alector*, 1560).

12 "La Farce de Regnault qui se marie à La Volée," owing to the discovery Jelle Koopmans describes in "Rabelais et l'esprit de la farce," in M.-L. Demonet and S. Geonget, eds., *Les Grands Jours de Rabelais*, pp. 299–311.

13 Michael Bakhtin, *Rabelais and his World*, H. Iswolsky, trans. (Boston: MIT Press, 1968) and Richard M. Berrong, *Rabelais and Bakhtin: Popular Culture in "Gargantua" and "Pantagruel"* (Lincoln: University of Nebraska Press, 1986).

14 See Michel Jeanneret, *Des Mets et des mots* (Paris: Corti, 1987).

15 Edwin Duval, *The Design of Rabelais's "Tiers Livre de Pantagruel"* (Geneva: Droz, 1997); Guy Demerson, *Rabelais* (Paris: Balland, 1986), p. 236; Jean Céard, introduction to his edition of *Le Tiers Livre* (Paris: Pochothèque, 1993), pp. xlii–xliii; and my discussion in "Les Textes et leur centre à la Renaissance: Une structure absente?" in Frédéric Tinguely, ed., *La Renaissance décentrée* (Geneva: Droz, 2008), pp. 158–73.

16 Ernst Kris, *Le Style rustique* (Paris: Macula, 2005 [1926]).

17 Gilles Polizzi, ed., introduction to *Le Songe de Poliphile*, Jean Martin, trans. (Paris: Imprimerie Nationale, 1994).

18 Among the many studies that deal with the topics of marriage and feminism in the age of Rabelais, see notably Michael Screech, *The Rabelaisian Marriage: Aspects of Rabelais's Religion, Ethics and Comic Philosophy* (London: Edward Arnold, 1958), and Kathleen Bauschatz, "Rabelais and Marguerite de Navarre on Sixteenth-Century Views of Clandestine Marriage," *The Sixteenth-Century Journal*, 34/2 (2003), pp. 395–408.

19 See Evelyne Berriot-Salvatore, *Les Femmes dans la société française de la Renaissance* (Geneva: Droz, 1990).

20 Paul J. Smith has demonstrated this new interpretation of this episode in "'Les Ames anglaises sont andouillettes': Nouvelles perspectives sur l'épisode des Andouilles (*Quart Livre*, ch. 35–42)," Cerisy Colloquium (2000) (Geneva: Droz, forthcoming).

21 Roland Antonioli, *Rabelais et la médecine* (Geneva: Droz, 1976).

22 Jean Céard, *La Nature et les prodiges: L'insolite au XVIe siècle*, 2nd edn. (Geneva: Droz, 1996) and Michel Jeanneret, *Le Défi des signes: Rabelais et la crise de l'interprétation à la Renaissance* (Orléans: Paradigme, 1994).

23 Levi ben Gerson (Gersonides) wrote a fourteenth-century pseudo-biblical text destined for *purim* (the Jewish carnival). It was edited in Italy in 1552, before the publication of *Book 4* (Marie-Luce Demonet, "Le Nom de Bacbuc", *Réforme, Humanisme, Renaissance*, 34 (1992), pp. 41–66).

24 The character of Panurge has been particularly studied by Myriam Marrache-Gouraud, *"Hors toute intimidation": Panurge ou la parole singulière* (Geneva: Droz, 2003), challenging Gérard Defaux's studies of Panurge as a Sophist, *Pantagruel et les sophistes: Contribution à l'histoire de l'humanisme chrétien au XVIème siècle* (The Hague: Nijhoff, 1973).

25 Lazare Sainéan, *La Langue de Rabelais*, 2 vols. (Paris: Boccard, 1922–3); Mireille Huchon, *Rabelais grammairien: De l'histoire du texte aux problèmes d'authenticité* (Geneva: Droz, 1981); Claude-Gilbert Dubois, *Mythe et langage au XVIe siècle* (Bordeaux: Ducros, 1970); François Rigolot, *Les Langages de Rabelais* (Geneva: Droz, 1972; reprint 1996); Jean Céard, "De Babel à la Pentecôte: La transformation du mythe de la confusion des langues au XVIe siècle",

Bibliothèque d'Humanisme et Renaissance, 42/3 (1980), pp. 577–94; Marie-Luce Demonet, *Les Voix du signe: Nature et origine du langage à la Renaissance, 1480–1580* (Paris: Champion, 1992), pp. 554 ff.

26 Teofilo Folengo, *Baldus*, 1st edn. (1517). The eponymous hero of this work counts among his followers the giant Fracassus and the roguish Cingar, a model for Panurge.

27 Pontus de Tyard will call Rabelais the "French Lucian" – not a compliment: *De recta nominum impositione* (Lyons: Roussin, 1603), p. 27; now in Jean Céard and Jean-Claude Margolin, eds. and French trans., *Œuvres complètes*, VII, *La Droite Imposition des noms* (Paris: Champion, 2007), p. 66.

28 The oldest copy known (Bibliothèque nationale de France) has no title-page.

29 On the legal aspects of this attitude, see Stéphan Geonget, *La Notion de perplexité à la Renaissance* (Geneva: Droz, 2006), pp. 119–28.

30 Lucianism and Cynicism in Rabelais have been studied by Christiane Lauvergnat-Gagnière, *Lucien de Samosate et le lucianisme en France au XVIe siècle: Athéisme et polémique* (Geneva: Droz, 1988) and Michèle Clément, *Le Cynisme à la Renaissance* (Geneva: Droz, 2005).

31 Translator's note: the French original contains an untranslatable pun at this point, "Pantagrué-lisant" ("Pantagruelizing" and "reading Pantagruel").

7

EDWIN DUVAL

Putting religion in its place

The two decades during which Rabelais wrote his four books of *Pantagruel* (1532–52) were a period of great religious ferment and strife. Framed by the dissemination of influential works by Erasmus and Luther in the 1520s and the outbreak of the Wars of Religion in 1562, these years witnessed the rise of biblical humanism and severe repressions by the Faculty of Theology in Paris (the Sorbonne), the creation of a Reformed Church in France and the convocation of the Council of Trent, and a Gallican crisis that nearly ended twelve centuries of papal authority in France. Rabelais's own personal experience placed him at the very center of this ferment. As a Franciscan monk in the monastery of Le Puy-Saint-Martin at Fontenay-le-Comte (before 1520–24) who ran afoul of his order for studying the language of the Greek New Testament, as a Benedictine monk at Maillezais in Poitou (1524–26?) who somehow incurred the charge of apostasy after leaving his monastery to study medicine in Paris and Montpellier, as a secular priest at the Abbey of Saint-Maur-des-Fossés which he himself helped to secularize (1536), as the holder of several benefices (Saint-Maur, Saint-Christophe-du-Jambet, Saint-Martin de Meudon), and as a doctor to Cardinal Jean du Bellay in his diplomatic missions to Rome, Rabelais was as familiar as anyone could be with all aspects – theological, institutional, political – of the religious currents and conflicts of his time.[1]

These currents and conflicts occupy a central place in Rabelais's satirical books, as do his polemical positions in religious matters. Such is the nature of satire, however, that these positions, while expressed with great vigor, have been understood in widely divergent ways. In his own lifetime Rabelais found himself condemned by both the Sorbonne and Calvin,[2] while readers of our own time have detected in his religious stance traces of everything from atheism to orthodox scholastic theology, with many strains and degrees of reformed Christianity in between. The modern consensus, now solidly established, is that Rabelais was a Christian humanist in the mold of Erasmus, whom he admired greatly.[3] Like Erasmus he tended to look upon the Greek and Hebrew texts of the Bible as the only authentic foundation of Christianity and, consequently, to view all beliefs, practices, doctrines, and institutions not expressly authorized by Scripture as spurious accretions, dilutions, and corruptions – what Erasmus called *constitutiones humanae*, or "human inventions." Because these "inventions" include many of the things most essential to the medieval Church – scholastic theology, monasticism and the papacy, canonical hours and the Mass, the cult of the saints and of the Virgin Mary, Lent – Rabelais, like Erasmus, tended to share with Protestant Reformers a fundamental hostility to Church orthodoxies and hierarchies. But, again like Erasmus, he opposed the Reformers too, in their radical break from the Church and especially in their elaboration of new theological orthodoxies to replace the old one, preferring instead the general ethical principles contained in what Erasmus called the "philosophy of Christ."

Rabelais's hostility to doctrinal orthodoxy and to various *constitutiones humanae* of the medieval Church is evident throughout his works and is relatively easy to interpret. Far more difficult is the task of inferring from his critiques a positive theological position, much less an unambiguous confessional stance. Several factors contribute to this difficulty. One is an all-pervasive, mercurial irony that constantly threatens to undermine even the most plausible positive expressions of religious belief. Another is Rabelais's practice of quoting and misquoting biblical and liturgical texts for comic effect, a practice that many modern readers have assumed, anachronistically, is necessarily subversive. Yet another is that Rabelais's religious stance evolved considerably from book to book, along with the religious climate and particular circumstances to which he was responding. In light of these difficulties it is prudent not to generalize too quickly about religion in Rabelais's books, but to consider the place and function of religious allusions within the immediate context and particular economy of each separate book, and the place of each book within the context of its own historical moment.

It is useful also for the purposes of analysis to distinguish three distinct types or modes of religious expression in Rabelais: satire, parody, and (for want of a better term) apologetics. Satire and parody are of course hallmarks of Rabelais's writing, but they serve different purposes and function in very different ways. While satire serves the entirely negative purpose of condemning through ridicule, parody is ideologically neutral. Contrary to what our modern sensibilities might lead us to assume, deformations of biblical and liturgical texts can be, in Rabelais as in the ambient culture, simply innocuous expressions of convivial hilarity. But Rabelais often uses parody functionally, as a narrative device, to suggest analogies that in turn convey precise meanings. In only rare cases do parodies carry any particular ideological weight of their own. As for the third type of religious allusion – "apologetics" in the sense of a positive representation of "correct" religious belief – this is by far the most difficult to interpret, since ideologies are rarely expressed directly and unproblematically in Rabelais, but tend to inhere in ironic structures and situations, requiring considerable interpretive tact.

Pantagruel (1532)

The first of Rabelais's books is, from the particular point of view that concerns us, the most complex and the most oblique. Satire is surprisingly rare here. The scholastic theologians most hostile to progressives like Erasmus, Luther, and Reuchlin are lampooned as authors of ponderous tomes on trivial pursuits, petty squabbles, and the lowest of bodily functions in the Library of St. Victor (chapter 7) and the medieval popes most notorious for expanding the temporal power of the papacy are sentenced to abject poverty and powerlessness in Hades (chapter 30), but such barbs are fleeting and incidental. The primary focus of the book is not religion at all, but reforms in higher learning as a means to social and political justice. The general idea is that "Gothic" learning is not only barbaric but deeply implicated in a culture of violence. Only a return to the pure sources of ancient learning, especially to the original texts of Roman law purged of their medieval glosses and interpreted with the aid of "moral and natural philosophy" and "history" (chapters 8 and 10), can save the world from murder and imperialism as represented by Werewolf and King Anarche. The program of Pantagruel is thus essentially secular, focusing on humanism as the necessary agent and foundation of a new ethical and political order.

Religion has an important place in this utopian scheme, however, as two "apologetic" passages clearly show. One occurs in Gargantua's famous letter spelling out a complete humanist program of study (chapter 8). In the place where we would expect to find theology in this program, Gargantua pointedly recommends daily study of the Bible in its original languages, and at the end he speaks of a strictly private, intimate relationship with God: "serve, love, and fear God, and in Him put all your thoughts and all your hope; and by faith formed of charity, be adjoined to Him, in such wise that you will never be sundered from Him by sin" (F162/H245). Gargantua's silences are as significant as his advice. By simple omission he in effect abolishes scholastic theology, the clergy, and all liturgical forms of worship, to make room for a direct, unmediated study of the original sources of Christianity and personal, unmediated communion with God. This is a clear expression of biblical humanism and evangelism as positive religious values.

A similar passage is found in the prayer uttered by Pantagruel in the last moments before his decisive duel with Werewolf (chapter 29). The hero addresses God directly here as his personal "Protector and Savior" in whom he places all his trust and hope: "en toy seul est ma totale confiance et espoir" (F227/H318–19). This last clause, omitted in Frame's translation, states the fundamental evangelical principle illustrated by the prayer itself – namely, that no clergy, ceremonies, saints, or sacraments are necessary for communion with God, much less for succor or salvation. In beseeching God's aid, moreover, the hero makes a solemn vow, not to perform the kind of "works" demanded by traditional Catholicism (donations to the Church, Masses) but, on the contrary, to abolish all such "Papist" works and replace them with the pure word of the Gospel: "I will have Thy Gospel preached pure, simple, and entire, so that the abuses of a bunch of hypocrites [*papelars*] and false prophets, who, by human institutions [*constitutions humaines*] and depraved inventions, have envenomed the whole world, will be driven forth from around me" (F227/H319). "Papelars et faulx prophetes" designate the clergy and the theologians, their "constitutions humaines" (a literal translation of Erasmus's *constitutiones humanae*) designate the Mass and theology. All are to be replaced by the Gospel in the utopian political and social order imagined in *Pantagruel*.

More conspicuous than either satire or apologetics in *Pantagruel* is parody. Whole episodes are in fact structured as parodies of well-known events in the Bible. These are not satirical but are nevertheless crucial to the meaning of the book. Parodies of the Fall, the Flood, and the genealogy of Christ in chapter 1 conspire to establish a strict analogy between the heroic gesta of Pantagruel and the redemptive mission of the Christian Messiah, but with a difference: Christ's role was to reconcile man to God by reversing the effects of man's original sin (Adam and Eve); Pantagruel's is to reconcile man to his fellow man by reversing the effects of the first murder (Cain and Abel). Far from mocking salvational history, the opening chapter of *Pantagruel* borrows the structure of that history to suggest, in comic but economical fashion, a parallel plot centered on humankind's tragic alienation from itself. According to this implicit analogy, the messianic role of the hero is to re-establish brotherly love in a "fallen" world of violence and bloodshed, in accordance with the second half of the Great Commandment, "love your brother as yourself" (Mt 22:39). The social and political utopia established at the conclusion of the book is founded on this principle.

Many other parodic elements scattered throughout the book corroborate this redemptive scheme, either by confirming the messianic identity of the hero or, as in the Hades episode (chapter 30), by literalizing the inversion of high and low estates fundamental to Christ's ethics of brotherly love: "The last will be first, and the first last," "Whoever exalts himself will be humbled, and whoever humbles himself will be exalted" (Mt 20:16, 23:12). Virtually all such instances of biblical parody contribute to a single analogy that lends remarkable force to a parable about the value of humanist learning in righting the wrongs of the world. In this sense religion, though not a primary subject, is an essential element of both the structure and the meaning of *Pantagruel*.[4]

The *Pantagrueline prognostication* (1532) and the *Almanachs* for 1533 and 1535

A striking feature of "religion" in *Pantagruel* is the total absence of anything resembling theology in the traditional sense. Metaphysical speculation is in fact firmly rejected – implicitly in the ridicule of Thaumaste's curious inquisitions into the arcane sciences (chapters 18–20) and explicitly in Gargantua's stern injunctions against the "abuses and vanities" of astrology (F161/H244). This anti-metaphysical bias is given emphatic expression in the *Pantagrueline prognostication*, a satirical parody of popular almanacs published the same year as *Pantagruel*, which debunks all pretenses to knowledge of the above and the beyond through a combination of devastating irony, denunciations of prognosticators, and exhortations to accept whatever happens as the inscrutable will of God. Even clearer expressions of this bias are found in the satirical *Almanachs* for 1533 and 1535, which consist almost entirely of direct quotations from the Bible condemning the impiety of all "curieuse inquisition" into God's hidden ways and holy will (*Almanach* for 1535; F761/H939) – what Erasmus called *impia curiositas* (impious curiosity). These minor texts confirm the implications of *Pantagruel*, defining Rabelais's religion as a profoundly skeptical form of Christianity indifferent to things that transcend human experience and hostile to metaphysical speculations of all kinds, whether scholastic, gnostic, reformed, or platonic.

Gargantua (1534?)

Gargantua repeats the basic plot of *Pantagruel* but the focus and mode of its religious message are very different. Satire now dominates and indeed overwhelms the narrative while functional parody is virtually absent, with the result that the book gains in polemical force what it loses in formal and ideological coherence. The two objects of Rabelais's harshest and most sustained satire here are the institutions most directly opposed to true Christianity as defined by Erasmus: the Faculty of Theology in Paris (the Sorbonne) and monasticism. Both are presented as bastions of ignorance, sloth, vanity, filth, and futility, and, more importantly, as preservers of a reactionary, anti-Christian orthodoxy.

Rabelais attacks the Faculty of Theology in two major episodes that greatly expand the discreet anti-scholastic satire of the Library of St. Victor in *Pantagruel*. The subject has a new urgency now because in 1533 the syndic of the Sorbonne, a rabid champion of orthodoxy named Noël Béda, had fomented a dangerous popular uprising against evangelicals like Gérard Roussel and King François I's own sister, Marguerite de Navarre. A pointed allusion to the general alarm caused by this episode suggests that Rabelais's satire is a direct response to it.[5] The attack focuses on stupidity and begins with Gargantua's primary education. The hero's first pedagogues are two "grands theologiens," "docteurs en theologie" (*F37–8/H42–3*, variant) – terms used in the first edition, not translated by Frame, emended in later editions to "sophistes," signifying the same thing less brazenly – incompetent bumblers whose harshness and witlessness are clearly indicated by their names: Maistre Thubal Holofernes and Maistre Jobelin Bridé. After a half century of instruction from these *magistri nostri* Gargantua is still an illiterate dunce. In the episode of the bells of Notre-Dame another *magister noster*, Janotus de Bragmardo, is selected by the "faculté théologale" itself as its most accomplished "theologien," and thus as the perfect representative and spokesman for the "Sorbone" (*F43/H49*, variant) – again terms used in the first edition, edulcorated in later editions. This jewel in the crown of the Sorbonne proves to be an unhygienic, ignorant, stupid, and selfish boor, interested only in the creaturely comforts provided by wine, sausages, and warm breeches. His laboriously prepared "harangue" brims with execrable Latin, faulty logic, misquotations of biblical and liturgical texts, and parodies of scholastic abstractions and syllogisms. The self-incriminating function of this speech is focused in the following chapter when Janotus denounces his own fellow theologians as "buggers, traitors, heretics, and seducers, enemies of God and of virtue" (*F48/H55*). The entire episode is a masterpiece of comic satire and one of Rabelais's most effective blows against the hated "Sorbonicoles."

As for monasticism, the most egregious of all *constitutiones humanae* from a Christian humanist's point of view, Rabelais focuses on the uselessness of the contemplative life as practiced by monks, and on the formalism of monastic observances. The subject is first introduced when Picrochole's undisciplined troops invade the Abbey of Seuillé, a real monastery situated next door to Rabelais's birthplace in La Devinière. Faced with imminent danger the cloistered monks find no better defense than to organize processions and chant formulaic litanies, all of which are of course ineffectual. The day is saved only by a cursing, mocking, truculent bon-vivant of a monk who, preferring action to prayer, single-handedly massacres the invaders using the "staff of the cross" as his weapon (*F67/H79*). Unlike the representatives of the Faculty of Theology, this representative of monasticism – Frère Jean – appears in an entirely positive light, serving to condemn his institution through his divergence from it. In fact Frère Jean is a highly paradoxical figure: an anti-monk in his taste for action, his spontaneity, and his good cheer, but at the same time a kind of super-monk in his devotion to his wine, his frock, and his breviary, in his ability to expedite a Mass in two shakes, and in his utter lack of learning – a "real monk if ever there was one," "a cleric to the teeth in breviary matter" (*F66/H78*). It can perhaps be said that in Frère Jean the futility and formalism of monastic orders are denounced while the traditional petty vices of monks – a taste for wine, women, and hunting, even ignorance – become positive traits because they are unaccompanied by hypocrisy.

This view is supported by one of the few apologetic passages of the *Gargantua*, where Gargantua and his companions discuss what distinguishes their friend Frère Jean from other monks, who are universally shunned (chapters 39–42). All agree that it is Frère Jean's atypical energy, good cheer, and candor that make him welcome in all company. An even more fundamental point to emerge from this discussion is that the prayers of monks are worse than ineffectual. As formulas recited by rote without understanding or feeling they are actually sacrilegious – not prayer at all but "mock-God." True prayer is something spontaneous, personal, and heart-felt, which can take place anywhere *except* in a liturgical setting like that of the monastery: "all real Christians, of all ranks, places, times, pray to God, and the Spirit prays and intercedes for them, and God takes them into His mercy" (*F93/H111*; cf. Rom 8:26). This vigorous statement is Erasmian in its terminology and clearly expresses the humanist case not only against monasticism but against liturgical formalism in general. According to this view, Holy Orders are worse than a false sacrament. They are an anti-Christian abomination.

The anti-monastic satire of the *Gargantua* culminates in the Abbaye de Thélème, an anti-monastery diametrically opposed to Seuillé and instituted "in the opposite way from all the others" (*F116/H137*). Not only is the Benedictine Rule of chastity, poverty, and obedience replaced by its opposite (marriage, wealth, and freedom), but all monastic rules and regulations concerning dress, diet, and observation of seasons, days, and hours are abolished. The single rule of Thélème is a non-rule: "Do what you will" (*F126/H149*). The essential but frequently misunderstood meaning of all this is to be found in the Pauline principle of Christian freedom, according to which all the dietary, vestimentary, and liturgical restrictions and prescriptions of Jewish law had been satisfied by Christ and superseded by the New Law of love. All such observances were henceforth theologically "indifferent" – that is, of no value in obtaining the grace of God or the salvation of the soul. Christians were by definition free to eat, drink, dress, and pray however, wherever, and whenever they wished, provided only that they love. Erasmus made this principle the basis for his most serious critique of *constitutiones humanae*, and of monasticism in particular, arguing that all such institutions are abominable because they reimpose precisely the kind of restrictions and prescriptions that Christ himself had removed. Worse still, the new restrictions and prescriptions, unlike those originally imposed on the Jews, were never sanctioned by God but are mere human inventions, and are even more onerous. Seen from this perspective nothing is more antithetical to Christianity than monasticism. This is precisely the point of Rabelais's vision of an anti-monastery as a deregulated – i.e., re-Christianized – community in which all are free to do as they wish, and in which each voluntarily defers to the whim and pleasure of the others. The point is driven home by the inscription above the entrance of Thélème, denying entrance to scribes, Pharisees, and hypocrites while welcoming those who preach the Gospel: "Enter, we'll found herein a faith profound, / And then confound ... / The foemen who oppose the Holy Word" (*F122/H143*). Coming at the end of a book preoccupied with monasticism, Thélème simply reveals the deeper theological basis of Rabelais's anti-monastic satire.

Other *constitutiones humanae* come in for occasional condemnation in the *Gargantua* as well, most notably pilgrimages and the cult of saints, satirized in chapter 38 and explicitly condemned by Grandgousier in chapter 45, and the Mass and canonical hours, omnipresent in the "Gothic" phase of Gargantua's education but entirely absent from the "humanist" phase, where they are replaced by readings from Scripture and spontaneous prayer (chapters 21 and 23). Satires and apologetics on themes like these develop a consistent view of the Church as corrupted, denatured, and enslaved by medieval traditions, and hint at a remedy in the return to the untrammeled freedom of a paleo-Christian evangelical community.

Parody in the *Gargantua* is for the most part a form of innocuous joking, the high-spirited "palaver of the potted" being an excellent example of this practice (chapter 5). Occasionally, however, parody serves a satirical purpose, as when the narrator misinterprets biblical passages in order to convince his readers to believe his implausible account of Gargantua's birth (chapter 6), or in the "prophetic riddle" where apocalyptic language is used to describe a game of tennis (chapter 58). In the first case Rabelais is drawing a crucial distinction between faith and credulity, in the second he is undercutting the pretensions of prophecy. Both reflect the skeptical strain that is integral to an unburdened, humanistic Christianity.

Book 3 (1546)

Book 3 is unique in Rabelais's *œuvre* in that it focuses not on princes, states, and institutions, but on the household of a single private individual, Panurge. Religion, being no longer necessary as the agent or foundation of a new social and political order, is hardly present. When it does appear, the Erasmian emphasis on biblical authority, interiority, and an ethics of freedom and love is as strong as ever, but the purposes served by religion – its function in the plot as well as its role in the world – are now completely different.

In the episode of Raminagrobis, for example, the monastic orders come in for harsh treatment as the dying poet denounces rapacious monks for troubling the minds of the dying with their intrusive rituals and their insistent solicitations of donations to their monasteries. Raminagrobis condemns these machinations not only because they presuppose that salvation can be bought and sold according to the orthodox principle of justification by works, but because they prevent a personal, direct communion of the individual with God (chapter 21). His invective is in fact perfectly congruent with Erasmus's colloquy on last rites, *Funus*. Apologetics is reinforced by satire when Panurge, now a staunch defender of orthodoxy, in turn condemns Raminagrobis as a blasphemer and a heretic, and defends the Dominican and Franciscan orders as the two indispensable pillars of the sacrosanct "Roman Church" (*F*320/*H*418). His approving mention of "Ichthyophagia" explicitly refers us to another of Erasmus's colloquies, the *Ichthyophagia* (on the "fish-eating" of Lent), thus anchoring the obvious satire of his violent diatribe in the Erasmian view of works as essentially indifferent. Similarly, in another episode Hippothadée, the evangelical Christian paradoxically designated by Pantagruel to represent Theology in counseling Panurge about marriage, quotes Saint Paul liberally and literally to present marriage as a legitimate, sanctified state for Christians (chapter 30).

But the religious positions expressed in such passages are not the primary object of the episodes. Nor are they integral to a broader ideology essential to the meaning of the book as a whole. Rather, they serve along with everything else to reveal the fundamental irrelevance of Panurge's quest, and thus a fundamental flaw in the quester himself. Theology – even the "correct" theology of biblical humanism – is no more capable of providing the kind of answer Panurge is looking for than are law, medicine, philosophy, or even crude divination, because Panurge's question is in part illegitimate, in part unanswerable by anyone other than himself. Hippothadée can tell him this in the language of religion, as others can do in the languages of other disciplines, but Panurge will not hear because he is paralyzed by a kind of superstition and blind trust in authority, as revealed by his response to Raminagrobis.

The one religious constant in *Book 3* is the idea, stated explicitly by Hippothadée, that the future cannot be known – that it is in fact sacrilegious to seek to know what God has deliberately kept hidden, and to presume to enter "God's privy council, ... the chamber of His petty pleasures" (*F350/H446*). Faced with uncertainty about the future consequences of present actions, the only legitimate course is to do the best one can and accept whatever may come of it, according to the Lord's Prayer: "thy will be done, on earth as it is in heaven" (Mt 6:10). All of Panurge's counselors repeat the same point in different terms, but Hippothadée's terms are especially significant because they reproduce exactly the language of the *Pantagrueline prognostication* and *Almanachs* espousing Christian skepticism and eschewing curiosity about things that transcend the human. Panurge's entire quest can perhaps be seen as an elaboration of this single skeptical principle. In this sense the only "religion" of *Book 3* is an anti-religion, or at least an anti-theology, "agnostic" in its absolute opposition to all forms of gnosis and prognosis, from the occult sciences (Her Trippa), to Platonism (divination by dreams), to Christian mysticism (dedication to Marguerite de Navarre).

In another respect, too, the primary function of religion in *Book 3* is to express something essentially non-religious: Rabelais again has recourse to the techniques of parody, this time as a means of revealing the nature of Panurge's peculiar paralysis of the will. At the beginning of his quest Panurge dons a Franciscan habit and a "Judaic" earring as effects of a "vow" and signs of his decision to marry (chapter 7), thus indicating, through a complex set of allusions to Deuteronomy, a desire to remain enslaved to the letter of a Mosaic law exempting newly weds from military service. This suggests, through a potent analogy, that for Panurge the legitimate sacrament of marriage functions like its polar opposite – the illegitimate, "Judaic" sacrament of monastic orders – not as a free state but as a guarantee of safety and happiness, as something like a "work of the Law." All efforts to disabuse him of this error, to lead him to the free exercise of his own will under something comparable to the New Law of Christian freedom, fail. Panurge's will remains "enslaved" to the very end.[6] As in *Pantagruel*, the language and fundamental structures of religion – here the opposition between Judaic law (including the new "Judaism" of Catholic *constitutiones humanae*) and Christian freedom – provide the analogy through which an essentially non-religious meaning is conveyed. In this sense religion is not an ideological end but a literary means in *Book 3*.

Book 4 (1552)

In *Book 4* religion returns, in tandem with politics, as a central preoccupation, but with a different emphasis – this time on the actual geopolitical effects of hardening orthodoxies in the real world of 1551–2, and on current events like the Gallican crisis and the reconvening of the Council of Trent. Satire is once again the dominant mode but is harsher than ever before and far more sharply focused on specific events, policies, and even theological doctrines. Hard-line Protestants like Calvin fare no better than hard-line Catholics, but the Church of Rome remains the principal target.

Two general themes underlie this satire. One is the antagonism that inevitably arises from mutually excluding beliefs, confessions, and churches. The paradigm for all such antagonisms is highlighted at the center of the book in the emblematic opposition between Lent and Carnival, familiar to Rabelais's readers from popular representations of the annual battle between Carême and Charnage, recast here as Quaresmeprenant (Fastilent) and the Andouilles (Chitterlings). This central opposition is significant not only because it is by definition irreconcilable, allowing no degree or mean term, but also because it involves one of the most notoriously "carnal" of all *constitutiones humanae*. To this, Rabelais adds another dimension by identifying Fastilent with Catholicism (and Charles V) and the Chitterlings with Protestants (and Swiss and German princes). The various implications of this central deadlock are developed in other episodes, most notably in the irreconcilable opposition between Papefigues (Popefigs) and Papimanes (Popemaniacs).

A second, related theme is the doctrinal hardening that makes all such antagonisms irreconcilable. Here the paradigm is found in the Council of Trent, satirized as the "council of Chesil" (Hebrew for "fool"). A chance encounter with a ship full of monks en route to Chesil to "scrutinize [sift]...the articles of faith against the new heretics" (F477/H581) gives rise to a violent sea storm in which the Pantagruelians nearly perish – an obvious allegory for the destruction wrought by such meticulous doctrinal "sifting." We learn later that even Fastilent and the Chitterlings were once close to a peace treaty until the council of Chesil intervened, exacerbating old hostilities by forbidding all treaties and anathematizing all compromisers (F513/H622). Clear definitions of orthodoxy serve only to destroy peace and breed violence.

Against the background of these general themes two specific attacks stand out. One involves the temporal power of popes, satirized in the episode of the Papimaniacs. Because the idolatrous Papimaniacs worship the Pope as their God they also revere the Decretals – the collection of papal decrees on which papal authority rests – as a sacred book containing divine revelation. In a brilliant paradoxical encomium Grosbeak, bishop of the Papimaniacs and a satirical representative comparable to Janotus de Bragmardo, extols the disastrous effects of papal power as so many blessings and miracles: holy wars against Christian nations, torture and execution of "heretics," and depletion of the treasuries of France by papal taxes on benefices and various dispensations. All of these calamities affected France directly, but the last – praised by Grosbeak as the effect of an occult "aurifluous energy" ("auriflue énergie") that magically transports vast quantities of gold each year from France to Rome ($F552/H663$) – was at the very heart of the Gallican crisis of 1551.

Another specific object of Rabelais's anti-Roman satire is the Mass, attacked here not simply as one of the ceremonies of an excessively ritualized Church, but also for its theological underpinnings, especially the idea of the Eucharist as a sacrifice. In the episode of Messere Gaster (Master Belly), idolatrous priests and monks – the Engastrimyths and Gastrolaters – perform degraded parodies of the Mass in which Eucharistic bread and wine are replaced by massive quantities of food offerings, which are repeatedly denounced by Pantagruel as abominable "sacrifices" to a carnal, ventripotent god (chapters 58–9). Implicit in this satire is the view, clearly articulated only by the most radical of Reformers like Zwingli, that Christ's redemptive sacrifice on the cross was unique, sufficient, and efficacious. The Mass denies the value and efficacy of that sacrifice by presuming to supplement, renew, and repeat it indefinitely in ritual sacrifices performed by mere mortals and asserted to be themselves efficacious and necessary for salvation. The pagan sacrifices of the Engastrimyths and Gastrolaters seem to suggest the sacrilege of the Mass thus conceived.

The implications of this satire are confirmed by rare instances of positive apologetics in *Book 4*. During the sea storm Pantagruel's fervent prayers, addressed directly to God as his unique "Savior" and based on Christ's own words in the Bible ($F479/H584$, $F482/H588$, $F484/H590$; cf. Mt 8:23–7, 26:39 and 42), stand in marked contrast both to Panurge's verbose, superstitious vows to saints and calls for confession and extreme unction, and to Frère Jean's fearless, cursing frenzy of activity. The hero's spontaneous prayers and synergistic piety are thus situated midway between the opposing extremes of superstitious trust in the magical efficacy of rites and irreverent self-reliance. Far more pointedly, at the very beginning of the book the sea voyage begins not with a Mass, as was customary, but with a paleo-Christian communion consisting of a sermon and prayer spoken by the layman Pantagruel, followed by the congregational singing of a complete Psalm in French translation and a communal banquet (F438/H538–9). This communion of the saved stands in direct opposition to the liturgical sacrifice of the Mass, which is by contrast carnal, "Judaic," and pagan.[7]

The "Ringing Island" and other episodes incorporated into the so-called *Book 5*, published posthumously in 1562 and 1564 respectively, are consonant with some of the religious positions staked out in earlier books. Of particular note are satires of monastic regulations and ceremonies and of Lent ("Ringing Island," chapters 1–8, and the "Semiquaver Friars," chapters 26–8). But these are relatively flat compared to Rabelais's other satires on similar themes, a fact that encourages doubts about their authenticity.

Conclusion

Looking back over Rabelais's four authentic books we may observe great differences in focus and modes of representation and a steady increase in the specificity and harshness of attacks against Catholic orthodoxy, but a remarkable consistency in underlying religious ideology. Critics are correct to insist on the serious Erasmian orientation of this ideology and on its strongly biblical, evangelical character. What has not always been sufficiently emphasized is the degree to which religion in these books is subordinated to political, social, and moral considerations and is indifferent, if not overtly hostile, to theological questions of divinity, salvation, and eschatology. This is an anthropocentric, non-theological ideology concerned almost exclusively with communal life here on earth. In this important sense Rabelais's religion, though profoundly Christian, is "secular" and "humanistic" even in the modern meaning of those words.

Realizing this removes one of the traditional obstacles to a proper understanding of religion in Rabelais – namely, our post-Reformation, post-Tridentine assumption that ribald, irreverent humor is necessarily incompatible with religiosity, and with Christianity especially. Given the particular nature and function of Rabelais's Christianity, we must view Rabelaisian humor, on the contrary, as integral and essential to it. As is clearly shown by the convivial banquets in Rabelais's prologues and books, ribald humor contributes directly to the good cheer and goodwill on which human communities depend. In this it actually engenders a *religio* that is, above all else, a binding together of human mortals.

NOTES

1 For the best documented account of Rabelais's religious career, see Richard Cooper, "Rabelais et l'Église," in Jean Céard and Jean-Claude Margolin, eds., *Rabelais en son demi-millénaire: Actes du colloque international de Tours (24–29 septembre 1984)*, Études Rabelaisiennes, 21 (Geneva: Droz, 1988), pp. 111–20, and *Rabelais et l'Italie*, Études Rabelaisiennes, 24 (Geneva: Droz, 1991).

2 *Gargantua* and *Pantagruel* figured on lists of books censored by the Sorbonne in 1543 and 1544. *Book 3* was added in 1546 and 1551. Calvin accused Rabelais of "atheism" in *De scandalis*, published in 1550.

3 The now-discredited view of an atheistic Rabelais was championed by Abel Lefranc in prefaces later collected in his *Rabelais*. For medieval elements in Rabelais's theology see especially Etienne Gilson, "Rabelais franciscain," in *Les Idées et les lettres*, 2nd edn. (Paris: Vrin, 1955), pp. 197–241, and "Notes médiévales au *Tiers Livre de Pantagruel*," *Revue d'Histoire Franciscaine*, 2 (1925), pp. 72–88. For various Erasmian, evangelical, and reformed aspects, see especially Lucien Febvre, *Le Problème de l'incroyance au XVIe siècle: La religion de Rabelais* (Paris: Albin Michel, 1942); Michael Screech, *L'Évangélisme de Rabelais: Aspects de la satire religieuse au XVIe siècle*, Études Rabelaisiennes, 2 (Geneva: Droz, 1959); Gérard Defaux, *Rabelais agonistes: Du rieur au prophète. Études sur "Pantagruel," "Gargantua," "Le Quart Livre,"* Études Rabelaisiennes, 32 (Geneva: Droz, 1997).

4 On this aspect of religious parody in *Pantagruel*, see Edwin Duval, *The Design of Rabelais's "Pantagruel"* (New Haven: Yale University Press, 1991).

5 See Gérard Defaux, "Rabelais et les cloches de Notre-Dame," *Études Rabelaisiennes*, 9 (1971), pp. 1–28, reworked in the same author's *Rabelais agonistes*, pp. 384–406.

6 See Edwin Duval, *The Design of Rabelais's "Tiers Livre de Pantagruel"* (Geneva: Droz, 1997), pp. 155–72.

7 See Edwin Duval, "La Messe, la Cène, et le voyage sans fin du *Quart Livre*," in Jean Céard and Jean-Claude Margolin, eds., *Rabelais en son demi-millénaire*, pp. 131–41.

8

ULLRICH LANGER

Pantagruel and *Gargantua*:
The political education of the king

The conception of monarchy in the early sixteenth century

At the time he was writing his books, by and large the humanist political thought Rabelais would have been familiar with did not see much of an alternative to monarchy, or rule by one person. This was the case even if political thinkers insisted on limits set upon the prince's powers, even if, in addition, the city of Venice provided a living example of a republic and although, finally, the other relatively recent republics of northern-central Italy had an immense impact on French artistic and intellectual culture. The intellectual justifications for monarchy were ultimately derived from Aristotle and Plutarch, and were founded not on a secular theory of justice or rights, nor even primarily on an empirical calculus of how to maximize human happiness, but instead on monarchy's resemblance to divine creation and to various phenomena in nature. Thus, the (good) monarch has some semblance of God (*imago deitatis*, or *dei simulachrum*): just as God alone is set above creation, so the king is placed above his subjects.[1] Erasmus, in his *Education of a Christian Prince* (1516), emphasizes how the divine analogy places responsibilities on the king:

> A beneficent prince, as Plutarch said with all his learning, is a kind of living likeness of God, who is at once good and powerful. His goodness [shows itself in that he wants] to help all; his power makes him able to do so . . . When you who are a prince, a Christian prince, hear and read that you are the likeness of God and his vicar, do not swell with pride on this account, but rather let the fact make you all the more concerned to live up to that wonderful archetype of yours; and remember that, though following him is hard, not following him is a sin. Christian theology attributes three principal qualities to God: total power, total wisdom, total goodness. You should master these three things as far as you can.[2]

The divine analogy which later in the sixteenth century, and especially in the seventeenth century, provides arguments for the king's absolute power, is thought by humanists to place moral restrictions on the exercise of power, to counter the willful, arbitrary nature of tyrannical rule. Other analogues used to justify monarchy are human organizations such as armies, fleets, ships, or the construction of buildings, which, when successful, are all commanded by one person, the family or household ruled by the *paterfamilias*, and finally various animals (e.g., deer, birds, and bees) that seem to be led by one single member. The human body itself is ruled by the head, or the mind.[3]

According to most political thinkers, monarchy is the best, most natural kind of political organization, and, given European politics of the time, admittedly the most frequent one. Aristotle claimed that while monarchy, for many of the above reasons, is superior to other kinds of states, the "perversion" of monarchy – tyranny – is certainly the worst.[4] Even if humanists had republican sympathies and were not equally enthusiastic about monarchy, they would all agree that despotic rule is to be avoided at all costs. The fundamental difference between the king and the tyrant, already enunciated by Aristotle, is the teleology of rule: the king acts in the best interests of his subjects, whereas the tyrant acts according to his own perceived best interests.[5] According to Erasmus, "he who looks to the common good is a king; he who looks to his own good is a tyrant."[6] The tyrant, in a frequently repeated simile, is someone who "devours his subjects" (Homer, *Iliad* I.231); in the mildest cases he discourages friendship among his subjects, one of the great ethical goods in life, and reduces his subjects to a form of slavery.

The etiology of tyranny is found in the ruler's own intemperance and his ignorance, the combination of which makes him vulnerable to corruption by flatterers. Castiglione provides a neat summary of how rulers develop into tyrants:

> The result of this [their own ignorance and the effect of flattery] is that apart from never hearing the truth of anything, princes become drunk with the power they wield, and abandoned to pleasure-seeking and amusements they become so corrupted in mind that (seeing themselves always obeyed and almost adored, with so much reverence and praise and never a hint of censure or contradiction) they pass from ignorance to extreme conceit. In consequence, they never accept anyone else's advice or opinion; and, believing that it is very easy to know how to rule and that successful government requires no art or training other than brute force, they devote all their mind and attention to maintaining the power they have and believe that true happiness consists in being able to do what one wants.[7]

The false definition of happiness (and freedom), as being able to do whatever pleases you,[8] leads tyrants not only to reject the constraints of the law but to feel that they should govern by force alone and, if the opportunity arises, wage wars of conquest on neighboring states. Their goal is the maintenance or the expansion of the power they possess, not the good of the subjects they rule.[9] Under this view, tyranny is seen as the consequence of a lack of certain moral qualities, foremost temperance, the controlling or moderating of one's emotions and pleasures, and also as a consequence of ignorance of the "art of ruling," of the legal, ethical and historical foundations of the social order. In other words, not only is a tyrant a certain kind of *person*, but his becoming this kind of person can be prevented by education. A sound moral education, and a sound education in the "letters," ranging from rhetoric to ancient and modern languages, and including the vast set of examples that is history, presumably can mold a boy into a good king. Hence the great concern voiced by humanists about the education of the royal successor.

Erasmus is a good example. The two sorts of princes he considers in *The Education of the Christian Prince* are elected or hereditary; he spends very little time discussing the first kind, since, as he notes rather acerbically, most princes are now simply successors to their station and the people have no say over who rules them:

> But when the prince is born to office, not elected, which was the custom among some barbarian peoples in the past (according to Aristotle) and is also the practice almost everywhere in our own times, then the main hope of getting a good prince hangs on his proper education, which should be managed all the more attentively, so that what has been lost with the right to vote is made up for by the care given to his upbringing.[10]

Education of the prince is, then, fundamental in preserving not only the well-being of subjects but also peace between Christian principalities. Rabelais's time witnessed the publication of humanist works devoted to this mixing of pedagogy and moral advice. His friend the poet Jean Bouchet wrote an epistle detailing the responsibilities of kings.[11] Erasmus's treatise and the fourth book of Castiglione's *Book of the Courtier* are notable examples, and during the sixteenth century they were followed in France by Guillaume Budé's *De l'institution du prince* (1547), Estienne Pasquier's *Pourparler du prince* (1560), and Pierre de Ronsard's poem on the education of Charles IX, "Institution pour l'adolescence du roy treschrestien Charles neufviesme de ce nom" (1561). Even, arguably, Montaigne's "De l'institution des enfans" (*Essays*, I.26; 1580) owes something to the humanist sense that education must be applied at the highest level.

That being said, monarchy is conceived as being healthiest when limited not simply by the virtuous disposition of the monarch himself, but by institutional or legal controls. Again, Erasmus states:

If it happens that your prince is complete with all the virtues, then monarchy pure and simple is the thing. But since this would probably never happen, although it is a fine ideal to entertain, if no more than an ordinary man is presented (things being what they are nowadays), then monarchy should preferably be checked and diluted with a mixture of aristocracy and democracy to prevent it ever breaking out into tyranny; and just as the elements mutually balance each other, so let the state be stabilised with a similar control. For if the prince is well disposed to the state, he will conclude that under such a system his power is not restricted but sustained.[12]

Similarly, Claude de Seyssel, in *La Grant Monarchie de France* (1519), speaks of the "bridles" of monarchy: religion, justice, and "polity" (the laws of the kingdom that the sovereign and his predecessors have confirmed and are intended to conserve the realm).[13] Even Machiavelli has praise for the "parlamento" in France (presumably, the "Estates General," the assembled representatives of the three estates: clergy, nobility, and the "Third Estate," the bourgeoisie) which gives the people a means of expression and controls the nobility.[14] When the disputes concerning a sovereign's absolute power are energized by the religious strife in France, the Roman law formula used to justify a sovereign's "absolute" status – that is, his freedom from constraint by the laws he has set down (*princeps legibus solutus*, *Digesta*, 1.3.31) – is counterbalanced by the sovereign's deliberate choice to submit himself to his own laws, thereby increasing his "majesty" (*digna vox maiestate regnantis legibus alligatum se principem profiteri* [it is a sentence worthy of majesty that the prince declare himself bound by the laws in force], *Codex*, 1.14.4). Even the most "absolutist" political thinkers concede that the sovereign is, in principle, bound by natural and divine law.

Pantagruel and *Gargantua* as educational manuals for the prince

Rabelais's first two books are situated in a period of relative hopefulness, as regards at least the possibility that an educated monarch will further the well-being of his subjects and the artistic and literary culture of his kingdom. This was especially true of Francis I,[15] although the French evangelical Reform movement, with which Rabelais showed great sympathy, was beginning to realize the limits of what the monarch was willing to do and was itself having to contend with more radical Lutheran elements ready to attack Catholic doctrine in ways that jeopardized any hope of royal support. But both of Rabelais's early books are suffused with a sense that the boy growing up to be king can do the job well, since his humanist education can make an immense difference, and they are replete with episodes not only detailing the development of the good prince, but also demonstrating his skills and virtues, and demonstrating, *a contrario*, the vices of the tyrant opposing him. In this sense *Pantagruel* and *Gargantua* are partial political allegories; I read them less as intervening directly in the political struggles of the French Christian humanists[16] than as fictions, many of whose episodes can be read as representations of the way a good prince, any good prince, should act. In the following pages I will give several salient examples; this is not meant to be an exhaustive account.

Pantagruel

Pantagruel is justly famous for its cheerful mocking of the epic tradition and its introduction of the character Panurge complete with his bag of tricks and his rhetorical and linguistic skills. It is equally famous for the letter written by Gargantua to his son and successor, Pantagruel, in which the king details the elements of a good humanist educational curriculum. These elements, as has been pointed out, correspond quite closely to the educational ideals of humanists intent on replacing the medieval scholastic curriculum,[17] and include in addition the military training necessary to defend the state and provide succor to allies. However, it is also worth pointing out that two features of the letter's exordium contain a political message consonant with the Erasmian–Aristotelian conception of monarchy I outlined above: the importance of a better successor and the reflection of the father's virtues in the mirror of the son. In *The Education of the Christian Prince*, the Dutch humanist emphasizes the importance of bequeathing the state to a son who is better than the father. This is, indeed, the responsibility of the reigning king:

> It is a fine and glorious thing to govern well, but it is no less meritorious to ensure that one's successor is not inferior; or rather, the chief responsibility of a good prince is this, to see to it that there cannot be a bad one ... There is no finer tribute to an excellent prince than when he bequeaths to the state someone by comparison with whom he himself seems little better than average ... [18]

Gargantua, in his exhortatory epistle to his son, emphasizes how his own father, Grandgousier, devoted much effort to his son's education; the times being what they were, Gargantua did what he could. The times having improved, all the more reason that his son Pantagruel can become wiser and more knowledgeable than Gargantua ever was:

> But even though my late father, of esteemed memory, Grandgousier, had devoted all his endeavor to having me profit in all politic perfection and learning, and my labor and application corresponded very well to his desire, indeed surpassed it, nonetheless, as you may well understand, the time was not so suitable or favorable for letters as it is at present, and I did not have

the abundance of such tutors as you have had. The time was still dark, and smacking of the infelicity and calamity of the Goths, who had brought all good literature to destruction; but, by God's goodness, in my day light and dignity has been restored to letters, and I see such improvement in these that at present I would hardly be accepted into the lowest class of little grammar-school boys, I who in my prime was reputed (not wrongly) the most learned man of the said century. (F160/H243)

Whereas the "rebirth" of letters is a commonplace in humanist writing of the fifteenth and sixteenth centuries, in this case it specifically supports the political finality of a (good) monarchy. Not only is it the duty of the king to educate his successor (as Grandgousier had done, despite the Gothic ignorance around him), but now it is even *easy* to do so: there is no reason, then, for the good king not to hand the state to an even better son.

Erasmus provides an additional incentive for the good king to prepare his successor for the job. An excellent son will remind everyone of the excellence of the father, who, in a sense, does not die, since the son is a living image of the father:

> However many statues he may set up and however much he may toil over the constructions he erects, the prince can leave no finer monument to his good qualities than a son who is in every way of the same stock and who recreates his father's excellence in his own excellent actions (*qui patrem optimum optimis factis repraesentet*). He does not die who leaves a living likeness of himself (*vivam sui reliquit imaginem*).[19]

The king's true glory does not consist in inanimate representations of himself (statues) or in stone edifices, but in the living representation that is his successor, and, unlike statues that remind people of the king's outward appearance, the good son resembles his father not simply physically, but through his moral excellence. The same development can be found in Gargantua's letter to his son:

> Wherefore, even as in you abides the image of my body, if the soul's behavior did not likewise shine out, you would not be judged the guardian and treasure-house of the immortality of our name... You may well remember how, to perfect and consummate this undertaking, I have spared nothing, but have assisted you just as if I had no other treasure in this world but to see you once in my life absolute and perfect both in virtue, honor, and valor, and in every liberal and praiseworthy branch of learning, and to leave you so, after my death, as a mirror representing the person of myself your father, and if not as excellent and such in fact as I wish you to be, assuredly indeed such in desire. (F159–60/H242–3)

Gargantua emphasizes his own efforts to render his son "perfect" in the moral virtues as well as in the liberal arts, thus preventing the seeds of tyranny from taking hold in the boy. Rather than accumulate gold and silver (or other states), presumably at the expense of his subjects or his neighbors, Gargantua has devoted his energies to the true treasure (*thésor*) that is his son.[20] The result will be a living representation of the dead father, as a "mirror" (*mirouoir*), a *speculum*, an example to other princes of the qualities necessary to the good king.

The serious tone of the letter to Pantagruel contrasts with the often burlesque narratives contained in other chapters, but even the presence of a character such as Panurge has political implications. In imitation of classical epic, the giant takes the versatile trickster as his *friend*.[21] Although in doing so Pantagruel refers explicitly to Aeneas and Achates, he is also demonstrating that the good (future) king enjoys the love of his subjects, in clear distinction to the tyrant whose regime allows no friendship between ruler and ruled,[22] and who discourages friendship among his subjects and needs to fear all those around him.[23] Pantagruel initiates the friendship with Panurge through an act of charity,[24] as Panurge, thirsty, hungry, and penniless, himself points out to the giant. The king helps even the weakest, and will be rewarded for his gesture by Panurge who proves to be an entertaining companion and most useful in defeating the 660 knights attacking the ship of Pantagruel and his companions, at the beginning of the war against the Dipsodes.[25] The more general principle, government by charity, is one that Christian princes should apply, and it is even in their own interest to do so, as Erasmus points out:

> Authority is not lost to him who rules in a Christian way; but he maintains it in other ways, and indeed much more gloriously and more securely . . . First, people you oppress with servitude are not really yours because it takes general agreement to make a prince. But in the end those are truly yours who obey you voluntarily and of their own accord. Next, when your subjects are impelled through fear, you do not possess even the half of them; their bodies are in your power, but their spirit is estranged from you. But when Christian charity binds prince and people together, then everything is yours whenever occasion demands.[26]

Not only is Pantagruel's helping out of Panurge an exemplary gesture of charity, but the fact that he accepts him as a friend also underlines the equality inherent in any human relationship, even if one of the friends is much more powerful (and physically much larger) than the other. Panurge, precisely, is not in Pantagruel's *servitude*. While much about Panurge's character remains problematic if it is read in straightforward moral terms, his very weaknesses, his trickery and cleverness, and his ability to amuse are a reflection of the giant's acceptance of humanness, and of his willingness to surround himself with friends, not flattering courtiers.

When, towards the end of the book, his father having died, the giant child has become a king and is leading his troups into battle, he begins to exhibit some of the characteristics of a prudent leader, one who chooses the best means towards a good end. He is persuaded by his friends to adopt strategies in warfare rather than relying on his own size and fortitude (chapter 25). As a good Christian prince he invokes the aid of God before his combat with Werewolf (chapter 29), and acknowledges the help of God both after the annihilation of the 660 knights (chapter 27) and when his triumph over the Dipsodes is complete and he is relating events to the narrator Alcofrybas, who emerges from a long voyage into the king's mouth (chapter 32). Furthermore, the good king demonstrates his virtue of (distributive) justice, rewarding those who helped him with banquets and punishing King Anarche (who instigated the invasion) and those who resist his rule, the Almyrodes. His triumph and restoration of a just order are so effective that his entry into the city of the Amaurots provokes a comparison to the return to the age of gold.[27]

These manifestations of Pantagruel's virtues as a king are set, of course, in contexts that are often wildly hyperbolic, funny, and parodic. An example is the beginning of chapter 32; Pantagruel's army is marching towards the city of the Almyrodes, and they are surprised by a rain storm:

> But on the way, passing over a great open field, they were caught in a heavy rain shower. At which they began to shiver and huddle close to one another. Pantagruel seeing this, he had them told by the captain that it was nothing and that he could see well above the clouds that it would be only a little dew, but at all events that they should fall into ranks and he intended to cover them. Then they lined up in good order and well closed up, and Pantagruel put his tongue out only a half way, and with it covered them as a hen does her chickens.   (F238–9/H330)

While the gesture of protecting men from the rain by sticking out one's tongue has medieval antecedents, and in a way it merely serves as a prelude to the more striking exploration of the giant's mouth by the narrator, who discovers within it another world, it also represents the king's *prudence*. The latter is defined as an intellectual virtue necessary to all others, since it involves choosing the best means to realize the other virtues. It is often analyzed (e.g., in Cicero, *De inventione*, 2.53.160) as a combination of knowledge of the past (*memoria*), an acute perception of the present situation (*intellegentia*), and foresight of future events (*providentia*). Pantagruel sees what is going on at the moment ("seeing this") and he foresees future events (it would only be a little shower), yet he judges that it would still be better to protect his men and so he has them line up in an orderly way. His superior prudence is incarnated by his towering stature that allows him to look beyond the present moment and the immediate situation, and to see that the skies are clearing soon. His knowledge of his men prompts him nevertheless to have them show discipline and seek cover underneath his tongue. The final comparison of Pantagruel to a hen protecting her chicks aptly summarizes both the loving concern the Christian king shows for his men and the superior virtues of the leader. The comparison is a "chicken" version of the *paterfamilias* analogy to good monarchy, and recalls Matthew 23:37, where Christ uses the same comparison to describe his assembling the "children" of Jerusalem.

Gargantua

Pantagruel combines many different strands of medieval and Renaissance literary traditions, and some consistent Christian humanist themes, including the "institution" of the Christian prince and a demonstration of the desirable virtues of a monarch. *Gargantua* is, in this political perspective at least, perhaps a more coherent work. The section of the book devoted to the education of the prince is significantly expanded, and above all the conduct of war, a test case for the good monarch, becomes an explicit theme during the second half of *Gargantua*. This is all the more apparent as Rabelais contrasts the behavior of the good humanist king with that of the tyrant Picrochole. It is by focusing initially on the outbreak of the war between Picrochole and Gargantua that the political allegory becomes clear. The setting is innocuous enough, and the dispute seems completely out of proportion with the war that follows. The elements of *peace* are set up with great care:

> At this time, which was the vintage season, and the beginning of the autumn, the shepherds of the region were busy guarding the vines and keeping the starlings from eating the grapes. At which time the *fouaciers* [bakers of a bread called *fouace*] of Lerné were passing by the great highway, taking ten or twelve loads of *fouaces* to town. (F62/H73)

Peace is evoked with each detail: it is the season of the wine harvest, which means that grapes have ripened all year long undisturbed. Autumn is the time of abundance, when nature bears its fruits. The shepherds are guarding the vines not against enemies, but to keep the grapes from being eaten by birds; they have no human beings to fear. The bakers are traveling to town to sell their bread, which means that commerce can be conducted and the highways can be traveled safely. In addition, both shepherds and bakers seem to belong initially to the same community – the shepherds are "de la contrée" and the bakers are from Lerné: one group is from the countryside, another from the village, as their professions dictate. It is only through the subtitle of the chapter and through subsequent events that we learn that Lerné belongs to the principality of Picrochole, whereas the shepherds are subjects of Grandgousier. In other words, a trading community and geographical proximity, indeed familiarity, exist between human beings artificially separated by political boundaries. Which is a measure of how strongly peace reigns (and how silly political boundaries are between Christians).

The confrontation between the shepherds and the bakers begins with a simple request:

> The shepherds asked them courteously to let them have some [*fouaces*] for their money, at the market price. For note that grapes with fresh fouace are a heavenly food to eat for breakfast... Not in the least inclined to grant their request were the *fouaciers*, but what is worse, they badly insulted them, calling them expendable, snaggle-teeth [etc.]... To this outrage one of them named Frogier, personally a very honorable man and a notable young fellow, replied mildly: "How long ago did you grow horns, that you've got so high-and-mighty? My word, you used to sell it to us, and now you refuse. That's not the way to treat good neighbors, and we don't treat you that way when you come here to buy our fine wheat from which you make your cakes and *fouaces*." (F62–3/H73–4)

The shepherds' request is made "courteously" and even when they are insulted, their representative, Frogier, answers not with insults but "mildly" (*doucettement*). It is all the more understandable a request in that the combination of bread and grapes is a *heavenly* one, recalling not only basic peasant fare but the Eucharist. The shepherds' mildness is a reflection of the peaceful setting, a proof of their humanity, and a manifestation of the Christian community that the Eucharist signifies. The shepherds offer to pay the market price for the bread, showing their respect for commutative justice (the fairness of exchanges), and Frogier also points out a related principle of justice that should govern contacts between neighbors, "treat others the way you want to be treated by them," since the bakers buy wheat from the shepherds but now refuse to sell the bread to them.[28] Commerce between neighbors is the normal situation, as he emphasizes ("you used to sell it to us"), and the bakers' refusal constitutes, in addition, an affront to custom. What's more, the bakers' refusal is not at all motivated by any *reason*, whereas Frogier advances all sorts of reasons for them to sell the bread.

In other words, the bakers are violating basic principles of human justice and Christian community, and, in so doing, they are refusing to engage in rational discussion. This makes them something less than human, and foreshadows the irrational behavior of Picrochole, their king. The subsequent "wasting and pillaging" of the countryside by Grandgousier's neighbors is an extension of this sudden and brutal irruption of the irrational and animalistic: Picrochole's hastily assembled troops are completely "without order or measure" (F65/H76), and they cause indiscriminate damage to the crops and livestock of Grandgousier's peasants, to rich and poor, sacred and profane alike.

Although the initial situation is trivial, it is a microcosm of a political situation that can be a *causa belli* (reason for war), on the level of states. Cicero summarizes succinctly the conditions under which a war can be fought:

> In the case of a state in its external relations, the rights of war must be strictly observed. For since there are two ways of settling a dispute: first, by discussion; second, by physical force; and since the former is characteristic of man, the latter of the brute, we must resort to force only in case we may not avail ourselves of discussion. The only excuse [*causa*], therefore, for going to war is that we may live in peace unharmed...[29]

The goal of a justified war, one with a *causa*, a rationale, is, then, above all the re-establishment of peace. The option of war should only be taken when rational discussion is no longer possible.

Grandgousier, in good humanist fashion and with a heavy heart, tries everything to avoid the resort to war: restitution, gifts, and diplomacy. In a letter to his son, calling him to return from his studies and prepare for war, he explains himself:

> My intention is not to provoke, but to appease [*apaiser*], not to attack, but to defend, not to conquer, but to protect my loyal subjects and hereditary lands, which Picrochole has invaded without cause or occasion, and from day to day pursues his mad enterprise [*furieuse entreprise*] with excesses intolerable to free men [*personnes liberes*].   (F71/H84)

Grandgousier's language is carefully chosen: the goal is pacification – *apaiser*, from *paix*, peace – not aggression. The good king protects what is already there (human beings and land), rather than acquires something new. His neighbor Picrochole has precisely not used discussion as a first resort, and his action seems devoid of any rationale (*cause*). He has become, literally, deprived of reason, *furieux*: the term stems from the Latin *furiosus*, which has the meaning of "being outside of oneself, not in possession of one's mind."[30] Just as the bakers all of a sudden become less than human, so does Picrochole, their king. His actions would be intolerable to any free persons – that is, persons who are masters of themselves (and not "furious"); all such persons, not simply the specific victims of this particular aggression, would agree with Grandgousier's judgment. Justification of war involves, then, a universal statement: part of the rationality of this resort to violence is the ability to generalize the justification to humanity as a whole. As a Christian humanist king, he adds a theological justification, God's withdrawal of grace from Picrochole; given his character, presumably only divine grace had kept him from invading his neighbors' kingdoms before. This theological explanation only comes after Grandgousier has gone through the steps provided to him by classical moral philosophy.

The counterpart to Grandgousier is obviously a tyrant. The good king refers to his opponent's "tyrannical anger" which needs to be moderated (*ibid.*). By his very name, Picrochole, we have an indication of his character: he is dominated by an excess of "bitter bile," which explains his reaction to the bakers' complaints:

> He instantly flew into a frenzied rage [*courroux furieux*], and, without asking himself what or how, he had the ban and the arrière-ban proclaimed throughout his country, summoning each and every man, on pain of the halter, to assemble under arms in the great square of the château, at the stroke of noon. (F64/H75–6)

Bitterness is the flavor of yellow bile, the choleric humor, and Picrochole's rage is a manifestation of his troubled internal state.[31] The very fact that one humor dominates, and that it is not the sanguine one, also means that the ruler is intemperate, that he has lost the ability to balance out the effects of his bodily sensations: he needs to be "moderated." It is essential that the good ruler not be swayed by his emotions.[32] Picrochole's intemperate reaction manifests itself also in the lack of any passage of time between receiving the news and his violent reaction (he "*instantly* flew into a frenzied rage").[33] As Bouchet puts it in his epistle to Louis XII, "It is fitting that a great king always possess gentleness, that is, that he not be moved too suddenly, that he not be irate and not seek vengeance."[34] Picrochole, in opposition to Grandgousier later on, seeks no understanding of what happened, and seeks no advice before making the fateful decision to call in his vassals to begin warfare. There is no one to "moderate" him. The amount of time he takes to decide to go to war is ridiculously short, and so too is the amount of time he gives his vassals to appear with their equipment and men.

Not only is Picrochole intemperate, he is also fundamentally bereft of prudence. We have seen that prudence requires knowledge of the past, accurate perception of the present, and foreknowledge of the future. Picrochole fails on all counts: he disregards the past friendly relationship with Grandgousier, he exaggerates wildly the importance of the incident, and then overestimates his own power and the weakness of his foe, Grandgousier. In looking to the future, he does not consider the consequences of his call to arms (indeed, the almost random way in which his army invades its neighbors makes it hard to calculate *any* outcome). The most glaring example of Picrochole's lack of *providentia* is given in chapter 33, when his advisors chart out an impossibly ambitious plan for imperial conquest. As the advisors list all of the countries his armies will conquer, they do not allow for any contingency, in the sense that not only do they take success of an initial enterprise for granted, but they go on to build their plans as if future events had already occurred ("once we conquer this, we go on to that, and then to that, etc."). This disregard for contingency is at the heart of imprudent deliberation, for it makes future events a simple consequence of the ruler's will, which by their very definition they cannot be. It is also a total perversion of the divine analogy underlying good monarchy.

When peace is re-established, it is time for distributive justice, the punishment of the wrong-doers and the reward of those who helped. The most striking example of the latter is the founding of the Abbey of Thélème. The chapters devoted to describing this "anti-monastery" have been the focus of intense critical scrutiny.[35] They seem to constitute a model society, similar to Thomas More's *Utopia* (1516). As a conclusion to the defeat of the tyrant Picrochole and the triumph of the humanist prince Gargantua, it is tempting to view the abbey as an incarnation of a Christian humanist political vision, centered on the sole precept, "Do what you will."[36] However, the abbey is hardly a systematic treatment of a possible society, in the manner of More, and Rabelais seems more interested in the luxurious building and in material details (such as the clothing of the residents) than in their social organization. Thélème is foremost a fine example of the liberality of the king, in a typically Rabelaisian economy of apparently infinite resources.

Whereas *Pantagruel* and *Gargantua* contain numerous episodes that can be read as humanist political advice, much about both works runs counter to the model of pacific governance. The conduct of Pantagruel's war against the Dipsodes is hardly an example of deliberation or negotiation and Pantagruel has no inclination to spare enemy lives. The most vivid episodes concern wholesale slaughter (the burning of the 660 knights, the drowning of the sleeping enemy, the slaying of the giants with Werewolf's corpse). Similarly, although in *Gargantua* the king Grandgousier, and his diplomatic efforts are admirable, the most salient character during the warfare episodes is Frère Jean whose glee in dispatching the soldiers pillaging the Abbey of

Seuillé's vineyards is less than Christian. The narrative at its most comical and energetic is full of the sort of bloody mayhem that precisely should not motivate a good king; with the exception of the initial dispute between the shepherds and the bakers, this mock-epic violence does not provoke dismay and sorrow in the reader or the characters. Political themes are not absent from Rabelais's later books, but Panurge's search for certainty concerning marriage, and the epic quest of the fourth (and fifth) books are less permeable to the political and moral intentions of Christian humanism and then, after all, the French political environment was undoubtedly less welcoming as well.

NOTES

1 See Plutarch, *Moral Essays*, "To An Uneducated Ruler," 780E, and Aristotle, *Politics*, 4.2 (1289b1). The analogy between royal power and God's governance of the world is integral to medieval political theory; see Ernst Kantorowicz, *The King's Two Bodies: A Study in Medieval Political Theology* (Princeton: Princeton University Press, 1957), and Francis Oakley, *Omnipotence, Covenant, and Order: An Excursion in the History of Ideas from Abelard to Leibniz* (Ithaca and London: Cornell University Press, 1984).

2 Erasmus, *Education of a Christian Prince*, N. M. Cheshire, M. J. Heath, trans., L. Jardine, ed. (Cambridge: Cambridge University Press, 1997[1516]), chapter 1, p. 22. See also p. 37: "Although there are many kinds of state [most commonly three viable ones: democracy, aristocracy, and monarchy] it is pretty well agreed among the philosophers that the most healthy form is monarchy; for, by analogy with the deity, when the totality of things is in one person's power, then indeed, in so far as he is in this respect in the image of God, he excels everyone else in wisdom and goodness, and, being quite independent, concentrates exclusively on helping the state."

3 See, for statements of these analogies, Baldassare Castiglione, *The Book of the Courtier*, G. Bull, trans. (Harmondsworth: Penguin, 1967 [1528]), 4.19, and Erasmus, *Education*, pp. 25, 29, 33–4. On the analogy to households, see Aristotle, *Nicomachean Ethics*, 8.10 (1160b23–8).

4 See Aristotle, *Nicomachean Ethics*, 8.10 (1160a31–b12), *Politics*, 4.2 (1289a28–b4) and 4.10 (1295a1–24), and for one of the numerous restatements of this distinction, Castiglione, *Courtier*, 4.21.

5 A succinct statement in *Nicomachean Ethics*, 8.10.2 (1160b1–3): "a tyrant studies his own advantage, a king that of his subjects."

6 Erasmus, *Education*, p. 53.

7 Castiglione, *The Book of the Courtier*, 4.7, p. 286. Much of the description of tyrants is taken from Plutarch, "To An Uneducated Ruler."

8 A definition recalling, among others, Cicero: "Such men have had the same aims as kings – to suffer no want, to be subject to no authority, to enjoy their liberty, that is, in its essence, to live just as they please" (*De officiis*, W. Miller, ed. and trans., Loeb Classical Library [Cambridge, MA: Harvard University Press, 1913], 1.20.70). The context in Cicero is anything but an incitement to tyrannical rule;

rather, it concerns the pleasure derived from retirement to one's estates and being untroubled by the worries of public life. See also Erasmus: "The tyrant's aim is to follow whatever takes his fancy" (*Education*, p. 27). The correct understanding of freedom is given by Castiglione's interlocutor a bit further on: "It should not be said that true freedom consists in living as one wishes but rather in living under good laws" (*Courtier*, 4.21, p. 298).

9 The position of the tyrant, as articulated in classical and humanist political thought, is thus equivalent in this respect to the initial point of view in Machiavelli's *The Prince* (composed 1513, published 1532): Machiavelli's advice-book shows the prince how to maintain the state that he has inherited or, more importantly, acquired, and although some of the measures take account of the well-being of the prince's subjects, the basic intention is for the prince to choose means to maintain his power. To the extent that the support of the subjects is a factor in holding on to a state, their well-being may be attended to. For example, in the case of principalities that are former republics, if the prince does not simply devastate them, he can choose to rule through the help of their citizens (*The Prince*, chapter 5).

10 Erasmus, *Education*, p. 5.

11 See Jean Bouchet, "Première épître aux Roys et Princes," dedicated to Louis XII, collected in his *Epistres morales et familieres du Traverseur* (1545), J. Beard, intr., facs. reprints (New York: Johnson Reprint Corp., 1969), part 2, fols. 1r–8v.

12 Erasmus, *Education*, p. 37.

13 Claude de Seyssel, *The Monarchy of France*, J. H. Hexter, trans., D. R. Kelley, ed. (New Haven: Yale University Press, 1981), pp. 51–7.

14 Machiavelli, *The Prince*, p. 19.

15 See A.-M. Lecoq, *François Ier imaginaire: Symbolique et politique à l'aube de la Renaissance française* (Paris: Macula, 1987), for an account of how the king, at least initially, was idolized by writers and artists.

16 Especially useful in charting the relations of Rabelais with his fellow Christian humanists and their political struggles is the work of Gérard Defaux (many of his studies are compiled in *Rabelais agonistes: Du rieur au prophète. Études sur "Pantagruel," "Gargantua," "Le Quart Livre,"* Études Rabelaisiennes, 32 [Geneva: Droz, 1997]).

17 Edwin Duval, *The Design of Rabelais's "Pantagruel"* (New Haven: Yale University Press, 1991), pp. 41–62.

18 Erasmus, *Education*, pp. 6–7.

19 *Ibid.*, p. 7.

20 This attentiveness to his successor is evident as well in the decision Gargantua eventually comes to in chapter 3, celebrating the birth of his son rather than mourning the death of his wife; given the realities of dynastic (and patrilineal) monarchy, the assurance of succession by a male heir is a far more important event for the kingdom than the death of a queen, as affectionate as the conjugal relationship might have been.

21 "I've already taken such a great liking for you that if you will grant me my will, you will never budge from my company, and you and I will form a new pair in friendship such as was that which existed between Aeneas and Achates" (F166/H249).

22 Aristotle, *Nicomachean Ethics*, 8.11.6 (1161a31–4).

23 See Castiglione, *Courtier*, iv.24.

24 Duval, *Design*, pp. 66–74.

25 The classic example is Aesop's fable of the lion and the mouse. See Erasmus, *Education*, p. 12: "the fable applies to the prince, telling him never to look down on anybody but to try assiduously to win over by kindness the heart of even the humblest of the common people, for no one is so weak but that he may at some time be a friend who can help you or an enemy who can harm you, however powerful you may be yourself." During the combat with Werewolf, Panurge, however, true to his increasingly cowardly nature, does not come to the aid of his friend, which complicates the relationship from a moral perspective. All the while Pantagruel does not seem to bear him a grudge.

26 Erasmus, *Education*, pp. 42–3. According to Machiavelli, governing only by Christian charity is impossible for a successful prince. In order to maintain his state he will on occasion be forced to go against good faith, charity, kindness, and religion (*The Prince*, chapter 18). On the whole, it is better for the prince to be feared than loved, although he must avoid being hated (chapter 17). In times of need the prince cannot rely on subjects who only love him and do not fear punishment.

27 "This news heard, there came out before him all the inhabitants of the city, in good order, and in great triumphal pomp, with divine gladness, and led him into the city; and fine bonfires were lit for joy all over the city, and fair round tables, garnished with victuals aplenty, were set up around the streets. It was a renewal of the golden age of Saturn, such a good time was had by all" (*F236/H327–8*). The institution of good government (symbolized by the "good order" of the Amaurots), and especially justice, are commonly described in terms of a return to the age of Saturn, which is evoked in Ovid, *Metamorphoses*, 1.89–112 (although no laws are necessary there); see Castiglione, *Courtier*: "[The good courtier gives to the prince] what is doubtless the greatest and rarest of all human virtues: the manner and method of good government. This alone would be enough to make men happy and restore to earth the golden age which is said to have existed once, when Saturn reigned" (4.18, p. 296).

28 See, among many sources for this principle, Seneca, *Letters to Lucilius*, 94.43: "You must expect to be treated by others as you yourself have treated them" (R. M. Gummere, ed. and trans., Loeb Classical Library [Cambridge, MA: Harvard University Press, 1925]).

29 Cicero, *De officiis*, 1.11.34–5. Compare Erasmus, *Education*, chapter 11, p. 103: "The truly Christian prince will first ponder how much difference there is between man, a creature born to peace and good will, and wild animals and beasts, born to pillage and war, and in addition how much difference there is between a man and a Christian."

30 According to Roman law, a "furiosus" cannot make wills or contracts because he does not understand what he is doing: see *Institutes*, 2.12.1 and 3.19.8.

31 On Picrochole as a choleric, see Emmanuel Naya, *Rabelais: Une anthropologie humaniste des passions* (Paris: Presses Universitaires de France, 1998), pp. 35–40. On the Gargantua–Picrochole contrast, see also the useful pages in D. Desrosiers-Bonin, *Rabelais et l'humanisme civil* (Geneva: Droz, 1992), pp. 119–27.

32 Erasmus comments on flattery consisting of calling the prince "invincible": "let him think how absurd it is to call invincible a man who is conquered by anger,

a slave to lust every single day, and the prisoner of ambition, which leads and drives him where it likes. He should think a man truly invincible only when he does not give in to any emotion and cannot be deflected from what is right by any circumstance" (*Education*, chapter 2, p. 59).

33 See the caution advised by Erasmus: "Although the prince will never make any decision hastily, he will never be more hesitant or more circumspect than in starting a war..." (*Education*, chapter 11, p. 102). The ironic mention of the adage "Festina lente" ("Make haste slowly") by Picrochole's foolhardy advisors (*F*78–9/*H*93) only underlines what this ruler lacks.

34 Bouchet, *Epistres*, part 2, Epistle 1, f. 4v (my trans.).

35 See Desrosiers-Bonin, *Rabelais*, pp. 131–41.

36 For the most recent review of interpretations of this precept, see Ullrich Langer, "Liberté chrétienne et liberté stoïcienne: L'abbaye de Thélème," in A. Tarrête, ed., *Stoïcisme et christianisme à la Renaissance* (Paris: Presses de l'École normale supérieure, 2006), pp. 59–70.

9

WES WILLIAMS

Histories natural and unnatural

"Let nothing be unknown to you"

Rabelais's capacious, encyclopedic, voracious imagination makes singular demands on his would-be readers; his text repays attention with the reward not only (or merely) of knowledge, but also of learning, of understanding, and of play. The embodiments of appetite, his principal characters are as monstrous in energy as they are in size, driven by a thirst for knowledge and experience which seems to encompass the whole of creation. The first two books, in detailing the educational programs followed by successive generations of giant, take us from "the dark . . . , the infelicity and calamity of the Goths," through to an age in which "light and dignity [have been] restored to letters," and to learning (*F160/H243*). Gargantua's letter to his son, in which this excitement is given voice as the new age dawns, reads as an emblem of that cultural moment which successive generations of scholars have described, discredited, and redescribed as the Renaissance. The Father's dream, translated into a curriculum, demands of the Son not only that he read books (and a good many, too), but also that he gain, through experiment and experience, a full and comprehensive understanding of "the works of nature":

> Let there be no sea, stream, or spring, whose fish you do not know; all the birds of the air, all the trees, shrubs, and bushes of the forest, all the herbs of the earth, all the metal hidden in the bowels of the depths, the precious stones of the entire Orient and Southern Hemisphere: let nothing be unknown to you.
> (*F161/H245*)

This is one of the shortest of Rabelais's many lists. Compared either to the list detailing the books in the Library of St. Victor immediately preceding the letter, or to the number of languages Panurge calls to mind in the chapter which follows this, it is by no means exhausting. But its scope is no less astonishing for all that, and the structure of the sentence itself enacts an exhaustive tour of the world as it moves through each of the life-giving elements (water, air, and earth), and each of the principal categories of natural creation (animal, vegetable, and mineral). The grammar of learning shifts from an initially negative aspect, establishing such places and things as are *not* to be left *un*known, through to a repeated insistence on *all* the creatures that are to be discovered (with the term *tout* in the original French acting both adjectivally and adverbially), before coming to rest again in that last, double negation, which serves as a powerfully positive command: "let nothing be unknown to you."

Gargantua's letter to Pantagruel further expresses the hope that his son and heir not be so fixated on acquiring knowledge of the created world that he forget to honor the Creator: "Science without conscience is but ruin of the soul," he warns, before signing off, "From Utopia" (F162/H245). Initially, the signs are that the son, even when he heads far, far from home, will keep both a Utopian vision of the world, and the early Renaissance program concerning the "works of nature" in mind. When in 1552 Rabelais (re)releases *Book 4*, he nominates as the travelers' first port of call an island called Medamothi: a displaced reworking of Utopia, in that it, too, bears the name of Nowhere Island. Here Pantagruel and his men set about acquiring, amongst other marvels, a number of never-before-seen beasts – the chameleon-like tarande, and three unicorns, two male and one female – so as to send them home (*Book 4*, chapter 2). These beasts (like the other objects for sale on Medamothi) are *adynata*: impossible objects, derived for the most part from Pliny's *Natural History*, books 8 and 10, where they figure such creatures as lie beyond credible representation. Rabelais's point is that here, now, in the New World of *Book 4*, nature (or perhaps the imagination) has extended itself such that ostensibly impossible wonders – far exceeding the earlier books' category and catalogues of "works of nature" – are openly on sale. As if to remind us of how far we have traveled in just a few days, Pantagruel and his followers are interrupted in their shopping spree by the arrival from home of a messenger, Squire Malicorne, bearing with him a homing pigeon (which Pantagruel sends swiftly back with a white ribbon, signifying that all is well), and a letter from the Father (the last words heard from the Old Man), signed and dated "from your paternal home" (F443/H545). This, the Father's second letter, while it enjoins the Son to further study, is principally concerned with the Son's well-being on the potentially perilous journey, and so encourages Pantagruel to read the "joyous books" ("livres joyeulx": Frame's translation unfortunately suppresses the adjective), brought by the messenger whose name makes him sound like he might himself be a species of old world mythological marvel...

The one generation wishes on the next all the knowledge in the world, and from the first to the fifth book, Rabelais takes his characters on a tour of the institutions and practices of Renaissance learning: from magic, medicine, and the law, through to animal husbandry, astronomy, book-making, botany, cake-baking, casuistry . . . The list is longer than that which makes up Gargantua's (as it turns out) modest program for understanding "the works of nature": with each successive generation of readers, new items are added to it, and with them are proposed new histories of the Renaissance which Rabelais is said to represent, together with new accounts of this text's relation to the worlds of "official" or "elite" institutional learning, or to the worlds of artisans, colporteurs (peddlers of tracts and books), and other figures of "popular" practice and culture.

In recent years one of the most productive responses to Rabelais (and to the early modern period) has been a reinvestigation of certain of those languages and practices which we now call science, and which were then known as natural history.[1] Pantagruel concludes *his* letter, sent back home to Gargantua with Squire Malicorne, with a promise to make of himself a model mid-century natural historian: he will send home all manner of "novelties in animals, plants, birds, and precious stones that I can find in this whole peregrination" (*F*446/*H*547). The list is both a brief reminder of the order of the "works of nature" outlined in Gargantua's very first letter, back in *Pantagruel*, and a promise of wonders to come later in the book. For Nowhere Island, for all its old-fangled play on words, and its studied recollection of classical texts and quotations, also takes its readers beyond the bournes of ancient understanding. Not only does it introduce us to a *mesnagerie* of *exotique* animals, it also introduces both of these words to the French language (or, at very least, to French print).

Rabelais's lexical innovations here bear witness to the fact that the mid-sixteenth century was a time in which the menagerie of exotic beasts and monsters thrived in print, particularly in the French vernacular. The pioneering work in the late 1540s and 1550s of Pierre Belon, and of Guillaume Rondelet (the latter the model for Rabelais's Rondibilis), to whom we shall return below, was followed, within a decade or two, by that of a whole brood of teratologists – from compilers of *Histoires Prodigieuses* such as Pierre Boaistuau, Guillaume Tesserant, and François de Belleforest, to cosmographer-travelers such as André Thevet, the prolific barber-surgeon and monster-theorist Ambroise Paré, Pliny's French translator and modernizer, Antoine du Pinet, and, in time, the essayist Michel de Montaigne – who populated their texts with images and accounts of encounters with creatures born both "beyond" (*outre*) and "against" (*contre*) nature. The history of science and the history of the book are also histories of encounter, of conflict, and of the imagination, as the text and images produced by these writers make plain. For the 1550s also seemed, to many of its contemporaries (particularly in retrospect), a time when nature turned against itself, when barbarism stalked the earth, and when the light of the Renaissance day gave way to darkening shapes, signifying schism, conflict, heresy, repression...

This chapter will concern itself with that texture of scientific knowledge in Rabelais's work and concentrate particularly on a number of beasts. Returning first to the early books and prologues, before revisiting *Book 4*, and in particular the encounter with the beast that is the Physeter, it will suggest ways in which Rabelais's writings of the 1550s signal a departure from the early Renaissance understanding of nature, her works, and our words. Drawing on, and – through a focus on beasts and monsters as figures for different kinds of reading – extending recent scholarship in fields related to natural history, what follows also seeks to assess the significance of the omission of the negative science of monsters from the early Renaissance learning program as exemplified by Gargantua's first letter to his son. It can be argued that at an early stage of the fiction (as of the Renaissance), nature, like the giants themselves, is extensible at will, creatively capable of including anything within her/their scope, such that, for instance, an entire race of pygmies can find itself farted into existence when Pantagruel is subject to a bad case of wind (*Book 2*, chapter 27). This argument understands voraciousness in the young giants to be not merely a metaphorical intensifier of their appetite for knowledge of the world and the beasts within it, but a sign of a broader Renaissance cultural practice: a kind of peacefully accommodating ingestion. A bear, several cows, some pill-encased servants, and the narrator are just some of the many creatures making up the world in Pantagruel's mouth.

Yet even in the early books, the physical comedy which animates Rabelais's world can be one of, at times, scabrous, brutish violence: words can become disturbingly animal flesh, as insults metamorphose themselves either into the hungry dogs in hot pursuit of the bacon-basted Panurge (*Book 2*, chapter 14), or, later, into the vengeful pack of hounds who, in pissing all over the Parisian lady as Panurge's surrogates, produce both "the dirtiest mess in the world" and, Pantagruel seems to concur (as it were), "a very fine and novel show" (F208/H296–7). As the story progresses, and particularly as we reach *Book 4*, the balance between the order of nature and the forces of disorder becomes radically unsettled, and unsettling. The sense of having entered a new, more dangerous, and difficult age is powerfully evoked in the narrative pairing of Pantagruel's discussion of the death of heroes (at once classical and Christian) with his startling, timely recollection of the haunting scene in which a group of old men – "Rabelays" among them – gather in terrified silence around the bed of their dying hero, the Lord of Langey, and note the "prodigies, portents, monsters, and other premonitory signs formed against all order of nature" which preceded his early death (F495/H602).[2] As the crew of the Thalamege sail further and further away from the "paternal home" (which used to call itself Utopia), so the Father's dream of "science with conscience"– knowledge with moral understanding – dissolves (as if in a film) into the Son's visions of a series of nightmare figures: conflict, heresy, disorder, and discord. And as allegorical beast follows (or tries to swallow) its counter-beast, all manner of monsters crowd into the book, and so warp the shapes of the natural histories through which the travelers find themselves moving.

Some dogs, an ox, a camel (and a motley colored slave)

The first animal the reader of Rabelais is likely to encounter is a monster: one of several beings pictured on the outside of the Sileni, or "little boxes, such as we see nowadays in apothecaries' shops," which, along with Socrates himself, figure in the Author's Prologue to *Gargantua* as part of a parable about reading (F3/H5). Each of the first few movements of the tale has its tutelary beast or monster: following the "harpies ... satyrs, bridled goslings, saddled ducks, flying goats ... and other such paintings" on the boxes, there is Prologue's dog, the "rats and moths, or (lest I tell a lie) other harmful creatures," which have eaten away the beginning of "The Anti-doted Frigglefraggles" (F8/H11) and, of course, there is Gargantua himself, whose monstrous birth (or "strange nativity") is made the more credible by reference to what we have seen to be the source text for most Renaissance marvels: Pliny's *Natural History* (F20/H22). Of these various beasts, it is the example of the most commonplace, the dog, that readers are enjoined to follow; it is the dog that serves to convey the Author's principal lesson. He might have said "Consider the lilies" or, perhaps, referred to camels and the eye of a needle for his parable about the nature of his text, and the quality of his readers. But instead, he draws our attention to the nature and qualities of the beast which is "as Plato says, Book 2 of *The Republic*, the most philo-sophic animal in the world": a dog tenaciously working away at a marrow bone. "If you have seen one" (a joke: dogs are hardly exotic marvels), you will have seen not only a beast in search of both nutrition and pleasure, but also a creature endowed with a host of qualities you might have mistakenly thought of as specifically human: devotion, care, fervor, prudence, affection, diligence, and hope (F4/H6).

Clearly it is not the beast itself that is the marvel, so much as the lesson it provides for us as readers, both of this Author's text, and of the "works of nature." For what matters is the dog's rhetorical function – both as exemplary figure for reading, and as evidence within a debate concerning the common qualities of animals and the specificity of humankind. The conjoining of these two themes had already been effected by the Author's rounding off the opening poem addressed to the readers with the silent appropriation of a line of thought from Aristotle's treatise *On the Parts of Animals*: "Laughter is proper to man" (*F2/H3*) (I have altered the translation here as it is somewhat mangled). The classical debate, at once philosophical and natural historical, is continued in the prologue, where following references to Plato, and to the medical authority, Galen (*On the Natural Faculties* and *On the Parts of the Body and their Functions*), the Author makes plain his own, contemporary perspectives and desire: I want you to read me like a dog "reads" a bone.

> After this example it behooves you to be wise enough to sniff out and assess these exquisite books, to be light footed in pursuit and bold in the encounter; then by careful reading and frequent meditation, break the bone and suck out the substantific marrow – that is to say what I mean by these Pythagorean symbols – in the certain hope of being made more astute and brave by the said reading: for in this you will find quite a different taste and more abstruse doctrine, which will reveal to you some very lofty sacraments and horrific mysteries, concerning both our political state and our domestic life. (*F4/H7*)

The prologue to *Gargantua* is perhaps the most frequently quoted passage in Rabelais's work. Its seemingly paradoxical injunctions (read my works doggedly for the "higher meaning"; don't think that I authorize you to overinterpret my text in the way that others have chewed hungrily over those of Homer and Ovid) have left readers bewitched, bothered, and bewildered for centuries. Nor does Rabelais let even satisfied dogs lie. For the prologue's dog returns, time and again throughout the five books, metamorphosing all the while into one of the principal figures in his bestiary, his menagerie of meaningful, instructive creatures. Each dog's appearance in the text is at once timely and exemplary. The sighting of a dog (or, more often, a pack of them) is always a meaningful event because the Rabelaisian animal derives its (at least dual) nature in what I have called his menagerie from the congruence of two distinct traditions: on the one hand the classical natural historical debate about the properties of animals and their difference from humans, and on the other hand the late antique and medieval bestiary, a tradition which explores animals as signs, figures for something other than themselves. The syncretism, or productive collaboration, of these traditions – and, as the text develops and as monsters crowd out the animals, their interaction with that other form at once classical and medieval, the metamorphic animal fable – is what underscores both Gargantua's educational program outlined above, and the play of the prologues.

The patrons of the classical traditions are displayed in the text itself: Plato, Aristotle, Galen, Lucian, and Ovid. The patron saint of the bestiary tradition, a discipline which originates in exegesis and in the training of priests, is Augustine, who explains, in book 2 of his treatise *On Christian Teaching* that difficulties in the understanding of Scripture may be caused by one of two reasons: obscurity and ambiguity. The first, and most straightforward point – which Augustine illustrates with the help (not of a dog but) of an ox – is that signs may be either literal or metaphorical:

> They are called literal when used to signify the things for which they were invented: as, for example, when we say *bovem* [ox], meaning the animal which we and all speakers of Latin call by that name. They are metaphorical when the actual things we signify by the particular words are used to signify something else: when for example we say *bovem* and not only interpret these two syllables to mean the animal normally referred to by that name but also understand, by that animal, "worker in the gospel," which is what scripture, as interpreted by the Apostle Paul means when it says, "You shall not muzzle the ox that treads out the grain" [1 Cor. 9:9 and 1 Tim. 5:18, quoting Deut. 25:4].[3]

This argument then supports another, in which the animal serves not as an example, but as itself the object of study. For if the method of "metaphorical" interpretation outlined here by Augustine is to work, then the qualities of what he calls "actual things" must be properly understood: "Ignorance of things makes figurative expressions unclear when we are ignorant of the qualities of animals or stones or plants or other things mentioned in scripture for the sake of some analogy".[4] It is the doctrine of analogy, then, that allows Augustine to set aside anxieties about an idolatrous overattachment to things of the world, and to replace them with a program of careful and attentive study (for the sake of the better understanding of Scripture) of what Gargantua will one day call the "works of nature."

What is true of the metaphorical legibility of dogs and oxen, beasts which we might recognize as natural, is perhaps all the more true of those creatures which are seen as "infamous monsters...the all-black Bactrian camel...and the motley colored slave" presented to the Egyptians, Rabelais tells us in the prologue to *Book 3*, by a Ptolemy hopeful of augmenting "by these novelties the people's love for him" (*F*258/*H*350). The Egyptians misread Ptolemy's intentions (or perhaps read them too well) and "the hope he had of pleasing them . . . slipped out of his hands." The exotic animals are dismissed as objects of ridicule rather than marvels; monstrous in a formal sense, they are not "beautiful, elegant and perfect" but seem to have been "created by an error of nature" (*ibid.*). Ptolemy's hopeful monsters themselves serve as analogies, of course, for Rabelais's own work; in this, they are kin to the monsters on the Sileni boxes in the earlier prologue to *Gargantua*. Monsters, it seems, can serve (at least in prologues) as second order signs. But is this flexibility of signifying function – the property of monsters as of certain species of writing – to be seen as a gift or a curse? Is it in any sense natural, or itself a further sign of the manner in which such monsters are beyond nature, and such texts work against the beauty, elegance, and perfection of what we might call natural historical narrative? The question is one asked again and again by Rabelais in the last two (or three) of his books as he investigates the possible shapes, forms, and (most of all) responses both to the monsters he has inherited from a range of traditions, and to those of his own times.

"Very like a whale": A monstrous encounter

As Abel Lefranc, one of the founding fathers of modern Rabelais criticism, wrote some time ago: "People have been all round the houses in an effort to find reasons for the anecdote with the Physeter." Railing against that "mania for outlandish allegorical interpretation" which made readers interpret this episode as yet another of Rabelais's assaults on the true Church, Lefranc argued that on the one hand the author's objective was both single and simple, while on the other hand the monster was meaningless: Rabelais's aim was "purely and simply to describe as exactly as possible, the capture of a whale."[5] His remark, part of a polemic with rival contemporary readers, is echoed in recent debates concerning conflicting interpretations of Rabelais's beasts and monsters, a debate which has been conducted, at times fiercely, in journals and books across the world, as well as across the interpretive, confessional divide, and in which the Physeter plays something of a starring role. The details of this interpretive drama need not detain us here.[6] What is of interest is the way in which the monster continues to reveal its readers' varied investments and anxieties, to figure forth the interpretive, confessional, and other allegiances of those of us who attempt to grapple with the beast. This is in a sense as it should be: that is what bestiaries do; this is what monsters are for.

It is in both the nature and the history of monsters that they find themselves explained by way of their capacity to generate interpretation. Where

Augustine argues in the *City of God* that a monster is something which shows – "*monstrum monstrat*" – others derived the sense of the monster from *monere* (to warn), and so related monsters to prodigies, having less to do with the past than with impending danger.[7] In either case, the monster itself is not the message (whether from the past or the future); it is not itself the thing shown, but is rather what the Augustine of *On Christian Teaching* calls a metaphorical sign: it points to something else. This means that a monster can, by definition, never be fully present, nor yet can you look directly at it and know it for what it – or he, or she – *really* is. For the monster's being and function are identical: *le monstre*, in early modern French, as in Latin, *monstre*. The first step on meeting an early modern monster, then, is to think of it as a meaningful phenomenon, to hypothesize a hidden content, and context, which is rendered legible by the form which the monster here takes on: don't fixate on the thing, ask what it reveals. Like Freud faced with a dream, or Marx with a commodity, if you find yourself face to face with a monster you should first recognize yourself as someone in the thrall of narrative: the monster is no mistake, but is rather a hint, a parcel of a larger story.[8] So, for instance, when Panurge sees the Physeter rising up out of the sea towards the travelers in their ship, he suggests that it is a creature from two possible prophetic grand narratives, the one sacred, the other classical: "it's Leviathian, as described by the noble prophet Moses... [it's] the very sea monster that was destined long ago to devour Andromeda" (*F508/H616*). Whether you read with Augustine, Freud, Marx – or Panurge – you are, effectively, reading in a similar tradition: you recognize the monster to be a poem, something made, a legend, something to be read; the moment of its appearance is less a chance event than an occasion.

The Physeter is in many respects an unlikely monster to attract readers' attention; indeed this seems, initially, the least interpretatively promising of the various encounters with monstrosity that occupy the exact center of *Book 4* (chapters 29–42). Unlike Fastilent, or Niphleseth, Queen of the Chitterlings, who take up positions either side of the two chapters in which it appears, the Physeter is not an immediately allegorizable figure: neither the ruler of an island community in crisis, nor double, nor enemy to another monstrously imagined creature. Interrupting the allegorical epic with a brief, diverting recollection of the possibility of a comprehensible world, one narratable as natural history, it seems rather to be very like a whale, one of those "works of nature," which has somehow strayed into the story from the learning program of the earlier books; or perhaps from recent accounts of travel to the New World (or both). The terms in which the narrative relates the initial sighting of the beast reinforce the sense that we have some-how both gone *back* in time, and *across* to another genre. Back, that is, to a point in the story when Pantagruel was still a giant, and across to natural historical travel writing; the technical realism of the description of life on board ship reinforces a mythic narrative of existential struggle, in which (Renaissance) man pits himself against nature, and survives.

The name "Physeter" comes from Pliny's *Natural History* (book 8, chap-ter 8, and again book 22, chapter 52), and the word had already appeared in a French text, a year before *Book 4*. The natural historian Pierre Belon, looking for the Latin name of a fish caught off the coast of Normandy and then displayed in Paris earlier that year, decides that "*Physeter*" will not do: "since it would (if what people write about them is true) have to be even bigger than this fish."[9] And the beast lives on beyond Rabelais's description into a host of other natural historical studies, in Greek, Latin, and French. Rabelais's Rondibilis, Guillaume Rondelet, for instance, devotes an entire chapter to the "ΦΥΣΗΤΗΡ in Greek, as if one were to say in French a spouter [*un souffleur*]."[10] The encounter with the beast in *Book 4* begins as Pantagruel, having first "sighted from afar a great and monstrous phy-seter" [I have altered Frame's translation here, as he changes "physeter" to "cachalot"], then "pointed it out" (the French reads "*le monstra*") to the captain and to Xenomanes (*F508/H616*). This gesture by Pantagruel, which motivates the narrator to turn an adjective (*monstrueux*) into a verb (*mon-stra*), a description into an action, is important, not least since it displaces the focus of the narrative away from the beast and towards the men in the boat. The narrative now shows not a potential monster, but men at work: Pantagruel points out the enormous fish to the chief professionals, and they call on the workers below them to deal with the problem in the standard manner "according to their orders and to naval practice." The beast is big, but it is not yet a monster in any malign, portentous, or revelatory sense. It is a danger, but not an unknown or unrecognized one, and there are estab-lished strategies for dealing with it: the sailors all adopt the Pythagorean Y position. The threat of danger unifies the disparate crew members, spurring them into action and making of them an orderly pattern. As if to stress that this is a natural response – that the sailors' human artifice has its analogue in nature, and that sea beast, men of the earth, and birds of the sky are part of some cosmic dance – the narrator notes how the sailors' position mirrors that which cranes adopt when flying. The individual char-acters, too, revert to type. Frère Jean returns to his former, and for some time forgotten, identity as the battling monk, taking his place, "valiant and ready for action," alongside the cannoneers on the poop deck (*F508/H616*).

It takes Panurge, and his habitual fear and excessively productive imagination, to refocus narrative attention on the beast, and in doing so to turn
the big fish into a meaningful monster:

> Bub-bub-babble-blubblub, he wailed, this is worse than ever. Let's run away!
> This, by gorry, is Leviathan as described by the noble prophet Moses in the
> life of that holy man Job [Job 40–1]. He'll swallow us all, men and ships,
> like so many pills...Look, here he is! Let's flee, let's go to land! I believe
> he's the very sea monster that was destined long ago to devour Andromeda.
> We're all done for! O if only there were here now to slay him some valiant
> Perseus! (*ibid.*)

Unlike the others on board, who respond to the beast by drawing on their
experience and professional skills, thereby giving "monstrous" the meaning
of just plain big, and seeking to keep the episode within the genre of natural
history, Panurge's imagination insists that the monster is for real, which is
to say that it has come from one of two possible master narratives (biblical
or classical), each of which exceeds their own, and so threatens to swallow
them up "like so many pills" and thus to end their story. Unless, that is, one
of them is prepared to use *their* imagination, to bring the Ovidian fable up
to date, to play Perseus to the crew's (or is it *his*?) Andromeda, and rescue
them all from the monster.

That monsters could be imagined into existence was clear to the man
who first introduced the Physeter to French print, Pierre Belon. In a number
of angry and polemical texts in the mid-1550s, Belon attacks his rivals
for claiming that they wish to "portray and represent things as they are"
but in fact add horns to whales which have none, and monsters to maps
where there are none: "Is it not altogether reprehensible to see such people
portraying so many sea monsters without any discretion whatsoever? Oh!
Inconstant spirits, why can they not turn their minds to such perfection as
nature presents?"[11] Belon is not thinking of Panurge here, but his conclusion
that it is the hyperbolic allegorical imagination of "inconstant spirits" that
is to blame applies as much to Rabelais's character as it does to the travel
writers who muddle the borders between fact and fiction that Belon has
in mind; it is their poetic impulse to fiction-making illusion (*feindre*), that
makes monsters of beasts which are, in truth, evidence of nature – "God's
handmaiden" – at work. Those who speak of monsters are "crooners of old
songs, singing only out of habit, without ever really acquiring any musical
skills." There are no monsters in nature, only in other people's readings
of it; and it is with the monsters of interpretation that Belon feels he must
do battle: "Since I am now engaged in this matter of monsters, I intend

to demonstrate that all manner of men have indiscriminately permitted the portrayal of monsters which have never existed, do not exist now, and never will."[12]

Pantagruel, for all that he may by now be tired of Panurge's overexcitable imagination, recognizes his companion's apparent wish that some Perseus might appear on the scene to be in truth a challenge. It is, I think, to this challenge to rhetorical self-fashioning, to playing a role within a fiction, a romance even – and not the challenge presented by the big fish – that Rabelais has his hero initially respond. Panurge is asking Pantagruel whether he can escape from the plot of the here and now, from the politics of the epic in which they are stuck, from the polar opposites of Lent and Carnival, popular and elite culture, lack and excess, and so on that have structured the journey so far, and from which this beast offers a welcome, and unexpected, diversion. The epic companion, tiring of his diminishing role, presents his friend with a monster by way of a question. It is a question that can be framed in a number of ways: Can you still do the hero thing? Are you still a giant? Do you measure up to the legends of the past? Do you fancy a role in a romance? Do you still love me enough to do this thing?

In a truly terrible pun – "*Persé jus* [pierced and on his back] by me he shall be" – Pantagruel both answers and avoids Panurge's question, before, as the new chapter starts, dispatching the beast with an impressive display of archery. He does not say: "Yes, I am that man. I am Perseus returned." It seems important that he avoids identifying himself completely with the hero of legend, avoids slotting himself into that systematizing tradition of reading Ovid (referred to in the prologue to *Gargantua* as noted above) which would make of him, for example, a stand-in for Christ and the monster an avatar of the devil. In other words, Pantagruel – and through him Rabelais – resists the kinds of readings to which many will later make him subject. This does not make these readings invalid; indeed, the text invites them. But it also resists endorsing them, and it is this resistance that interests me here, not least for what it might itself reveal.

For all his initial reluctance to play the hero, Pantagruel does, of course, kill the beast. The narrator, with evident relief, shifts into the epic present tense to narrate the slaughter, noting that "Pantagruel, considering the occasion and the need, unfolds his arms [i.e., returns to his gigantic size for the first time since the conclusion of *Pantagruel*] and shows [*monstre*] what he could do" (*F509/H618*). Committing his body and mind to the task in hand, with a knowledge of arms and a sense of timing and identity appropriate to the situation – with, in other words, a due sense of decorum – Pantagruel takes on the status of a legendary giant and reduces the monster to the past.

No longer a present danger, the fish is described by the narrator in terms of the natural historian, terms which are pure Pliny: an object of natural history, "the physeter, dying, rolled over on to its back, belly up, as do all dead fish" ($F511/H620$).

The subsequent chapter starts in the past, narrating how the crew dragged the fish ashore and, like a group of overeager medical students proceeded to anatomize it, to dissect it. In other words, what had happened rhetorically to Fastilent, that metaphorical monster, now happens literally to the big fish. The dead Physeter returns to its status as a very big thing, though not so big as to merit Pantagruel's attention – "Pantagruel took no account of it, for he had seen enough others like it, indeed even more enormous, in the Gallic Ocean."[13] The beast is reduced to an assemblage of parts, one of which – "the fat of the kidneys" – is said to have healing properties, curing "a certain malady they called Lack of Money" (*ibid.*). The monster, once dead, becomes subject to the twinned discourses of medicine and of money, and the narratives of cure and debt which have structured much of this story thus far are shown to be related to all those contemporary polemicists – priests, lawyers, doctors, cosmographers, and the rest – who make a living out of fear, and money out of monster parts.

This sad structure, a recurrent double movement whereby the "works of nature" are first inflated into monsters and subsequently destroyed, is assimilable to one of the most enduring grand narratives about Renaissance culture, and about Rabelais as an exemplar of that culture: each new port of call in *Book 4*, from Medamothi onwards, stages an encounter with a different form of difference, a new form of "novelty"; or, as some would have it, promotes the value of the same old novelty, namely the Reform. In each case, the otherness thus encountered is at first feared, and then either destroyed or sent home to be hung on the wall, stored in curiosity cabinets, or otherwise subjected to the related cultures of domestication, dissection, and display. As we saw above, Pantagruel promises to participate in this culture, by sending home all the novelties he can find in the course of his peregrination; and Rabelais plays the game, by suggesting that some of them – such as the painting bought on Medamothi, a copy of the tapestry which Philomela wove after being raped by the brute Tereus – can still be seen hanging on the walls of Thélème, "on the left hand, as you enter the high gallery" ($F440/H541$). This process of domestication, of bringing the novelty, or the monster, home to those forms of knowledge, understanding, and polemical argument with which we are already familiar, can also be understood as operating at the level of interpretation. Critical readings of Rabelais's monstrous tales all too often follow an uncannily similar set of moves to those which the travelers here perform: the monsters in the text are shown to be "nothing but" metaphorical signs for Catholics, Reformers, polysemites, phallic mothers...

Rabelais's monsters are all of these things, and more. His heroes – if Pantagruel is indeed a hero in any sense that *Book 4* can sustain – can, and must, be productively read in conjunction with those of contemporary political and religious history, as of legend, of psychoanalysis, and of whichever interpretive forms our culture develops. Not least since the text itself, precisely through the dramatization of differing responses to crisis that I have been following here, asks, goads, challenges us to make such connections, and to read the monsters according to our own designs and fears. It is only by risking repeated close encounters with the hybrid, motley *mesnagerie* that is Rabelais's writing, that we can allow his monsters to do their vital work: that of teaching us about the "works of nature," all the while provoking reaction, and so challenging the conventions both of interpretation and of community.

NOTES

1 See, in addition to Jean Céard's magisterial *La Nature et les prodiges: L'insolite au XVIe siècle*, 2nd edn. (Geneva: Droz, 1996), the very differently accented, but nonetheless related, studies of Dudley Wilson, *Signs and Portents: Monstrous Births from the Middle Ages to the Enlightenment* (London: Routledge, 1993) and Lorraine Daston and Katharine Park, *Wonders and the Order of Nature, 1150–1750* (New York: Zone, 1998), and the following: Marie-Hélène Huet, *Monstrous Imagination* (Cambridge, MA: Harvard University Press, 1993); Marina Warner, *From the Beast to the Blonde: On Fairy Tales and their Tellers* (London: Vintage, 1995); C.-C. Kappler, *Monstres, démons et merveilles à la fin du Moyen Age* (Paris: Payot, 1999); Ian Maclean, *Logic, Signs and Nature in the Renaissance: The Case of Learned Medicine* (Cambridge: Cambridge University Press, 2001). Still immensely useful is Lazare Sainéan, *L'Histoire naturelle dans l'œuvre de Rabelais* (Paris: Champion, 1921).

2 For a persuasive account of this crucial scene, see Terence Cave, *Pré-histoires: Textes troublés au seuil de la modernité* (Geneva: Droz, 1999), pp. 87–93.

3 Augustine, *On Christian Teaching*, R. P. H. Green, ed. and trans., World's Classics (Oxford: Oxford University Press, 1997), pp. 37–8.

4 *Ibid.*, p. 44.

5 Abel Lefranc, *Les Navigations de Pantagruel* (Paris: Leclerc, 1905), pp. 137–8.

6 See (amongst others) Michel Jeanneret, "Rabelais, les monstres et l'interprétation des signes (*Quart Livre* 18–42)," in R. C. La Charité, ed., *Writing the Renaissance: Essays on Sixteenth-Century French Literature in Honor of Floyd Gray* (Lexington, KT: French Forum, 1992), pp. 65–76; Frank Lestringant, "L'Insulaire de Rabelais, ou la fiction en archipel (pour une lecture topographique du *Quart Livre*)," in *Écrire le monde à la Renaissance: Quinze études sur Rabelais, Postel, Bodin et la littérature géographique* (Caen: Paradigme, 1993), pp. 159–84; Gérard Defaux, *Rabelais agonistes: Du rieur au prophète. Études*

sur "Pantagruel," "Gargantua," "Le Quart Livre," Études Rabelaisiennes, 32 (Geneva: Droz, 1997); Edwin Duval, *The Design of Rabelais's "Quart Livre de Pantagruel"* (Geneva: Droz, 1998), pp. 135–7; and, for a fine analysis of the whole question, Timothy Hampton, "Signs of Monstrosity: The Rhetoric of Description and the Limits of Allegory in Rabelais and Montaigne," in L. Knoppers and J. Landes, eds., *Monstrous Bodies/Political Monstrosities in Early Modern Europe* (Ithaca and London: Cornell University Press, 2004), pp. 179–99.

7 Augustine, *City of God*, XVI.8 and XXI.8; for the best account of the meanings of monsters from Aristotle to Augustine, see Céard, *La Nature et les prodiges*, pp. 3–30.

8 See Slavoj Žižek, "How Did Marx Invent the Symptom?," in *The Sublime Object of Ideology* (London: Verso, 1989), pp. 11–54.

9 Pierre Belon, *L'Histoire naturelle des estranges poissons marins* (Paris: Chaudiere, 1551), f. 23v [actually 31v]).

10 Guillaume Rondelet, *De piscibus marinis* (Lyons: Bonhomme, 1554), translated by Laurent Joubert as *L'Histoire entiere des poissons* (Lyons: Bonhomme, 1558); the Physeter passages are found at: Latin, pp. 485–7; French, pp. 355–6.

11 Belon, *L'Histoire naturelle*, f. 16v. One author worthy of Belon's criticism is Olaus Magnus, whose *Carta marina* (Venice: De Rubis, 1539), with its image of a horned Physeter blowing alongside a boat off the Faroe Islands, Rabelais might have read before dreaming up this episode.

12 Belon, *L'Histoire naturelle*, f. 16v.

13 Pantagruel has clearly read Pliny, whose words about whales in the "Ocean Gallique" he echoes; perhaps the Physeter did not match the expectations reading Pliny had given him.

to popular theatrical genres such as farce, fools' plays (*soties*), and paro-dic sermons (*sermons joyeux*), enacted at banquets, carnival, epiphany, or student revels. Critics generally agree that the first two books would have been accessible to contemporary readers nurtured on such a vernacular diet of plays, short stories, mock-epic, and romance, and that their printing in octavo format (nowadays standard book size) and old-fashioned gothic type corresponds to the presentation of books in these genres. Does the intended readership change with the runaway success of the chronicles, when the place of publication shifts from Lyon to Paris, when Rabelais starts to sign his books, and when the format goes up-market from gothic type to roman (considered more modern)? The presentation of the last three books is much more akin to that of serious works of erudition or of novels like the *Amadis*, and the contents imply in the imagined public a much wider range of read-ing, including Latin works on medicine, law, philosophy, and history, to such a degree that Rabelais, or his printer Fezandat, included the *Brief Dec-laration*, a detailed seventeen-page glossary of recondite terms in *Book 4*. For the first time, the obscurity of Rabelais becomes an issue.

Rabelais's prologues and epilogues make much of his potential readers, both good and bad. While inviting good readers into Thélème or to drink from his barrel, the author complains loudly about unlaughing detractors who misread and distort him, among whom loom large the censors of the Sorbonne and the Parlement, who condemn Rabelais's writings, Protestants like Calvin who besmirch his character, or Catholic disparagers like Dupuy Herbault, who attack both the immoral man and his pernicious book. Within his own lifetime Rabelais was branded a Lucianic atheist – that is, a mocker of all things serious. The comic epitaphs written for him by the Pléiade poets balance this image of the universal mocker, a jester destined to entertain the spirits in the Underworld, against the growing – and more sympathetic – legend of Rabelais the universal boozer and glutton, wallowing among the barrels, sausages, and hams, a character derived from the literary persona of the prologues, who veers between salesman's patter to sell his scribblings and imprecations against his treacherous enemies and detractors, or yet against the reader (who is no more sober than he, and is riddled with pox and gout).

Within 10 years of his death, whilst sales of his books continued to flour-ish, Rabelais was being radically reinvented. Some, like François de Billon, were seeing him as a diehard antifeminist, identified with voices like that of Rondibilis; for Louis Le Caron he was an Epicurean philosopher. For the Paris publisher of the *Songes drolatiques de Pantagruel* (1565) he was an embodiment of monstrous excess, whether in food, drink, or sex, to whom one could attribute a collection of caricatural images derived from Breughel, Bosch, or Cock. And for some Huguenots, despite Calvin's hostility, he was a potential ally in his exposure of the faults of the Catholic Church, as witness the publication of *Book 5* during the early stages of the religious wars: Huguenots sought to exploit Rabelais's name for propaganda purposes, and the numerous editions of Rabelais printed from 1552, and especially after 1564, in which his attack on Calvin is suppressed, fit in with Rabelais's being enlisted in the Protestant cause.

By the end of the sixteenth century, the legendary image of Rabelais is virtually complete, as seen in the list of epithets associated with him by Maurice de La Porte (1571):

> Rabelais, facetious, biting, usefully pleasing, scoffing, second Epicurus, joyful ridiculer, French Lucian, deriding doctor, Epicurean paunch, amusing mocker, pantagruelist.[4]

His reputation had by now spread beyond the confines of France. Germany was the first country to produce a translation of the chronicles, by the lawyer Johann Fischart (1575), adapted to German taste.[5] In England "the great jester of France" had found many admirers and imitators[6] in writers like Francis Bacon, Sir John Harington, Thomas Nashe, or Gabriel Harvey, and in the lexicographer Randle Cotgrave, who drew abundantly on the wealth of Rabelais's vocabulary. British readership of Rabelais was to climax in the translation by the Scottish knight Sir Thomas Urquhart (1653 and 1693), which developed the fascination of earlier English writers with Rabelaisian linguistic fantasy, and was completed by Peter Le Motteux (1693–4), who enriched the book with an elaborate commentary privileging an allegorical reading of the text.

In the first half of the seventeenth century in France, editions of his works continued to appear, and echoes of his style and humor can be found in comic writers like Sorel and Scarron (and later Molière and La Fontaine), in *libertin* poets like Saint-Amant and Sarazin, or in pastiches like the *Rabelais ressuscité* of Nicolas de Horry (1611); episodes were even turned into ballets which were performed at court. By contrast, Catholic apologists such as Père Garasse composed tracts against the "damned and pernicious" Rabelais (1619–23), identifying his work as the bedside book of free-thinkers, the "enchiridion of libertinism," and condemned it as a "plague and gangrene" for devout believers; Catholics were not slow to burn their copies of such a damned book. These so-called libertine readers included writers and wits like Gabriel Naudé, Pierre Gassendi, Gui Patin, and Guillaume Colletet, whose circle included a defender of Rabelais, Antoine Leroy, who carried support to the frontiers of adulation: he lived in Rabelais's own presbytery in Meudon, worked in his very library, and composed exhaustive panegyrics which present him as a prodigy in every discipline, from mathematics to medicine, architecture to astrology, magic to music, politics to painting.

The middle of the century marked a turning-point, with a decline in editions and an increase in hostility. The editor of the first Elzevir edition (1663) remarked that, up till then, every man of the world owned a copy, knew the text, and quoted it over the dinner table; but with the passage of time the allusions became more obscure, and the language more archaic, detracting from the pleasure of reading Rabelais. Whence the need for more and more critical apparatus, as seen in editions like that of the Huguenot exile Jacob Le Duchat (1711), who converted Rabelais's chronicles into six luxury illustrated volumes, copiously annotated to bring out the linguistic curiosities, the sources, and the historical context, but deliberately stopping short of identifying any arcane allegorical message hidden under the comic veil.[7] Le Duchat's philological notes are still of enduring value to any editor of Rabelais. Of less enduring value are the so-called keys to Rabelais, which appeared in many seventeenth-century editions, and which sought to portray the work as political satire, and to identify the major comic characters as leading figures at the courts of François I and Henri II.[8]

The change in fortune signaled by the 1663 editor is exemplified in the above-mentioned judgment of La Bruyère (1690). Whilst the moralist concedes that Rabelais may have good points, natural talent, and a subtle morality, these are outweighed by the obscurity and the obscenity of the work. A watershed has been reached, with, on the one side, those like La Bruyère who condemn Rabelais for purveying vulgar, gutter humor; and, on the other side, editors and critics like Jean Bernier, Le Motteux, or Le Duchat, who seek to reclaim him as a serious, edifying, encyclopedic author, worthy of scholarly attention.

This same ambivalence prevails throughout the Enlightenment.[9] Some judgments were resolutely hostile, whether to the immoral man, "clown, scoffer, debauchee, drunkard, apostate, womanizer,"[10] or to the corrupting book, which Voltaire described as "a pile of the most crude and impertinent filth that a drunken monk can spew up."[11] The work is obscene, chaotic, fantastic, obscure, and pedantic:

> In his extravagant and unintelligible book Rabelais has dispensed great merriment and greater still immorality; he has poured out pedantry, filth and tedium.[12]

The only people who read it are dismissed as libertines with a bizarre, lewd taste for obscenities.

Some critics pleaded mitigation, seeking to replace the book in its Renaissance context, and to attribute the scatology not to Rabelais's character but to "the barbarism of his age," to the barbarous, semi-Gothic taste of his readers; or arguing that Rabelais might have prudently worn the mask of folly to protect himself from the censors. Nicéron in particular rejected the many accretions to Rabelais's biography, making use of his letters from Rome and supplications to Paul III to show that he was not the drunken atheist buffoon of legend.[13] In this process of rehabilitation Rabelais was increasingly viewed through Enlightenment glasses, praised for his erudition (so different from Renaissance monks or eighteenth-century curés), for his qualities of attic wit and finesse, of charm and *enjouement*, for his "concise and flowing style," for his irony and satiric verve. Besides being a salon wit, Rabelais was recast as a *philosophe avant la lettre* (even if a "philosopher in drunkenness"),[14] a satirist who railed against the vices of the Ancien Régime. His work was a coded allegory, to which access was provided by the keys of seventeenth-century editions, regularly reprinted. He was seen as a forerunner of the Enlightenment (and indeed the Revolution) for what were perceived as sustained anti-clericalism and attacks on the monarchy, especially in a 1791 tract by Ginguené, purportedly printed in Thélème,[15] where he was repackaged as a prophet of popular uprising, ridiculing royal extravagance and warmongering, ecclesiastical privilege and repression, as well as the corruption and venality of the legal and fiscal systems.

Despite the strictures of detractors, the public's appetite for Rabelais was very healthy, and was amply supplied by the printing trade, though almost exclusively outside the borders of France. Rabelais was evidently too hot for French publishers. New documents appeared, such as his letters and supplications, while Le Duchat's monumental philological edition was reprinted three times, embellished with abundant engravings and supplemented by Le Motteux's more allegorical annotations. Le Motteux's apparatus emerged triumphant in the final luxury edition of the century (1798), for which Bastien commissioned a whole new set of explicit and fantastic engravings. These reveal an evolving taste reflected equally in a new 1797 edition of the *Songes drolatiques*, richly illustrated and interpreted as authentic drawings by Rabelais, made in Italy to satirize "the foremost figures of his time, and especially the Court of Rome."

In order to balance the demand for Rabelais against concern for public morality, two abbés undertook in the same year (1752) to bowdlerize and modernize the text. The rival editions of *Le Rabelais Moderne* by Abbé de Marsy (in six volumes!), and of *Œuvres choisies de M. François Rabelais* by Abbé Pérau (in three volumes) modernized the spelling, cut out lists, tirades, archaisms, improprieties, and lewd material, some of which was simply moved to the bottom of the page. It is striking to see the Catholic clergy attempting to promote a purified Rabelais, in (unequal) competition with the weighty, unexpurgated versions produced by Protestant scholarship. Despite all the emasculations, neither of the Catholic versions was printed in France, unlike the abridgement carried out for the *Bibliothèque universelle des romans*, which produced for lady readers a predigested synopsis of Rabelais, some forty pages long, which would save them the trouble – and the danger to their innocence – of reading the original.[16]

Writers like Diderot, who deplored the impoverishment and regularization of classical French, looked with nostalgia on the wealth of Rabelaisian vocabulary and the playful fantasy of his style. Rabelaisian pastiche was practiced throughout the century, especially among Parisian *philosophes* like Diderot and Galiani, who exchanged letters parodying his style and signed by his characters. Various bogus works were written under Rabelais's name and circulated as political pamphlets, especially during the Revolution. Wholly fictitious *Confessions* were attributed to him by Lesuire, supposedly translated from the original Gaulois, and recounting his ribald and wildly improbable adventures with clysters, the Inquisition, and Columbus, and his affairs with royalty, including Marguerite de Navarre.[17] Such tales were the stuff of theater, and there is an abundance of burlesque ballet and comic opera loosely based on the chronicles, including a very successful *Panurge dans l'isle des Lanternes* (*Panurge in Lantern Island*) with music by Grétry (1785), which had almost 250 performances. Comedies and vaudevilles also abounded, placing Rabelais on the stage as a boozy spendthrift monk, battling against his enemy Ronsard, a penniless swaggering hack, and supported by a chorus of drinkers, and these continued to be written throughout the nineteenth century.

After an eclipse in the late seventeenth century, therefore, Rabelais's star was in the ascent throughout the Enlightenment, as witness the volte-face of Voltaire: from having damned Rabelais as a lewd pedant, he came in his later writings to see him as the most learned man of his age, an apostle of anti-clericalism and republicanism, who only escaped execution by donning the motley. One contemporary even saw him as a forerunner of Voltaire himself:

> We may conclude (much to Rabelais's credit), that had he been alive today, he might have been the author of *Candide* and *Zadig*.[18]

The Romantics were largely enthusiastic about Rabelais, with the curious exception of Lamartine who, with a latter-day neoclassical purism, dismissed him as "a filthy genius of cynicism, a scandal to the ears, to the mind and taste, a fetid poisonous mushroom sprung from the manure of the medieval cloister, a grunting Gallic pig."[19] They knew his text thoroughly: Nodier was said to have copied it out three times, and had planned to write a commentary; George Sand intended to publish an expurgated edition, with the obscenities removed; and writers like Flaubert delighted in filling their fiction and correspondence with allusions, quotations and imitations. Balzac, who saw him not only as "the master of us all," but as a fellow citizen of Tours, wrote a lot of Rabelaisian pastiche in the early 1830s, especially in the *Contes drôlatiques* (1832 – purportedly published "for the merriment of Pantagruelists") and in the banquet of Taillefer in the *Peau de Chagrin* (1831), as did Gautier in *Grotesques* (1844) and in *Capitaine Fracasse* (1863). Some, like Chateaubriand, saw him as the writer who had created French literature, from whom stemmed Montaigne, Molière, and La Fontaine; George Sand judged him to be "much more so than Montaigne, the great emancipator of the French mind during the Renaissance" (letter of 1847); Michelet held him to be greater than Aristophanes, Cervantes, and Voltaire, and as great as Shakespeare; while for Balzac he was "the greatest mind of modern humanity" (*Cousin Pons*, 1846–7).

Others attributed to him an epic status, calling him "an Homeric clown" (Nodier), "an Homeric buffoon" (Sainte-Beuve), "this mocking Homer" (Gautier), and "the Homer of laughter" (Hugo). Although Hugo rarely refers to his writing in detail, he classifies Rabelais among his fourteen geniuses of humanity, the only Frenchman so honored, attributing to this "great laugher," "this scoffer at the whole compass of things human," a vision which encompasses the whole world "in a barrel," or in a vast stomach, which earns him the title "the Aeschylus of grub" (*William Shakespeare*, 1864). Rabelais fits perfectly Hugo's concept of the hero as enormous, exaggerated, monstrous, and grotesque, in keeping with the illustrations of the much-read and republished *Songes drolatiques* (1791, 1823, 1869), with the engravings produced by Gustave Doré (1854) and with Michelet's own definition of Rabelais:

> A sphinx or chimera, a hundred-headed, hundred-tongued monster, harmonious chaos, a boundless farce, a wonderfully lucid drunkenness, a profoundly wise folly. (*Histoire de France*)

The public's growing demand for Rabelais was satisfied both by forgers and by scholarly editors. The forger Vrain-Lucas is said to have faked some two thousand letters by Rabelais, and a number of others addressed to him, including from the emperor Charles V, Copernicus, Nostradamus, Columbus, and Amerigo Vespucci describing their voyages, not forgetting one from Raphael.[20] Weighty editions of the chronicles and minor works continued to appear, including the exhaustive nine-volume *Editio variorum* by Esmangard and Johanneau (1823), which uncritically accumulated all existing commentaries. German readers were treated to a four-volume translation with superabundant annotations by Gottlob Regis (1832–41), which, among the broad swathes of footnotes, contains some valuable and original material, which has been little exploited since. Two more large French editions followed, by Burgaud des Marets and Rathéry (1857) and by Marty-Laveaux in six volumes (1868–1902), with elaborate indices and concordances but few new insights.

Surprisingly, George Sand's intention of purging Rabelais was not untypical of the age, which continued to see edulcorated texts being produced by admirers who sought to combat prejudices against their author. The critic Eugène Noël tried to adapt the text to take account of modern sensibilities, publishing a modernized anthology of choice morsels with some of the racier elements omitted.[21] His initiative was supported by Alfred Talandier, who published two versions aimed at different readerships, *Le Rabelais populaire* and *Le Rabelais classique, édition modernisée et expurgée à l'usage des écolières et écoliers*: "the one expurgated for girls' as well as boys' schools; the other for all those who refuse to miss any discussion of asswipes, any criticism of nitpicking cranks of yesteryear, any trumpetings from the posterior or any fuddling of the mind, etc."[22] What Noël and Talandier did not censor has been left to the scissors of two much more recent and prudish vulgarizers for the educational market, Lagarde and Michard, whose intervention is all the more furtive because the cuts were not acknowledged.[23]

The twentieth century saw an enormous expansion and internationalization of Rabelais criticism. The foundation in 1902 by Lefranc, Boulenger, and Clouzot of the *Revue des Études Rabelaisiennes* provided a forum for discussion of all aspects of Rabelais's life, work, and influence, with particular attention paid to unpublished documents, to literary sources, to historical context, and to linguistics and philology. The expansion of the scope of this journal, first into the *Revue du seizième siècle*, then into *Humanisme et Renaissance* and finally *Bibliothèque d'humanisme et Renaissance*, has allowed scholarship on Rabelais to appear in a broader European Renaissance context, although specifically Rabelaisian material more commonly now appears in the companion series *Études Rabelaisiennes*. The 1902 team, augmented by scholars like Plattard and Sainéan, undertook a totally new edition of the five books to replace the recent but unsatisfactory editions of Burgaud des Marets and Marty-Laveaux. From 1913 to 1955 six volumes of this Critical Edition appeared, going as far as *Book 4*, chapter 17, and providing an extraordinary wealth of critical apparatus and historical, humanist, and linguistic commentary. Spin-offs from this team were Plattard's biography (1928) and his *Œuvre de Rabelais* (1910), and Sainéan's magisterial *La Langue de Rabelais* (1922–3). Although never completed, the Critical Edition maintained its authority until the appearance of the TLF editions by Saulnier, Screech, and Marichal, most of whom opted to take as the base text the initial rather than the final state of each book. By common consent, the most satisfactory edition currently available is that by Mireille Huchon in the Pléiade series (1994), whilst a broader range of readers has been won over by the parallel-text edition by Guy Demerson (1973).

The Critical Edition took a stand on certain central issues which have been the subject of debate ever since. Lefranc set great store by the realism of Rabelais, seeking to identify autobiographical and topical allusions throughout the five books. He and Plattard focused on the material relating to Poitou and to Touraine,[24] and in particular the local fishing dispute, which Lefranc thought had inspired the war chapters in *Gargantua*; *Book 3* was interpreted in the context of the contemporary "Querelles des Femmes" and of the revival of neo-Platonism; and *Book 4* in the context of contemporary voyages of discovery.[25] Lefranc carried this idea of topicality into the realm of politics, seeing Rabelais as an agent of royal propaganda and of the du Bellay brothers.[26] The idea of realism was contested by Spitzer, who, in "Le prétendu réalisme de Rabelais," placed greater stress on the fantasy and surrealism of Rabelais. Similarly, the idea of Rabelais as a propagandist, supporting Valois ambitions in Italy, was contested by writers like Kaiser, who applied analysis of the mock encomia to argue that passages like the praise of war in the *Book 3* prologue were ironic.

Lefranc's group also took a stand on Rabelais's religion, seeking to reveal his "secret thoughts":[27] in an analysis influenced by the anti-clericalism of the Third Republic, and picking up on Rabelais's earlier reputation as a Lucianic scoffer, they deduced from his many irreverent jokes that he was a crypto-atheist, who parodies speeches and miracles of Christ, who mocks the Mass, and who doubts the afterlife; such devout material as there is can be dismissed as a prudent smokescreen put up by a man aware of the threat of persecution and prepared to defend his ideas as far as the stake (but not "inclusively"). This theory was reinforced by Busson, who sought to link Rabelais with Italian rationalists from Padua,[28] and was widely accepted until the intervention in 1942 by Lucien Febvre, who distinguished irreverence from atheism, and dismissed the views of Lefranc and Busson as anachronistic. Febvre's position has been supported by both Krailsheimer, who found parallels for Rabelais's irreverence in Franciscan writings and sermons, and by Screech who has firmly established the author among a group of Erasmian evangelicals, associated with Marguerite de Navarre, who believed in reform of the Catholic Church from within, and who found themselves attacked by both the Sorbonne and by Protestants like Calvin. Much of his criticism of the Church is common to humanists over two centuries, who call for reform of the cults of saints, pilgrimages, relics, fasting, indulgences and other superstitions, the wealth of monasteries, the ignorance and debauchery of monks and friars, and so forth.

This negative, satirical material is counterbalanced by positive arguments put into the mouths of the giants and some companions, which commend evangelical preachers, bible-reading and direct prayer to God – common-places in the writings of Christian humanists – flavored with a nationalist Gallican view that the King of France should reform his own Church. From *Book 3* onwards, Panurge becomes associated with a superstitious creed, which fears devils, and which believes in justification by works alone, such as invoking saints, or vowing to found a chapel if preserved from the storm (*Book 4*, chapter 19). The narrator of *Book 4* also distances himself from the Calvinist doctrine of predestination (prologue and chapter 32), preferring to show man enjoying a measure of free will and being justified by a combina-tion of faith and activity. Various episodes illustrate this position, notably the battle with Werewolf (*Pantagruel*, chapter 29), the story of Couillatris (*Book 4*, prologue) and the storm scenes (*ibid.*, chapters 18–24): the giants in particular are seen to reaffirm their faith in God before going into vigorous action, a doctrine close to St. Paul's synergism, or cooperation with grace. Although some critics sense a Lutheran flavor in passages in *Pantagruel*, most are agreed on Rabelais as a Christian humanist, whose giants live out a pantagruelistic creed of active, muscular, joyful, charitable faith, seeking salvation through cooperation with grace, and through stoic indifference to fortune. Saulnier has added a nuance by suggesting that, by the 1540s, the political climate in France had turned against evangelism, which had gone underground, and was expressed by Rabelais in increasingly veiled terms; in *Le Dessein de Rabelais*, Saulnier labels this *hésuchisme*.

Lefranc's team also made much of the erudition of Rabelais, presenting him as a man of vast reading, which percolated into his writing. Both the Critical Edition and Plattard's monograph on *L'Œuvre de Rabelais* were at pains to identify echoes and borrowings from a wide range of classi-cal, medieval, and humanist writing in all genres, and especially in law and medicine. Most recent critics and editors have gone along with this approach, and have identified other sources. One note of caution has, however, been sounded: Rabelais's erudition does not necessarily derive from first-hand knowledge, but from the work of polygraphs like Erasmus, Calcagnini, Cœlius Rhodoginus, and Ravisius Textor. A case in point comes in the Her Trippa or Bridlegoose episodes (*Book 3*, chapters 25 and 39–43), where, Derrett argues, the erudition derives not from classical sources but from compilers like Cardano and Calcagnini in the first instance,[29] and in the sec-ond from legal cribs like *Brocardia juris*, or Tiraqueau's tract *De nobilitate*.[30]

The influence of a treasure house like Erasmus's *Adages* is evident through-out Rabelais's writings, as it is in so many of his contemporaries.

The picture of a Christian, royalist, erudite Rabelais has not gone unchal-lenged. Marxists critics like Lefebvre, and especially the Russian Bakhtin, presented Rabelais as fascinated by the language and culture of folklore, carnival, and the market-place. Bakhtin's book was widely translated, influ-encing critics like Beaujour and Paris who, in the wake of the events of May 1968, dressed Rabelais up as a subversive revolutionary, who espoused the cause of the people against the establishment. The apparent dichotomy between the intellectual and the intestinal, between high and low in Rabelais, was explained by means of the image of carnival, when the king is upturned and loses his crown. The inverted monarch, whose ass is now above his head, is seen to represent Rabelais's alleged preference for the things of the body – guts, excrement, sex – over things intellectual; for the popular over the privileged; for the pagan over the Christian; and for the sound of words over their meaning. Rather than ideal figures, the giants are tyran-nical oppressors, Thélème is a prison, and Panurge represents the aspira-tions of the proletariat. As to the erudition of Rabelais, these critics accuse Screech and other editors of inventing sources, asserting Rabelais had not read half the books they claim. Critical support for this schematic opposi-tion between the *id* of Alcofribas Nasier and the *superego* of the revered Dr. Rabelais has ebbed away; but the carnival analogy has served a useful purpose in focusing critical attention on elements of folklore and popular culture.[31]

This approach contrasts directly with another reading of Rabelais, which sees him as a writer of riddles and codes, a purveyor of a higher, hid-den, wisdom stemming from Italian Neo-Platonism. For critics like Péladan, Naudon, or Mettra, Rabelais was linked with underground brotherhoods (including freemasonry) and with orphic writers such as Hermes Trismegis-tus, Leonardo da Vinci, or Colonna's *Hypnerotomachia*, with writers on alchemy and patapsychology.[32] This rather eccentric approach was treated in a more scholarly fashion by Weinberg and Mallary Masters, who argued for the authenticity of *Book 5*, which they saw as the key to Rabelais's Hermetic philosophy, interpreting the references to wine and to ritual as evidence of his fascination with Bacchic and other mysteries.[33] A variation on this has been provided by critics who see Rabelais as a mathematician and numerologist, combing the text for significant numbers.[34] The recent critical edition by Mireille Huchon has provided persuasive arguments for an alchemical inspiration in some of Rabelais's writings.

The authenticity of *Book 5* continues to divide critics and readers. The circumstances of the posthumous publication, the relative absence of humor and dialogue, the long translations from Colonna, led many, including the early readers like Tabourot, Du Verdier, and Leroy, to suspect that the book was a pastiche; modern critics like Villey, Plattard, Screech, Rigolot, and Glauser have been of the same view. A second group of readers have unquestioningly accepted the book as authentic, and as the summation and solution of Rabelais's enigmatic, esoteric thought, whether alchemical, orphic, or dionysiac. Other readers, while recognizing the hand of Rabelais in the material of the book, doubt that he had any part in any of its final three states, *The Ringing Island*, the manuscript, and the 1564 edition. A majority of critics, led by Mireille Huchon, now hold, on the basis of stylistic and orthographic analysis, that the book was inexpertly stitched together from two sets of rejected Rabelaisian drafts, one dating from before *Book 3* and one planned as a continuation of the 1548 *Book 4*, and was published by Huguenot sympathizers at the beginning of the Wars of Religion. The consequence of this theory is that *Book 5*, as we have it, cannot be read as the continuation of the *Book 4* of 1552, the conclusion of which is Rabelais's final statement. Despite the richness and complexity of *Book 5*, it is surprising that so little critical attention was paid to it, until a major conference in Rome in 1998 organized by Giacone.

Modern readers, less obsessed with classical canons of order, consistency, clarity, and propriety, have felt less uncomfortable with the perceived disorder and excess of the five books. Erich Auerbach's brilliant essay argues that Rabelais's aesthetics are specifically anti-classical, an approach developed by Terence Cave in his study of the abundance, discontinuity, and plurality of a work which never concludes.[35] Some, such as Coleman, have labeled this unique kind of fiction as a Menippean Satire after the manner of Lucian, a disjointed medley of prose and verse and of high and low registers; others prefer the term anti-novel, as if Rabelais already had in mind the way prose fiction would evolve, and was out to parody it. In either case, he is playing with the traditional relationship between narrator, text, and public, by adopting a protean persona, and by presenting an ambiguous text to a caricatured reader.

How ambiguous? Some critics, like Beaujour, Paris, and Greene, present Rabelais as a play spirit whose deliberately enigmatic text defies interpretation, and is fundamentally unreadable.[36] They imagine the author rolling with laughter in his grave at readers' attempts to make sense of nonsense. The idea that Rabelais wrote words, but had nothing to say, has since fallen out of fashion. Critics may continue to disagree about just what the marrowbone jelly might be which, in the prologue to *Gargantua*, we are invited to suck out after gnawing through the bones of the book, or about how the wine might taste in the barrel of the *Book 3* prologue, but they generally believe that the book means something, and embark on ever more ambitious quests for overarching patterns and design.[37]

No pretext for comedy seems taboo, as Rabelais tests his reader with scatalogical vocabulary, with jokes about fortifying Paris with female pudenda, about the ideal ass wipe, or with irreverent mimicking of material from the Gospels. Intervening centuries have felt it necessary to apologize for, or to deplore, Rabelais's bawdiness, which the modern reader finds less shocking. However, the tone of the humor evolves over the five books, and whereas in the earliest stories the giants contribute to the comedy, in the later ones they distance themselves from the clowns, and we see Pantagruel reproving his companion for a sacrilegious joke (*Book 4*, chapter 50).

Modern critics have given greater attention than before to Rabelais's language, following the lead given by Huguet, Sainéan, and Spitzer.[38] Rather than continuing to focus on the vocabulary, they have examined his creative style, and his use of registers and imagery, while Mireille Huchon's study of norms of grammar and orthography in Rabelais has revolutionized understanding of the development of his text.[39] The degree of inventiveness in language, which goes beyond the simple communication of meaning, has suggested the idea of a certain verbal drunkenness, whether in terms of abundance or fantasy, or in the dithyrambic rhythms of certain passages. Words, of course, are not always necessary: Rabelais seems to be just as interested in signs, which are variously interpreted in *Book 3*, while in the last two books we are shown pictures and portents, storms and monsters, and a whole series of clues, mysterious names, and parables, to which no key is given: the companions debate but rarely resolve, and the signs remain enigmatic.

George Steiner has applied to Rabelais the term "poetic prose," in the sense of language free from the constraints of syntax and meaning, and Rabelais often seems as interested in the words themselves (*signifiant*) as in any message they might convey (*signifié*). Examples of this are not only the lists, but experiments in nonsense such as bogus languages (including Lanternois), enigmatic poems, riddles like the "Antidoted Frigglefraggles" (*Gargantua*, chapter 2), and especially the celebrated frozen words (*Book 4*, chapter 56), where sounds emitted in the past have been solidified in the arctic air and, now divorced from their original context, are thawed out in the hands of the giant and his companions, or preserved in oil or straw like ice. This focus on aural effect is characteristic of Rabelais's writing, and takes modern readers back to the idea that many of Rabelais's first readers were actually listeners, to whom the books were read aloud, as they were to François I by his librarian. Rabelais's interest in rhetoric is not in doubt – we have many examples of monologue, of varied sorts of dialogue, of formal speeches and letters – but recent critics would add a dimension of performance art to our appreciation of Rabelais, thinking of his books being delivered orally to an audience well used to hearing lawyers pleading, academics debating, or actors performing at banquets or in street theatre. The adaptation of the chronicles for theatrical performance by Jean-Louis Barrault[40] brought Rabelais to the attention of a wide range of enthusiastic listeners and viewers. Their experience may have come close to that of the very first readers, with whose expectations Rabelais sported, chopping and changing register, switching from prose to verse, from gigantic to trivial, disrupting the narrative, interweaving realistic and fantastic, and inviting them to save up their laughter in this endless comic carnival for a future seventy-eighth book (*Book 3*, title-page).

NOTES

1 Voltaire, *Œuvres complètes*, Louis Molland, ed., 54 vols. (Paris: Garnier frères, 1877–85), vol. 8, p. 577.

2 See S. Rawles and M. Screech, *A New Rabelais Bibliography* (Geneva: Droz, 1987), pp. 95, 304.

3 See the testimony of Gilles de Gouberville, *Journal*, E. Robillard de Beaurepaire, ed., 2 vols. (Caen: H. Delesque, 1892–3), vol. 1, p. 156.

4 Maurice de La Porte, *Les Epithetes* (Paris: Buon, 1571), p. 347.

5 Lazaire Sainéan, "Les Interprètes de Rabelais en Angleterre et en Allemagne," *Revue des Études Rabelaisiennes*, 7 (1909), pp. 137–258.

6 In addition to A. L. Prescott, *Imagining Rabelais in Renaissance England* (New Haven and London: Yale University Press, 1988), see H. Brown, *Rabelais and English Literature* (Cambridge, MA: Harvard University Press, 1933; repr. London: Frank Cass & Co., 1967).

7 See T. P. Fraser, *Le Duchat, First Editor of Rabelais* (Geneva: Droz, 1971).

8 Marcel de Grève, "Les Erudits du XVIIe siècle en quête de la clef de Rabelais," *Études Rabelaisiennes*, 5 (1964), pp. 41–63.

9 Richard Cooper, "'Charmant mais très obscène': Some French Eighteenth-Century Readings of Rabelais," in Giles Barber and C. P. Courtney, eds., *Enlightenment Essays in Memory of Robert Shackleton* (Oxford: Voltaire Foundation, 1988), pp. 39–60; also, "Le Véritable Rabelais déformé," in Paul Smith, ed., *Éditer et traduire Rabelais à travers les âges* (Amsterdam: Rodopi, 1997), pp. 195–220.

10 H.-J. Du Laurens, *Compère Mathieu*, 3 vols. (London: n.p., 1766), vol. 2, p. 77.

11 Voltaire, *Œuvres complètes*, vol. 26, p. 470.

12 *Ibid.*, vol. 22, p. 174.

13 J.-P. Nicéron, *Mémoires pour servir à l'histoire de la république des lettres*, 43 vols. (Paris: Briasson, 1727–45), vol. 32, pp. 367–71.

14 J.-F. Marmontel, *Éléments de littérature*, 2 vols. (Paris: Verdière, 1824–5), vol. 1, p. 525.

15 P.-L. Ginguené, *De l'autorité de Rabelais dans la Révolution présente et dans la constitution du clergé ou institutions royales, politiques et ecclésiastiques* (Paris: Gattey, 1791).

16 *Bibliothèque universelle des romans*, March 1776, pp. 81–128.

17 R.-M. Lesuire, *Confessions de Rabelais* (Paris: Louis, 1797).

18 *Bibliothèque universelle des romans*, March 1776, pp. 127–8.

19 Lamartine, *Cours familier de littérature* (Paris: author, 1856).

20 E. Charavay, *Faux autographes, affaire Vrain-Lucas* (Paris: J. Charavay aîné, 1870).

21 Eugène Noël, *Le Rabelais de poche* (Alençon: Poulet-Malassis, 1860).

22 Alfred Talandier, *Le Rabelais populaire* (Paris: Librairie populaire, 1883), x.

23 *Textes et littérature, XVIe siècle*, A. Lagarde and L. Michard, eds. (Paris: Bordas, 1960).

24 Abel Lefranc et al., eds., *Œuvres de François Rabelais*, Édition Critique, 5 vols. (Paris: Garnier, 1913–31), vol. 1, l–lxxxvii; Jean Plattard, *L'Adolescence de Rabelais en Poitou* (Paris: Les Belles Lettres, 1923).

25 Abel Lefranc, *Les Navigations de Pantagruel* (Paris: Leclerc, 1905).

26 Abel Lefranc, "Rabelais et le pouvoir royal," *Revue du seizième siècle*, 17 (1930), pp. 191–202; G. Lote, "La politique de Rabelais," *Revue des cours et conférences*, 37 (1935–6), pp. 64–79, 332–47, 464–80.

27 Lefranc et al., Édition Critique, vol. 3, xl–lxx.

28 Henri Busson, *Les Sources et le développement du rationalisme dans la littérature française de la Renaissance (1533–1601)* (Paris: Letouzet and Ané, 1922); also, "Rabelais et le miracle," *Revue des cours et conférences*, 30 (1929), pp. 385–400.

29 Michael Screech, "G. Cardano's *De sapientia* and the *Tiers Livre*," *Bibliothèque d'Humanisme et Renaissance*, 25 (1963), pp. 97–110.

30 Michael Screech, "The Legal Comedy of Rabelais in the Trial of Bridoye in the *Tiers livre de Pantagruel*," *Études Rabelaisiennes*, 5 (1964), pp. 175–95.

31 See Carol Clark, *The Vulgar Rabelais* (Glasgow: Pressgang, 1983); Claude Gaignebet, *A plus hault sens: L'ésotérisme spirituel et charnel de Rabelais*, 2 vols. (Paris: Maisonneuve et Larose, 1986).

32 J. Péladan, *Le Secret des corporations, la clé de Rabelais* (Paris: Scripta brevia, 1905); P. Naudon, *Rabelais franc-maçon* (Paris: La Balance, 1954); *Rabelais pataphysicien*, special number of *Cahiers du Collège de Pataphysique*, 13/14 (1954); C. Mettra, *Rabelais secret* (Paris: Grasset, 1973).

33 G. Mallary Masters, *Rabelaisian Dialectic and the Platonic-Hermetic Tradition* (Albany: State University of New York Press, 1969); Florence Weinberg, *The Wine and the Will: Rabelais's Bacchic Christianity* (Detroit: Wayne State University Press, 1972).

34 Alfred Glauser, *Fonctions du nombre chez Rabelais* (Paris: Nizet, 1982).

35 Erich Auerbach, in "The World in Pantagruel's Mouth," in *Mimesis: The Representation of Reality in Western Literature*, W. R. Trask, trans. (Princeton: Princeton University Press, 1953), pp. 262–84; Terence Cave, *The Cornucopian Text: Problems of Writing in the French Renaissance* (Oxford: Clarendon Press, 1979).

36 Michel Beaujour, *Le Jeu de Rabelais* (Paris: L'Herne, 1969); Jean Paris, *Rabelais au futur* (Paris: Seuil, 1970); Thomas Greene, *Rabelais: A Study in Comic Courage* (Englewood Cliffs, NJ: Prentice-Hall, 1970).

37 Edwin Duval, *The Design of Rabelais's "Tiers Livre de Pantagruel"* (Geneva: Droz, 1997); V.-L. Saulnier, *Le Dessein de Rabelais* (Paris: SEDES, 1957); Paul Smith, *Voyage et écriture: Étude sur le "Quart Livre" de Rabelais* (Geneva: Droz, 1987); Gérard Defaux, *Rabelais agonistes: Du rieur au prophète. Études sur "Pantagruel," "Gargantua," "Le Quart Livre,"* Études Rabelaisiennes, 32 (Geneva: Droz, 1997).

38 Edmond Huguet, *Étude sur la syntaxe de Rabelais* (Paris: Hachette, 1894); Lazare Sainéan, *La Langue de Rabelais* (Paris: Boccard, 1922–3); Leo Spitzer, *Die Wortbildung als stilistisches Mittel exemplifiziert an Rabelais* (Halle: Niemeyer, 1910).

39 Respectively, Floyd Gray, *Rabelais et l'écriture* (Paris: Nizet, 1974); François Rigolot, *Les Langages de Rabelais* (Geneva: Droz, 1972, reprint 1996); François Moreau, *Les Images dans l'œuvre de Rabelais* (Paris: SEDES, 1982); Mireille Huchon, *Rabelais grammairien: De l'histoire du texte aux problèmes d'authenticité* (Geneva: Droz, 1981).

40 Jean-Louis Barrault, *Rabelais, jeu dramatique* (12 Dec. 1968) (Paris: Gallimard, 1968).

GUIDE TO FURTHER READING

Works by Rabelais

Rabelais, *Les Cinq Livres*, G. Defaux, J. Céard, and M. Simonin, eds. Le Livre de Poche (Paris: Librairie Générale Française, 1994).

The Complete Works of François Rabelais, D. M. Frame, trans. (Berkeley: University of California Press, 1991).

Gargantua and Pantagruel, Sir Thomas Urquhart and Pierre Le Motteux, trans., with an introduction by T. Cave, Everyman's Library (London: David Campbell Publishers, 1994) (a modern reprint of a seventeenth-century English translation; contains all five books).

Gargantua and Pantagruel, Sir Thomas Urquhart and Pierre Le Motteux, trans., with an introduction by R. Cooper, Wordsworth Classics of World Literature (Ware: Wordsworth, 1999) (content as previous item).

Gargantua and Pantagruel, M. A. Screech, trans. and ed. (London: Penguin Books, 2006) (a new annotated translation into modern English offering the five books, plus the Almanacs and the *Pantagrueline Prognostication*).

Œuvres complètes, M. Huchon with F. Moureau, eds. Bibliothèque de la Pléiade (Paris: Gallimard, 1994).

Reference works

Cotgrave, R. *A Dictionarie of the French and English Tongues*, reproduced from the first edition, London, 1611, with an introduction by W. S. Woods (Columbia: University of Carolina Press, 1950).

Dixon, J. E. G. and J. L. Dawson. *Concordance des Œuvres de François Rabelais* (Geneva: Droz, 1992).

Huguet, E. *Dictionnaire de la langue française du XVIe siècle* (Paris: Champion-Didier, 1925–67).

Rawles, S. and M. Screech. *A New Rabelais Bibliography* (Geneva: Droz, 1987).

Zegura, E. C., ed., *The Rabelais Encyclopedia* (Westport, CT, and London: Greenwood Press, 2004).

Selective critical reading

Antonioli, R. *Rabelais et la médecine* (Geneva: Droz, 1976).

Auerbach, E. "The World in Pantagruel's Mouth," in *Mimesis: The Representation of Reality in Western Literature*, W. R. Trask, trans. (Princeton: Princeton University Press, 1953), pp. 262–84.

Bakhtin, M. *Rabelais and his World*, H. Iswolsky, trans. (Boston: MIT Press, 1968).

Bauschatz, K. "Rabelais and Marguerite de Navarre on Sixteenth-Century Views of Clandestine Marriage," *The Sixteenth-Century Journal*, 34/2 (2003), pp. 395–408.

Beaujour, M. *Le Jeu de Rabelais* (Paris: L'Herne, 1969).

Berrong, R. *Rabelais and Bakhtin: Popular Culture in "Gargantua" and "Pantagruel"* (Lincoln: University of Nebraska Press, 1986).

Boulenger, J. *Rabelais à travers les âges* (Paris: Le Divan, 1925).

Bowen, B. C. *The Age of Bluff: Paradox and Ambiguity in Rabelais and Montaigne* (Urbana: University of Illinois Press, 1972).

"Rire est le propre de l'homme," in *Rabelais en son demi-millénaire: Actes du Colloque International de Tours (24–29 septembre 1984)*, Jean Céard and Jean-Claude Margolin, eds., Études Rabelaisiennes, 21 (Geneva: Droz, 1988), pp. 185–90.

ed., *Rabelais in Context* (Birmingham, AL: Summa, 1993).

Enter Rabelais, Laughing (Nashville and London: Vanderbilt University Press, 1998).

Brown, H. *Rabelais and English Literature* (Cambridge, MA: Harvard University Press, 1933; reprint London: Frank Cass & Co., 1967).

Busson, H. "Les Eglises contre Rabelais," *Études Rabelaisiennes*, 7 (1967), pp. 1–81.

Carron, J.-C., ed., *François Rabelais: Critical Assessments* (Baltimore: Johns Hopkins University Press, 1995).

Cave, T. *The Cornucopian Text: Problems of Writing in the French Renaissance* (Oxford: Clarendon Press, 1979).

"Panurge and Odysseus," in K. Aspley, D. Bellos, and P. Sharratt, eds., *Myth and Legend in French Literature: Essays in Honour of A. J. Steele* (London: MHRA, 1982), pp. 47–59.

"Reading Rabelais: Variations on the Rock of Virtue," in P. Parker and D. Quint, eds., *Literary Theory/Renaissance Texts* (Baltimore: Johns Hopkins University Press, 1986), pp. 78–95.

Pré-histoires: Textes troublés au seuil de la modernité (Geneva: Droz, 1999).

Pré-histoires II: Langues étrangères et troubles économiques au XVIe siècle (Geneva: Droz, 2001).

"Thinking with Commonplaces: The Example of Rabelais," in G. Ferguson and C. Hampton, eds., *(Re)Inventing the Past: Essays on French Early Modern Culture, Literature and Thought in Honour of Ann Moss* (Durham: Durham Modern Languages Series, 2003), pp. 34–50.

Cave, T., M. Jeanneret, and F. Rigolot. "Sur la prétendue transparence de Rabelais," *Revue d'Histoire Littéraire de la France*, 86/4 (1986), pp. 709–16.

Céard, J. "Rabelais, lecteur et juge des romans de chevalerie," in J. Céard and J.-C. Margolin, eds., *Rabelais en son demi-millénaire: Actes du colloque international de Tours (24–29 septembre 1984)*, Études Rabelaisiennes, 21 (Geneva: Droz, 1988), pp. 237–48.

La Nature et les prodiges: L'insolite au XVIe siècle, 2nd edn. (Geneva: Droz, 1996).

Céard, J. and J.-C. Margolin, eds., *Rabelais en son demi-millénaire: Actes du colloque international de Tours (24–29 septembre 1984)*, Études Rabelaisiennes, 21 (Geneva: Droz, 1988).

Clark, C. *The Vulgar Rabelais* (Glasgow: Pressgang, 1983).

Clément, M. *Le Cynisme à la Renaissance* (Geneva: Droz, 2005).

Cohen, G. "Rabelais et le théâtre," *Revue des Études Rabelaisiennes*, 9 (1911), pp. 1–72.

Coleman, D. *Rabelais. A Critical Study in Prose Fiction* (Cambridge: Cambridge University Press, 1971).

Cooper, R. "'Charmant mais très obscène': Some French Eighteenth-Century Readings of Rabelais," in G. Barber and C. P. Courtney, eds., *Enlightenment Essays in Memory of Robert Shackleton* (Oxford: Voltaire Foundation, 1988), pp. 39–60.

"Rabelais et l'Église," in *Rabelais en son demi-millénaire: Actes du colloque international de Tours (24–29 septembre 1984)*, Études Rabelaisiennes, 21 (Geneva: Droz, 1988), pp. 111–20.

Rabelais et l'Italie, Études Rabelaisiennes, 24 (Geneva: Droz, 1991).

"Le Véritable Rabelais déformé," in P. Smith, ed., *Éditer et traduire Rabelais à travers les âges* (Amsterdam: Rodopi, 1997), pp. 195–220.

"Les Lectures italiennes de Rabelais: Une mise au point," *Études Rabelaisiennes*, 37 (1999), pp. 25–49.

"L'Authenticité du *Cinquiesme livre*: État présent de la question," in Franco Giacone, ed., *Actes du colloque international de Rome: Rabelais, le "Cinquiesme Livre"* (Geneva: Droz, 2001), pp. 9–22.

Cornilliat, F. "L'Autre géant: Les *Chroniques gargantuines* et leur intertexte," *Littérature*, 55 (1984), pp. 85–97.

"On Words and Meaning in Rabelais Criticism," *Études Rabelaisiennes*, 35 (1998), pp. 7–28.

Daston, L. and K. Park. *Wonders and the Order of Nature, 1150–1750* (New York: Zone, 1998).

Defaux, G. "Rabelais et les cloches de Notre-Dame," *Études Rabelaisiennes*, 9 (1971), pp. 1–28.

Pantagruel et les sophistes: Contribution à l'histoire de l'humanisme chrétien au XVIe siècle (The Hague: Nijhoff, 1973).

"Rabelais et son masque comique: *Sophista loquitur*," *Études Rabelaisiennes*, 11 (1974), pp. 89–135.

Le Curieux, le glorieux et la sagesse du monde dans la première moitié du XVIe siècle: L'exemple de Panurge (Ulysse, Démosthène, Empédocle), French Forum Monographs 34 (Lexington, KY: French Forum, 1982).

"D'un problème l'autre: Herméneutique de l'*altior sensus* et *captatio lectoris* dans le prologue de *Gargantua*," *Revue d'Histoire Littéraire de la France*, 85/2 (1985), pp. 195–216.

"Sur la prétendue pluralité du prologue de *Gargantua*," *Revue d'Histoire Littéraire de la France*, 86/4 (1986), pp. 716–22.

Marot, Rabelais, Montaigne: L'écriture comme présence (Paris: Champion, 1987).

Rabelais agonistes: Du rieur au prophète. Études sur "Pantagruel," "Gargantua," "Le Quart Livre," Études Rabelaisiennes, 32 (Geneva: Droz, 1997).

Demerson, G. "Paradigmes épiques chez Rabelais," in *Rabelais en son demi-millénaire: Actes du colloque international de Tours (24–29 septembre 1984),* Études Rabelaisiennes, 21 (Geneva: Droz, 1988), pp. 225–36.

Rabelais (Paris: Fayard, 1991).

Humanisme et facétie: Quinze études sur Rabelais (Orléans: Paradigme, 1994).

L'Esthétique de Rabelais (Paris: SEDES, 1996).

Demonet, M.-L. *Les Voix du signe: Nature et origine du langage à la Renaissance, 1480–1580* (Paris: Champion, 1992).

"Le Nom de Bacbuc," *Réforme, Humanisme, Renaissance*, 34 (1992), pp. 41–66.

"Les Textes et leur centre à la Renaissance: Une structure absente?," in F. Tinguely, ed., *La Renaissance décentrée* (Geneva: Droz, 2008), pp. 158–73.

"Trois vies de Rabelais: Franciscain, bénédictin, médecin," in C. Tottmann and F. La Brasca, eds., *Vie solitaire, vie civile* (Paris: Champion, forthcoming).

ed., *Rabelais et la question du sens* (Geneva: Droz, forthcoming).

Demonet, M.-L. and S. Geonget, eds., *Les Grands Jours de Rabelais en Poitou* (Geneva: Droz, 2006).

Derrett, J. D. M. "Rabelais's Legal Learning and the Trial of Bridoye," *Bibliothèque d'Humanisme et Renaissance*, 25 (1963), pp. 111–71.

Desrosiers-Bonin, D. *Rabelais et l'humanisme civil* (Geneva: Droz, 1992).

Dupèbe, J. "Remarques critiques sur la date de la naissance de Rabelais," in J. Lecointe, C. Magnien, I. Pantin, and M.-C. Thomine, eds., *Devis d'amitié: Mélanges en l'honneur de Nicole Cazauran* (Paris: Champion, 2002), pp. 732–7.

Duval, E. M. "Interpretation and the 'Doctrine absconse' of Rabelais's Prologue to *Gargantua*," *Études Rabelaisiennes*, 18 (1985), pp. 1–17.

"La Messe, la Cène, et le voyage sans fin du *Quart Livre*," in *Rabelais en son demi-millénaire: Actes du colloque international de Tours (24–29 septembre),* Études Rabelaisiennes, 21 (Geneva: Droz, 1988), pp. 131–41.

The Design of Rabelais's "Pantagruel" (New Haven: Yale University Press, 1991).

The Design of Rabelais's "Tiers Livre de Pantagruel" (Geneva: Droz, 1997).

The Design of Rabelais's "Quart Livre de Pantagruel" (Geneva: Droz, 1998).

"De la Dive Bouteille à la quête du *Tiers Livre*," in M. Simonin, ed., *Rabelais pour le XXIe siècle* (Geneva: Droz, 1998), pp. 265–78.

Febvre, L. *Le Problème de l'incroyance au XVIe siècle: La religion de Rabelais* (Paris: Albin Michel, 1942). English version: *The Problem of Unbelief in the Sixteenth Century: The Religion of Rabelais*, B. Gottlieb, trans. (Cambridge, MA: Harvard University Press, 1982).

Frame, D. *François Rabelais: A Study* (New York: Harcourt Brace Jovanovich, 1977).

Fraser, T. P. *Le Duchat, First Editor of Rabelais* (Geneva: Droz, 1971).

Freccero, C. *Father Figures: Genealogy and Narrative Structure in Rabelais* (Ithaca and London: Cornell University Press, 1991).

Gaignebet, C. *A plus hault sens: L'ésotérisme spirituel et charnel de Rabelais*, 2 vols. (Paris: Maisonneuve et Larose, 1986).

Geonget, S. *La Notion de perplexité à la Renaissance* (Geneva: Droz, 2006).

Giacone, F., ed., *Actes du colloque international de Rome: Rabelais, le "Cinquiesme Livre"* (Geneva: Droz, 2001).

Gilson, E. "Notes médiévales au *Tiers Livre de Pantagruel*," *Revue d'Histoire Franciscaine*, 2 (1925), pp. 72–88.

"Rabelais franciscain," in *Les Idées et les lettres*, 2nd edn. (Paris: Vrin, 1955), pp. 197–241.

Glauser, A. *Rabelais créateur* (Paris: Nizet, 1966).

Le faux Rabelais ou de l'inauthenticité du Cinquième Livre (Paris: Nizet, 1975).

Fonctions du nombre chez Rabelais (Paris: Nizet, 1982).

Gray, F. "Ambiguity and Point of View in the Prologue to *Gargantua*," *Romanic Review*, 56 (1965), pp. 12–21.

Rabelais et l'écriture (Paris: Nizet, 1974).

Rabelais et le comique du discontinu (Paris: Champion, 1994).

Greene, T. M. *Rabelais: A Study in Comic Courage* (Englewood Cliffs, NJ: Prentice-Hall, 1970).

"The Unity of the *Tiers Livre*," *Études Rabelaisiennes*, 21 (1988), pp. 293–309.

Grève, M. de. *L'Interprétation de Rabelais au XVIe siècle* (Geneva: Droz, 1961).

Hampton, T. "Signs of Monstrosity: The Rhetoric of Description and the Limits of Allegory in Rabelais and Montaigne," in L. Knoppers and J. Landes, eds., *Monstrous Bodies/Political Monstrosities in Early Modern Europe* (Ithaca and London: Cornell University Press, 2004), pp. 179–99.

Helgeson, J. "'Ce que j'entends par ces symboles pythagoricques': Rabelais on Meaning and Intention," *Études Rabelaisiennes*, 42 (2003), pp. 75–100.

Hoffmann, G. "Neither One nor the Other and Both Together," *Études Rabelaisiennes*, 25 (1991), pp. 76–90.

Huchon, M. *Rabelais grammairien: De l'histoire du texte aux problèmes d'authenticité* (Geneva: Droz, 1981).

"Variations rabelaisiennes sur l'imposition du nom," in *Prose et prosateurs de la Renaissance: Mélanges offerts à Robert Aulotte* (Paris: SEDES, 1988), pp. 93–100.

"La Poétique dévoyée du *Tiers Livre*," in E. Kotler, ed., *Rabelais et le Tiers Livre* (Paris: CNRS, 1996), pp. 97–115.

Jeanneret, M. "'Ma patrie est une citrouille': Thèmes alimentaires dans Rabelais et Folengo," *Études de lettres*, 2 (1984), pp. 25–44.

Des Mets et des mots (Paris: Corti, 1987). English version: *A Feast of Words: Banquets and Table Talk in the Renaissance*, J. Whiteley and E. Hughes, trans. (London: Polity Press, 1991).

"Rabelais, les monstres et l'interprétation des signes (*Quart Livre* 18–42)," in R. C. La Charité, ed., *Writing the Renaissance: Essays on Sixteenth-Century French Literature in Honor of Floyd Gray* (Lexington, KY: French Forum, 1992), pp. 65–76.

Le Défi des signes: Rabelais et la crise de l'interprétation à la Renaissance (Orléans: Paradigme, 1994).

Kaiser, W. *Praisers of Folly: Erasmus, Rabelais, Shakespeare* (Cambridge, MA: Harvard University Press, 1963).

Kenny, N. "Plautus, Panurge, and 'les aventures des gens curieux'," in G. Ferguson and C. Hampton, eds., *(Re)Inventing the Past: Essays on French Early Modern Culture, Literature and Thought in Honour of Ann Moss* (Durham: Durham Modern Language Series, 2003), pp. 51–71.

Koopmans, J. "Rabelais et l'esprit de la farce," in M.-L. Demonet and S. Geonget, eds., *Les Grands Jours de Rabelais en Poitou* (Geneva: Droz, 2006), pp. 299–311.

Krailsheimer, A. J. *Rabelais and the Franciscans* (Oxford: Clarendon Press, 1963).
Rabelais (Bruges: Desclée De Brouwer, 1967).

La Charité, R. C. *Recreation, Reflection, and Re-Creation: Perspectives on Rabelais's* Pantagruel (Lexington, KY: French Forum, 1980).
"Lecteurs et lectures dans le prologue du *Gargantua*," *Études Rabelaisiennes*, 21 (Geneva: Droz, 1988), pp. 285–92.

Langer, U. *Divine and Poetic Freedom in the Renaissance: Nominalist Theology and Literature in France and Italy* (Princeton: Princeton University Press, 1990).
Perfect Friendship: Studies in Literature and Moral Philosophy from Boccaccio to Corneille (Geneva: Droz, 1994).
"Liberté chrétienne et liberté stoïcienne: L'abbaye de Thélème," in A. Tarrête, ed., *Stoïcisme et christianisme à la Renaissance* (Paris: Presses de l'Ecole normale supérieure, 2006), pp. 59–70.

Lauvergnat-Gagnière, C. *Lucien de Samosate et le lucianisme en France au XVIe siècle: Athéisme et polémique* (Geneva: Droz, 1988).

Lauvergnat-Gagnière, C. and G. Demerson, eds., with the collaboration of R. Antonioli, C. Bonilauri, M. Huchon, J. Lewis, and B. Teyssot, *Les Chroniques gargantuines* (Paris: Nizet, 1988).

Lazard, M. *Rabelais l'humaniste* (Paris: Hachette, 1993).

Lefebvre, H. *Rabelais* (Paris: Editeurs français réunis, 1955).

Lefranc, A. *Les Navigations de Pantagruel* (Paris: Leclerc, 1905).
Rabelais: Études sur Gargantua, Pantagruel, le Tiers Livre, Avant-propos de R. Marichal (Paris: Albin Michel, 1953).

Lefranc, A. *et al.*, eds., *Œuvres de François Rabelais*, Édition Critique, 5 vols. (Paris: Garnier, 19–31).

Lestringant, F. "L'Insulaire de Rabelais, ou la fiction en archipel (pour une lecture topographique du *Quart Livre*)," in *Écrire le monde à la Renaissance: Quinze études sur Rabelais, Postel, Bodin et la littérature géographique* (Caen: Paradigme, 1993), pp. 159–84.

Lewis, J. "Quelques aspects de la littérature para-rabelaisienne d'avant 1562," in *Rabelais en son demi-millénaire: Actes du colloque international de Tours (24–29 septembre)*, Études Rabelaisiennes, 21 (Geneva: Droz, 1988), pp. 357–64.

Losse, D. N. *Rhetoric at Play: Rabelais and Satirical Eulogy* (Bern and Las Vegas: Lang, 1980).

Marichal, R. "L'Attitude de Rabelais devant le néo-platonisme et l'italianisme," in *François Rabelais: Ouvrage publié pour le quatrième centenaire de sa mort (1553–1953)* (Geneva: Droz, 1953), pp. 181–209.
"*Quart Livre*: Commentaires," *Études Rabelaisiennes*, 5 (1964), pp. 65–162.

Marrache-Gouraud, M. *"Hors toute intimidation": Panurge ou la parole singulière* (Geneva: Droz, 2003).

Miernowski, J. "Literature and Metaphysics: Rabelais and the Poetics of Misunderstanding," *Études Rabelaisiennes*, 35 (1998), pp. 131–51.

Moreau, F. *Les Images dans l'œuvre de Rabelais* (Paris: SEDES, 1982).

Mounier, P. *Le Roman humaniste* (Paris: Champion, 2007).

Naya, E. *Rabelais: Une anthropologie humaniste des passions* (Paris: Presses Universitaires de France, 1998).

"'Ne scepticque, ne dogmatique, et tous les deux ensemble': Rabelais 'on phrontistere et escholle des Pyrrhoniens'," *Études Rabelaisiennes*, 35 (1998), pp. 81–129.

O'Brien, J. and M. Quainton, eds., *Distant Voices Still Heard: Contemporary Readings of French Renaissance Literature* (Liverpool: Liverpool University Press, 2000).

Paris, J. *Rabelais au futur* (Paris: Seuil, 1970).

Plattard, J. *L'Œuvre de Rabelais: Sources, invention et composition* (Paris: Champion, 1910).

François Rabelais (Paris: Boivin, 1932).

Polizzi, G. "Thélème ou l'éloge du don: Le texte rabelaisien à la lumière de l'*Hypnerotomachia Poliphili*," *Réforme, Humanisme, Renaissance*, 25 (1988), pp. 39–59.

"Le Voyage vers l'oracle ou la dérive des intertextes dans le *Cinquième Livre*," in F. Giacone, ed., *Rabelais, le "Cinquiesme Livre": Actes du colloque international de Rome* (Geneva: Droz, 2001), pp. 577–96.

Prescott, A. L. *Imagining Rabelais in Renaissance England* (New Haven and London: Yale University Press, 1988).

Randall, M. *Building Resemblance: Analogical Imagery in the Early French Renaissance* (Baltimore: Johns Hopkins University Press, 1996).

Regosin, R. "Opening Discourse," in J.-C. Carron, ed., *François Rabelais: Critical Assessments* (Baltimore: Johns Hopkins University Press, 1995), pp. 133–47.

Rigolot, F. *Les Langages de Rabelais* (Geneva: Droz, 1972; reprint 1996).

"Cratylisme et Pantagruélisme: Rabelais et le statut du signe," *Études Rabelaisiennes*, 13 (1976), pp. 115–32.

Poétique et onomastique (Geneva: Droz, 1977).

"Rabelais, Misogyny, and Christian Charity: Biblical Intertexuality and the Renaissance Crisis of Exemplarity," *PMLA*, 109/2 (1994), pp. 225–37.

"'Service divin, service du vin': L'équivoque dionysiaque," in M. Bideaux, ed., *Rabelais-Dionysos* (Montpellier: Laffitte, 1997), pp. 15–28.

Russell, A. P. "Epic *Agon* and the Strategy of Reform in Folengo and Rabelais," *Comparative Literature Studies*, 34 (1997), pp. 119–48.

Sainéan, L. "Les Interprètes de Rabelais en Angleterre et en Allemagne," *Revue d'Études Rabelaisiennes*, 7 (1909), pp. 137–258.

L'Histoire naturelle dans l'œuvre de Rabelais (Paris: Champion, 1921).

La Langue de Rabelais, 2 vols. (Paris: Boccard, 1922–3).

L'Influence et la réputation de Rabelais (Paris: Gamber, 1930).

Saulnier, V.-L. *Le Dessein de Rabelais* (Paris: SEDES, 1957).

Rabelais dans son enquête, 2 vols. (Paris: SEDES, 1982–3).

Schwartz, J. *Irony and Ideology in Rabelais* (Cambridge: Cambridge University Press, 1990).

Screech, M. A. "Some Stoic Elements in Rabelais's Religious Thought," *Études Rabelaisiennes*, 1 (1956), pp. 73–97.

The Rabelaisian Marriage: Aspects of Rabelais's Religion, Ethics and Comic Philosophy (London: Arnold, 1958).

L'Évangélisme de Rabelais: Aspects de la satire religieuse au XVIe siècle, Études Rabelaisiennes, 2 (Geneva: Droz, 1959). English translation: *Rabelais and the Challenge of the Gospel: Evangelism, Reformation, Dissent* (Baden–Baden: Koerner, 1992).

"The Legal Comedy of Rabelais in the Trial of Bridoye in the *Tiers livre de Pantagruel*," Études Rabelaisiennes, 5 (1964), pp. 175–95.

Rabelais (London: Duckworth, 1979).

"Celio Calcagnini and Rabelaisian Sympathy," in G. Castor and T. Cave, eds., *Neo-Latin and the Vernacular in Renaissance France* (Oxford: Oxford University Press, 1984), pp. 26–48.

Laughter at the Foot of the Cross (London: Allen Lane, 1997).

Smith, P. J. *Voyage et écriture: Étude sur le "Quart Livre" de Rabelais* (Geneva: Droz, 1987).

ed., *Éditer et traduire Rabelais à travers les âges* (Amsterdam: Rodopi, 1997).

"'Les Ames anglaises sont andouillettes': Nouvelles perspectives sur l'épisode des Andouilles (*Quart Livre*, ch. 35–42)," Cerisy Colloquium (2000) (Geneva: Droz, forthcoming).

Spitzer, L. "Le prétendu réalisme de Rabelais," *Modern Philology*, 37 (1939–40), pp. 139–50.

"Rabelais et les rabelaisants," *Studi francesi*, 4 (1960), pp. 401–23.

"Ancora sul prologo al primo libro del *Gargantua* di Rabelais," *Studi Francesi*, 9 (1965), pp. 423–34.

Stephens, W. *Giants in those Days: Folklore, Ancient History, and Nationalism* (Lincoln: University of Nebraska Press, 1989).

Tetel, M. *Étude sur le comique de Rabelais* (Florence: Olschki, 1964).

Rabelais et l'Italie (Florence: Olschki, 1969).

Tournon, A. "Ce qui devait se dire en utopien (*Pantagruel*, IX)," *Michigan Romance Studies*, 7 (1987), pp. 115–35.

"'Le Paradoxe ménippéen dans l'œuvre de Rabelais," in *Rabelais en son demi-millénaire: Actes du colloque international de Tours (24–29 septembre)*, Études Rabelaisiennes, 21 (Geneva: Droz, 1988), pp. 309–17.

"En Sens agile": Les acrobaties de l'esprit selon Rabelais (Paris: Champion, 1995).

Weinberg, F. *The Wine and the Will: Rabelais's Bacchic Christianity* (Detroit: Wayne State University Press, 1972).

Rabelais et les leçons du rire: Paraboles évangéliques et néoplatoniciennes (Orléans: Paradigme, 2000).

Wilson, D. *Signs and Portents: Monstrous Births from the Middle Ages to the Enlightenment* (London: Routledge, 1993).

Zaercher, V. *Le Dialogue rabelaisien: Le "Tiers Livre" exemplaire* (Geneva: Droz, 2000).

Zhiri, O. *L'Extase et ses paradoxes: Essai sur la structure narrative du "Tiers Livre"* (Paris: Champion, 1999).

INDEX

Cambridge Companions to ...

AUTHORS

TOPICS